C0-AUA-449

Healing Our
Differences

Healing Our Differences

THE CRISIS OF GLOBAL HEALTH AND THE POLITICS OF IDENTITY

Collins O. Airhihenbuwa

ROWMAN & LITTLEFIELD PUBLISHERS, INC.
Lanham • Boulder • New York • Toronto • Plymouth, UK

RA
441
.A347
2007

ROWMAN & LITTLEFIELD PUBLISHERS, INC.

Published in the United States of America
by Rowman & Littlefield Publishers, Inc.
A wholly owned subsidiary of The Rowman & Littlefield Publishing Group, Inc.
4501 Forbes Boulevard, Suite 200, Lanham, Maryland 20706
www.rowmanlittlefield.com

Estover Road
Plymouth PL6 7PY
United Kingdom

Copyright © 2007 by Rowman & Littlefield Publishers, Inc.

All rights reserved. No part of this publication may be reproduced, stored in a
retrieval system, or transmitted in any form or by any means, electronic, mechanical,
photocopying, recording, or otherwise, without the prior permission of the publisher.

British Library Cataloguing in Publication Information Available

Library of Congress Cataloging-in-Publication Data

Airhihenbuwa, Collins O.
  Healing our differences : the crisis of global health and the politics of identity / Collins
O. Airhihenbuwa.
    p. ; cm.
  Includes bibliographical references.
  ISBN-13: 978-0-7425-3981-5 (cloth : alk. paper)
  ISBN-10: 0-7425-3981-4 (cloth : alk. paper)
  ISBN-13: 978-0-7425-3982-2 (pbk. : alk. paper)
  ISBN-10: 0-7425-3982-2 (pbk. : alk. paper)
  1. World health. 2. Social medicine. 3. Identity—Social aspects. I. Title.
  [DNLM: 1. World Health—Africa. 2. Culture—Africa. 3. International
Cooperation—Africa. 4. Social Identification—Africa. 5. Social Medicine—Africa.
6. Socioeconomic Factors—Africa. WA 530 HA1 A298h 2006]
  RA441.A357 2006
  362.1—dc22   2006017494

Printed in the United States of America

∞™ The paper used in this publication meets the minimum requirements of American
National Standard for Information Sciences—Permanence of Paper for Printed Library
Materials, ANSI/NISO Z39.48-1992.

To Yannick
Today's beacon for tomorrow's humanity

University Libraries
Carnegie Mellon University
Pittsburgh, PA 15213-3890

Contents

PART 3 REMAPPING THE TERRAIN ON HEALTH

Preface

My Final Prayer: Oh my body, make of me always a man who questions.

—Frantz Fanon

Fifteen years ago during a class discussion in a graduate seminar I taught on global health, a debate ensued between two of my students on the intersection of identity and public health. The topic of the day was on the question of identity—what it means and how it influences the ability to respond effectively to health problems of minorities in general and Africans and African Americans in particular. I had raised the question in the context of the politics of representation in the tradition of Stuart Hall, and how our perception of sameness and/or differences of identity often color our ways of seeing and acknowledging different forms of identities and consequently our understanding of how these identities influence and shape health behavior. In class were a mixed representation of twelve males and females, African Americans and White students. In responding to my question, an African American female in class lamented the negative representation of the Black body, Black identity, in all spheres of life, notably in the media, and she wondered how we could effectively interrogate the question of identity and health as long as the negative representation of the Black body persisted. A female White student responded immediately that when she looked at this African American female, she did not see her as Black—which is to say, in her further explanation, she (as a White woman) did not see her as different but simply as a woman. The African American female, both shocked and incensed at the remark, asked, "How can you look at me and not see that I am Black?" The White female responded that she believed everyone was equal and did not see her as different.

Thus began the debate on identity and health. In my role as the instructor, I resisted what typically occurs in this kind of situation, which is to intercede to prevent a verbal conflict. The desire to avoid conflict, even when such a conflict may be a most productive process of producing knowledge, has become a common instructional norm in the classroom. In the other students' collective silence, I could feel the tension of discomfort radiating from the class as they hoped that I would end this exchange. They wished that this issue would go away. I found comfort in my personal mantra: *be comfortable with being uncomfortable*. Apparently so did my two female students. Credit to them, they were not to be silenced in a space where they have been allowed to come to voice. Intellectually charged as the exchange may have been, to them it was as professional as it was personal. Beyond the discourse on global health crisis from which the debate was launched, it was clearly about the politics of identity. I allowed the debate to continue because in my view, this was the proverbial teachable/learnable moment. Two very open-minded women, two progressive young scholars, two equally passionate voices had succeeded in bringing to the fore of the class discussion the question of when should a difference make a difference.

After more than thirty minutes of the debate, it came to a closure when the class ran out of time. Before we left the classroom, I gave an assignment that every student was to complete for class discussions in the following week. The assignment was simple, at least in its instruction: "When do you see Black and see Black, and when do you see Black and not see Black?" The central issue here of course was the question of the meaning of Blackness as an identity in the United States compared with Blackness as an identity globally, and how these identity representations intersect with public health. An extension of this question was really "When do you see the identity of an 'Other' for who they are, and when do you see them for what they do, and who framed your perception of them?" Stated differently, "When do you separate what one does from whom one is, and how do you see whom one is without knowing where one is?" "When do you see a person of different identity as a representation of 'healthy identity,' and when do you see one as a representation of a 'diseased identity?'" In a nutshell, "When do you see a difference and acknowledge a difference, and when do you see a difference and see no difference?"

The philosopher Williams James believed that the difference that makes no difference is no difference. Fifteen years later, the two women, now university professors, would seek out each other, inviting my input to process how that experience made a positive mark on them as learners and scholars. As professors assigned to teach a course on diversity and health in their respective universities, they must now interrogate the interface of culture, identity, and health revealed in the question, When does a difference make a difference?

In this era of globalization and the crisis of global health inequity, a new vision is needed to guide directions for addressing health as a political as well as a cultural project. Such a vision should provide the platform from which to question limitations of identity-neutral behavior change strategies that have become ubiquitous in promoting health and preventing diseases. Central to an examination of failed behavior change strategies is a concomitant advancement of the meanings and functions of identity as a cultural as well as political production in forming and shaping health behaviors and decisions. Thus, a new vision for addressing public health must employ a critical analysis informed by an understanding of culture, capable of contextualizing behavior and health as inseparable spaces where the politics of identity must be discursively engaged.

The present investigation is undertaken with the premise that the public health mission and the question of cultural identity are inseparable. Such a premise expands the intellectual and programmatic spaces for interrogating the apolitical and acontextual analyses that have devalued culture and behavior of communities that are evidently bearing the heaviest burden of inequity and inequality in health outcomes. The intersection of politics and identity in health, communication, and education discourses engages the questions of scholarship that "Otherizes" and silences African and African American voices in their various behavioral and cultural expressions and meanings.

On the question of identity and health, race has often served as a frame, albeit proven to be an unscientific marker, for a politically defined representation of identities. Where race serves as a fuse for the identity debate, culture orders the rule of engaging a solution, as will be discussed in chapter 5. Cultural identity defines forms of social interactions that allow us to understand health behavior within different historical and political spaces and times. In other words, culture is neither a totality of unquestioning values and practices, nor is it some archival relics that have fossilized at a particular point in history and thus are impervious to contemporary realities. Cultural identity links the present with the past to establish trails for the future. Failure to engage the historical and political trajectories of cultural identity and its relations to a range of positive to negative health behaviors has led often to the binarism, the twoness of either blaming cultures for certain ill-understood health practices at one extreme of the identity discourse or exalting culture for imagined past glory at the other extreme. The opportunity presented in this book is one that allows scholars and practitioners to move beyond the individualized notion of identity expressed in "I think, therefore I am" by counterposing a collective notion of identity articulated in "I am because we are."

The intent here is not to suggest that one form of identity is superior to the other but to direct public health to a cultural landscape where differences that make differences are promoted and encouraged. Such a cultural landscape promotes multiple truths rather than a universal truth. It is such understanding of multiple truths that frees our minds from the straitjacket of mechanization of knowledge—knowing without questioning. As we question theoretical assumptions that are often apolitical and acontextual in their foundation, we must begin to examine intellectual traditions that have created and nurtured a notion of universal truth. These traditions have directly and indirectly left us with models and theories in global health intervention that treats identity and behavior as neutral and indifferent. For these theories, when identity and behavior are acknowledged to be different, it is for their deficits rather than their possibilities.

A central theme of this book is an examination of how the theoretical tools used to neutralize identity and apoliticize health have been deployed to address perceived deficits in the behaviors of Others. These tools are based on presumed identity deficit behaviors of Africans on the continent and in the diaspora, producing a continuous misallocation of intervention strategies that relegate African agencies and their cultures to the margin of their lived experiences. Using historical and philosophical contributions of scholars addressing African and African American ways of knowing, I examine the serious limitation of these theoretical tools and how they continue to produce and reproduce a universalist public health from the identity-neutral model of constructing health behavior. These universalist assumptions of identity and behavior have continued to be employed globally, to the extent that many Africans subscribe to them even as they question and bemoan the inadequacy and irrelevancy of these assumptions, as demonstrated in part 2. I argue that the present condition of poor health among Africans and African Americans cannot be resolutely addressed without an analysis of how health has been rendered apolitical in public health training, research, and policy, resulting in identity-neutral responses to health interventions.

In this book, questions of cultural identity and health behavior are critically examined to produce a framework for examining what I refer to as the social cultural infrastructures of health behaviors. By *social cultural infrastructure*, I refer to systems and mechanisms of culture that nurture, for example, Senegal's ability to maintain a relatively low level of HIV and AIDS compared with other African countries like South Africa, Botswana, and Ivory Coast that have a relatively superior physical infrastructure. To engage a discourse that examines the value of a society's social cultural infrastructure is to begin to question the old questions. As in my earlier work, I focus on the question rather than the answer, since the question can be posed in a manner that makes the answer inevitable. In other words, focusing on the answer rather than the question on identity and health does not allow us to examine the question of when and how a difference matters.

The book is presented in three parts. In part 1, I focus on philosophical, historical, and literary discourses on politics and identity as they remain a strong foundation for assumptions that are held and theories that are formulated about different forms of cultural identities. I then interrogate social science contributions in the scientific representation of these identities in the process of translating and transmuting the meanings of identities in general and those of Africans and African Americans in particular.

In chapter 1, I explore the construction and representation of identity through literature, history, and philosophy. I examine the notion of cultural construction of identity and the contexts of a related construction of racial identity.

In chapter 2, I question the notion of globalization and the myth of oneness and the concomitant universalization of solutions. I raise questions about the language and premise of globalization that subordinates African cultural identities at the same time that it invites Africans to partake in the global market.

In chapter 3, I critique the language of intervention that has circumscribed scholarship in public health and health communications interventions, at the levels of both theories that frame the education direction of training institutions and practice that invites community members to be a part of the implementation of what has been defined and planned. One very effective method of normalizing a model or strategy has been to locate it in a training language that conditions the learner to assume that the question is self-evident and thus never to question the questions.

In chapter 4, I examine the issue of professionalism and the appearance of neutrality in social science construction of health and identity. I question the ethics of continuing to employ theoretical assumptions that are known to be of limited or no value particularly to people of African descents. I argue that many professionals know and have acknowledged the limitation of certain theories and models but still continue to use them because their professional values are defined and circumscribed by the funding politics of their scholarship rather than any presumed politics-neutral assumptions of their research hypotheses.

In chapter 5, I critique notions of identity, particularly with reference to the debate around whether identity markers in the United States should employ race or ethnicity constructs. This debate around the definition of race is central to developing a new strategy for addressing public health and health communication interventions. The politics of identity are perhaps more charged in the construction of racial identity than any other form of identity in the United

States and South Africa. Although the presumed biological and genetic representation of race has always been global, albeit unscientific, its identity politics in national population policies have always been more visible in countries like the United States and South Africa compared with other African countries where race is rarely present in national policy.

In part 2, I examine specific population groups that deserve attention in the politics of identity and the global health crisis. I address the health concerns of children and youth in chapter 6. The sociocultural condition of youth within the African context has become increasingly problematic. Health conditions of children and youth are presented to underscore the way in which the silencing of youth by adults has contributed to their poor health even as youths are blamed for their collective state of hopelessness.

In chapter 7, women's health issues are examined as the intersection of key relationships. These relationships include those of women to women, women to men, and African women to White women. The degree to which these combined forces attempt to silence the voices of African women and thus compromise their health status and health concern is explored. Indeed, when women are oppressed in Africa, it is considered to be a function of culture, whereas the same oppression in the United States is considered to be a function of gender. I interrogate the politics of identity that differentially define womanhood in similar cultural and racial spaces.

In chapter 8, I examine the historical and cultural contexts of traditional medicine with examples of how this modality can be strengthened from within its cultural space to maximize its benefit for global health. Traditional healers, as cultural workers, have often been demonized for their failures but never acknowledged for their successes and contributions to health care. As the cultural emblem of the suspicion and uncertainty of medical science and public health about culture, traditional healing has come to symbolize the politics of identity inscribed in the crisis of global health.

I conclude this part with a chapter that pays tribute to the late Brazilian Paulo Freire for his tireless efforts to promote a scholarship that embraces differences. In chapter 9, I examine the question of critical consciousness and the influence of Freire's scholarship in grounding educational interventions to address the crisis of health and the politics of identity. Indeed, his scholarship exemplifies the confluence of the various disciplinary contributors to health behavior.

While I engage the politics of identity in the contexts of public health in parts 1 and 2, in part 3, I offer my vision of ways in which health and identity assume their meanings by erasing disciplinary boundaries to produce a collective response to healing our differences. Beyond identity analysis, I extend the process of raising questions by offering strategic approaches to addressing health issues and problems.

In chapter 10, I examine the issue of spirituality and the moralization of behavior as produced and embraced by Africans and non-Africans. Spirituality, as many agree, is central to understanding the central value of behavior. However, spirituality is often articulated only through the prism of morality and behavioral deviance as judged commonly within the doctrines and codes of organized religions.

In chapter 11, I introduce a contextual approach to communications strategies for HIV/AIDS prevention, care, and support. This strategy is based on a collaborative effort with the Joint United Nations Programme on HIV/AIDS (UNAIDS), in which I led a team of 103 health communications and public health researchers and practitioners globally to critically examine the utility of conventional behavioral science theories and models. After three years of this process (1997–1999), we developed a new framework for HIV/AIDS communication intervention that debunked conventional social-psychological theories and models.

In chapter 12, I offer a direction for the future in the application of a cultural model by examining questions of identity and politics in the cultural production of health. This is a rearticulation of the cultural model (PEN-3) that has been presented in my earlier work, including my previous book *Health and Culture: Beyond the Western Paradigm*. In this chapter, I offer a detailed strategic approach to engaging the community in a "polylogue" whereby communities have spaces within which they collectively frame the questions and responses to health issues and problems. A central theme in this process is the recognition of the location of power and the affirmation of community members' collective identity and their cultural and political space relative to health. This chapter offers an opportunity to link theory with practice in developing health promotion and disease prevention programs. The model provides a programmatic approach that offers educators and researchers the opportunity to understand and evaluate culture from multiple dimensions instead of appropriating culture only as a barrier. This is the process of affirming and healing our differences.

In chapter 13, I discuss a futuristic space that holds possibilities and promise for global health, politics, and identity. I offer insights into why politics and identity serve as points of departure and reentry for global health. Such a challenge requires that public health draws from the theory and practice of critical intellectual projects typically offered in African studies, gender studies, cultural studies, and other transdisciplinary scholarly spaces. By examining the public health theoretical and programmatic landscapes of knowledge production and translation, I challenge public health and communications workers and scholars to question the conventional questions. It is by questioning the question that we can collectively heal our differences by affirming our identities. Such discursive projects of transforming conventions in approaches to public health, health promotion, and communication are intended to challenge us to find comfort in a space where, like Fanon, our body could make us always people who question.

Acknowledgments

A debt of gratitude is owed to many people for their encouragement and support in completing this project, especially my wife, Angele Kingue, for her love and unwavering support. I have been very fortunate to benefit from comments on earlier drafts of this manuscript from close friends and colleagues who have continued to be very supportive of me over the years: Shiriki Kumanyika, Olive Shisana, Cheikh Ibrahim Niang, James B. Stewart, Bunmi Makinwa, Arvind Singhal, Rafael Obregon, and the late Everett Rogers. We miss you, Ev. I thank Oyeronke Oyewumi for her intellectual generosity. I also extend many thanks to some emerging scholars whom I have been privileged to mentor directly or indirectly, particularly DeWitt Webster, Aranthan Jones III, and Titilayo Okoror; and to colleagues like Kathleen Roe and Mohan Dutta-Bergman, whose contributions to our understanding of culture radiates through their students. I thank Lenora Johnson for her quiet strength and being the nexus for many likeminded scholars with an interest in African American health issues.

At a time when some publishers have disengaged from projects that invite critical thoughts, I remain grateful to Henry Giroux not only for showing me the way to connect with publishers that matter but for always being encouraging and remaining fresh and insightful in his scholarly productions.

I am thankful to my previous publishers for their permission to revise and update some of my previous publications for inclusion in this book. I am grateful to Sage Publications for the permission to use revised and updated chapters from my previous book, *Health and Culture: Beyond the Western Paradigm*—specifically, chapter 6 on children and chapter 8 on traditional medicine. Chapter 12 on culture and the PEN-3 model have been totally revised with new insights from Africanists' perspectives.

I also want to thank colleagues with whom I have collaborated to develop two of the chapters. For chapter 11 on the communications framework, I want to thank specifically Arvind Singhal, Bunmi Makinwa, and Rafael Obregon for their detailed contributions to and critique of the chapter. Thanks to Michael Ludwig for his collaboration in the original article on Paulo Freire that was revised and updated in chapter 9. A heartfelt thanks to Titilayo Okoror for indexing this book.

Finally, I would like to thank my editors at Rowman and Littlefield, Alan McClare, Molly Ahearn, and Laura E. Larson for her detailed copyedits. As always, I am honored by the support I have received from so many; however, any mistakes in this book are solely mine.

1

QUESTIONING THE QUESTIONS

1

The Cultural Politics of Identity

The difference which we are seeking to define between European and African drama as one of man's formal representation of experience is not simply a difference of style or form, nor is it confined to drama alone. It is representative of the essential differences between two world-views, a difference between one culture whose very artifacts are evidence of a cohesive understanding of irreducible truths and another, whose creative impulses are directed by period dialectics.

—Wole Soyinka (1976:38)

Two gentlemen went to the cemetery to pay respect to their late wives. The first, an American, had a bouquet of roses; the second, a Nigerian, had a pot of soup. As they knelt side by side in front of their wives' graves, the American asked the Nigerian, "When do you expect your wife to eat the soup?" The Nigerian responded, "As soon as your wife begins to smell the roses."

This anecdote exemplifies two cultural values practiced by two men from two different cultures. Neither practice had any practical significance for the beneficiary. However, both practices have such profound cultural value that the practical irrelevance to the foreign eye is unimportant. The study of culture is a study of ideas and values. No one culture is more important than another, just different. Cultural differences are not meant to exalt one over another but to celebrate cultures' differences even as we value their similarities. It is the value and richness of cultural differences that William James embraces when he postulates that "the difference that makes no difference is no difference." The differences in culture are as important, and sometimes more so, than the values that are shared.

Culture is a collective sense of consciousness active enough to influence and condition perception, judgment, communication, behavior, and expectations and the location of power in a given society. Culture may render itself neutral, but its power to define identity and knowledge is expressed through institutions such as families and schools as well as in communications. For Henry Giroux, identity and difference within the contexts of power, agency, and history foregrounds the political dimensions of culture; hence, power and the context of culture must be interrogated as intellectual and practical projects. Culture must be understood within the context of its values, which offer possibilities ranging from positives that should be promoted to negatives that should be overcome.

A culture is never so unique and different that it shares nothing with the world outside it. However, that it shares certain elements with the outside world is no invitation to universalize all of its values and qualities. The challenge often faced by educators engaged in promoting strength in diversity is how to legitimate the coexistence of unique as well as shared values in a culture. The context for experiencing such a journey is the challenge undertaken in this book. In *Myth, Literature, and the African World*, Nobel laureate Wole Soyinka (1976) argues that the African world shares with other worlds the total contexts of the complementarity of myth, history, and mores. That these basic values are shared among different worlds should be no excuse to devalue the ways in which the African world produces and reproduces its cultures through this complementarity of contexts, nor is it an excuse to engage in cross-cultural comparative discourse that privileges Western culture as the point of reference. Such privileging of the West has been and continues to be used to explain African identity and ideas.

THE CONTOURS OF KNOWING AND BEING

The experience that produces the virtue of humanity from birth to death and all the lived experiences between them are anchored on the confluence of myth, history, and mores as they evolve and are nurtured over generations through dramatic events and natural transformations. In the domain of health and identity, the interpretation of the meaning of this complementarity is often constructed through the prism of the non-African interpretations of culture and behavior that are bounded by the beginning and end of life. Health is thus framed in the labyrinth of cultural production of behaviors that make meanings of mores (not myth or history, unless such history were a voyeuristic interpretation of African behavior) in life between birth and death. It is in response to these impoverished representations of African identity that a new method of addressing behavior about health within the context of culture must be engaged. Such methods for Africans should be anchored in African ways of knowing (including myth) within an authentic and organic historical experience of knowledge production and acquisition that inform behavior change—authentic and organic in the sense of representing behavior from the point of view of subjects within their natural and evolving contexts.

In a sense, producing an authentic and organic representation of identity and behaviors within social contexts may be viewed as building a new house. In order to accomplish this feat successfully, one must heed Audre Lorde's (1984) caution to not use the master's tools in dismantling the master's house. That is, one cannot construct a new way of addressing health behavior based on the tools of the old strategy, which do not represent the identity and experience of the households and their communities. An old tool may be used to produce a different shape and dimension of a new house, but the new house is in fact an old house in a new structure because it retains the history, value, and myth of the old house. These characters are transmitted through the tools for constructing the house. An authentic and organic representation of a new house begins with the development of new tools—new theories and models that are anchored in the myth, mores, and history of the people. It is through these tools that the cultural meanings of people's behavior can be represented in their health and their identity can be produced, first for the people and their progeny and then for the global community.

The debate about the potentials and pitfalls on the health and cultural implications of globalization has become even more critical. Discourse on transcultural health and behavior has entered a new phase as the boundaries of identity (individual and collective) and cultural sovereignty are increasingly being questioned and redefined. The new language of this debate necessitates an interrogation of some hitherto exalted notions of globalization that cast a shadow on the voices of scholars and cultural agencies in regions and cultures of the world that are considered to be marginal. By this I refer not only to scholars from non-Western countries but also to scholars from Western countries who are engaged in the struggle to transform certain dominant but retrogressive languages of health behavior. The pursuit of a common global mission has slowly been translated to mean an expectation of unquestioning cooperation (in the name of partnership) from, for example, African colleagues in addressing what has been determined in the Westernized academies to be issues of health priority. This hegemonic policy of determining African health priorities outside Africa is even more evident in the work of some experienced and productive African researchers whose scholarship serves to promote the health issues and priorities that are determined outside their resource-poor environment. These health priorities and issues are often determined by funding agencies of government and major philanthropic foundations in the West. A resulting Western hegemonic blow received by Africans was to be softened by the United Nations corporate language. *Technical cooperation*, for example, is considered to be a preferred term to *technical assistance* (more on this in chapter 3), even though the latter better reflects the relationship between Western ideology and recipient partners. *Technical assistance* conveys language of paternalism and is thus too revealing of its intent to be acceptable in the discourse on partnership for global health with no serious interests in questions of identity and cultures as determinants of health behavior. The Malian sage/thinker Amadu Hampate Ba once noted that the hand that gives always stays on top. In a partnership that separates a giver from a receiver, the receiver must interrogate his or her voiceless position if his or her cultural identity is to have any role in the meaning of such partnership.

The study of culture is shrouded in identity politics. Culture is so much a part of identity that the two words are often coupled to produce *cultural identity*. What is certain is that for identity to have meaning, it is directly or indirectly associated with culture. The meanings that are ascribed to one's group identity, therefore, have a strong historical and social meaning that goes beyond individual choice of identity. For example, knowing one's racial or ethnic identity in the United States and South Africa reveals more of the societal arrangements and identity politics than any text of individual understanding of one's biological being. It is the strength and salience of social arrangements, often anchored in the politics of difference, that necessitate a globally relevant and inclusive definition of group identity—culture. Culture is what defines our identity. Even when we claim dual or multiple cultures, our primary culture of reference is where we seek refuge in times of difficulty.

In its various meanings, health behavior is defined in terms of interpersonal relationships and social functioning, but identity and culture are insufficiently recognized as a part of the equation. In other words, health behavior is commonly defined on the basis of our alignment or misalignment with others, whether at the individual, family, or societal level. However, how we interpret health in relation to a person within a group, a family within a community, or a nation within a region is based on identity and culture. The challenge is how to represent culture in the global context. Moreover, the confluence of culture and identity define who we are and how we see our health and behavior. In normalizing our identity in social relationships, naming one's cultural space often reveals one's context in ways that are often political even when it is not intended. For example, being asked simply "Where are you from?" usually well intentioned, is a function of identity representation that echoes "who you are not" rather than "who you are." African (and African American) identity is often marked by representations that consign those who people the continent to voiceless objects that need others to speak for them. They are commonly not seen as having the capacity to speak for themselves.

This marginal representation is often coded linguistically in phrases such as "sub-Saharan Africa," which the philosopher Charles Mills (1997) concluded is a product of the racial contract (more on this later). Emmanuel Eze (2001), also a philosopher, further unveils the racialism of identity in European's construction of its own identity as "white" by "the conception of African continent as dark simultaneously made it possible to articulate its own spaces as enlightened" (17). Thus, racism and other forms of systemic oppression produce ways of asserting one's identity not by self-analysis (individual and collective) but by learning to define one's identity in terms of the comparative differences (read: deficits) with others' behaviors. These behaviors could be expressed in their language, history, health, and other forms of behavior that conflate to represent identity and culture.

Stuart Hall (1991) concludes that the British (Whites) are not racist because they hate Blacks but because they do not know who they are without Blacks. This point is very true of identity construction in the United States. In fact, much of the discomfort and resistance to engage a discourse on identity involve the fear and inability to articulate one's identity through self-analysis (individual and collective) where one has always been taught to do so through analysis of others' behaviors. Ngugi wa Thiong'O (1993) describes language as a cultural bomb because of its ability to represent and misrepresent identity and culture. Cheik Anta Diop (1991), the Senegalese Egyptologist and thinker; Frantz Fanon (1958), the late Algerian psychiatrist and thinker; and others have written about the importance of history in cultural construction of identity. This is particularly central to meanings of health as I have argued previously (Airhihenbuwa 1995b). In the final analysis, culture must be studied within its historical contexts in a language that expresses its experiences. This is the way to overcome the representation of African cultures that is often negatively juxtaposed against Western culture to produce victims and villains in what is often characterized as a clash of cultures.

In Soyinka's (1975) *Death and the King's Horseman*, the king's horseman was to honor the king's death by "committing death"—that is, sacrificing his own life, not unlike the Christian missionary who turns a child against his family, community, and culture in the name of moral rescue in Chinua Achebe's (1958) *Things Fall Apart*. The missionary in this case, the White district officer, convinces the king's horseman that it is sacrilege for the king's horseman to sacrifice his life for the king even though his entire world has been nurtured under this virtue. At the brink of capitulating to the external invasion of values that is being forced on his father under Western eyes, the king's horseman's son hears about the news and returns from Europe to save his father from the impending cultural abrogation. He confronts the missionaries' hypocrisy in exalting, as the penultimate form of leadership and character, a ship captain who knowingly goes down with the ship in the name of valor. For the son, it would appear that Western culture values the ultimate sacrifice—"committing death"—if such a sacrifice is in the interest of honoring a property (a boat) rather than a cultural institution (royalty). Thus, it is not possible to understand the value of life and death intraculturally unless they are understood from within the identities that cultured these values.

Culture is central to the meanings and interpretation of development. A. Escobar (1995) believes that traditional cultures should not be succumbed to notions of "development" and "modernity" as a marker for "progress." Rather as a continuously renovative base of identity, culture should be represented in its hybrid culmination of multiple values, characters, and relationships to produce its identity. Identity should be studied within culture and the meaning ascribed to a given behavior. Stated differently, although the same behavior may be practiced across cultures, the meaning ascribed to such a behavior in each culture may be totally different.

Cultural identity around food is one of the most salient anchors for maintenance of identity. For example, it has been argued that it is the disengagement from the cultural practice of cooking one's cultural food and the embracing of a practice of buying food in a new culture (a borrowed concept) that serves as a threat to the health identity of recent Latino immigrants in the United States. Consumption patterns and their relations to group interaction, for instance, are shaped by cultures. Food, tobacco, and alcohol all have cultural meanings that are often expressed through the prisms of daily rituals and habits. Thus, an event such as visiting a new mother and her baby may require distinctly different cultural expressions of joy and celebration in two cultures, such as food for one group and flowers for another. Furthermore, even when two cultures use food to express love and care, such expression may be very different. The same presentation of food can signify different meanings between two different groups where one group may experience the meal as having religious or healing qualities, while the other sees it merely as a momentary repast or social event. I recall a Brazilian colleague who once expressed serious concern over her American colleagues' misunderstanding of the cultural significance of sharing food. To offer goodwill and a personal get-well wish to a sick colleague, the Brazilian suggested, and her colleagues agreed, to visit the sick colleague and bring some food to be shared. Upon arrival at the sick colleague's house, she discovered with amazement that her colleagues had bought prepackaged food from the grocery store instead of coming with home-cooked food as she had done. In the Brazilian tradition, bringing prepackaged food to a sick colleague would be an aberration. In this case, such behavior was culturally normal in mainstream America and hence the behavior of her colleagues.

Culture as a processor and regulator of behavior goes beyond consumption patterns. Indeed, medical standards for treating the same disease (e.g., cancer) and procedure (birth by cesarean section) differ among countries with comparable resources such as the United States, France, and England. However, approaches to the human body as a diseased entity with propensity for deviance are similar. In her book *Medicine as Culture*, Deborah Lupton (1994) argues that the practice of medicine is a cultural production. It is based on the conception of the body as a habitat for disease, in which case the body must be controlled. In public health and medicine, "the body is regarded as dangerous, problematic, ever threatening to run out of control, to attract disease, to pose imminent danger to the rest of society" (30). At the same time, society is often represented as a social body, such that a racial or cultural group is also viewed as a habitat for deviant activities, in which case the group also needs to be controlled. Disease is thus constituted in the social (subgroup) body rather than the individual body, and deviant types should be identified as needing to be controlled for the sake of the health of the entire population. In addition to examining the social contribution of the body as deviance, we also focus on the body as underdeveloped and definitely underresourced. Thus, social economic status (SES) becomes a rallying indicator for marking progress for the body as culture and cultures as bodies.

Measures of SES are often seen as a proxies for what is considered to be the richness or poorness of a culture. Indeed, SES may reflect buying power and opportunity, but it does not always explain or predict behavior. In fact, the notion of poverty as a function of culture is meaningless since cultures (in their historical, linguistic, and lineage sense) do not derive from economic resources. The collective experience (positive or negative) of a people, regardless of income levels, shapes the meaning and behavioral response to an illness and defines the value attached to diseases' seriousness, whom to visit for treatment, and how the treatment encounter is to be evaluated by both the provider and patient. Even if the resource base of individuals or collectives were related to health behavior, the notion that such a resource base could be measured by income is flawed, as will be discussed in chapter 3. However, historical attempts to define a people by the deficits society has allocated them lead to the production of race as an identity even though it is scientifically inaccurate.

Race as both a production of individual identity and an institutional mechanism for control is constructed to influence various contexts of behavior. In fact, it is not always the case that race or racism manifests itself in the discourse on culture. This is particularly true because culture as an international discourse often hides racism because racism is most often observed in countries that have a history of racialized politics, as in South Africa and the United States. Race is a regular feature in the relationships of the subjects and actors convening to address issues of identity such as culture. During an international workshop on communication and social context (see chapter 11 for full details) in Geneva in July 2000, a UN agency participant invited a Kenyan she had met on the bus to discuss the role of Massai culture in HIV prevention. The only factor she used in offering her invitation was this Kenyan's Massai attire. Never mind the yearlong planning and careful selection of speakers invited to address different aspects of HIV/AIDS prevention, care, and support. This participant, a senior professional with an international development agency, decided that her time would be given to addressing culture by a stranger she had met on a bus in the belief that being an authority on culture only requires an "exotic" appearance and representation of "otherness." Beyond the arrogance of race and the privilege of Whiteness inscribed in her invitation to this unsuspecting stranger to speak authoritatively on a subject that requires expertise, was the expectation for the unsuspecting Massai also to be an expert on feminism in her culture. The impromptu guest delivered her speech to the pleasure of her guest and her culture voyeurs, while others, including Africans and progressive Whites, were left to wonder whether to challenge the speaker's obvious naiveté, knowing that she too had been unknowingly victimized, or to remain silent, knowing that the true instigator would end up looking innocent in her voyeuristic gaze. Of course, the protection of innocence was deemed to be the right cause of action, and so it was. Race operates institutionally in ways that render itself neutral in the discourse on identity, which is to say that the racial processes do not announce themselves to the onlooker. In some cases, the agents of a racialized project may seriously believe in the naive neutrality of their actions. The intention or naiveté of the race agent does not neutralize the effect on its victim.

In the racial contract, Charles Mills (1997) offers three principles on which race has been constructed and nurtured globally. The first is the naturalization of White supremacy, which he refers to as the existential principle; the second is the affirmation of this White supremacy as a political system, which he refers to as the conceptual principle; and the third is the production of theories that normalize White supremacy as a contract among Whites, which he refers to as the methodological principle. I have argued elsewhere that if health is the "outcome measure" for the statuses of societies and individuals, then identity construction is the "input measure." Unfortunately, most public health scholars have not given much attention to the input measure, even though salutary reference is made to the role of social context in individual health behavior outcomes.

Using Mills's (1997) three principles of the racial contract as input measures, one could construct outcome measures along three similar principles to explicate the historical foundation and professional currents in public health training and practice. The first principle holds that the health of Whites (see Dyer 1991; Gabriel 1998) is existentially and universally central and must be the referent for all others. The second principle, as an extension of the first principle, holds that the White body (i.e., the ubiquitous published comparative health studies on racial differences in the medical literature), particularly the White male body (even though White males suffer higher mortality than White females), is the standard against which all must be conceptually measured as a political system. The third principle holds that the first two principles must be naturalized and universalized through theories and models and that systemic allocation of funds should uphold this "health contract." Thus, funding allocations should support the methodological principles to absolutize and essentialize this last principle since the first two are dependent on it. With the first two principles as a given, the practice of health promotion and public health tend to remain, for the most part, in strengthening the methodological principles by focusing mostly on the "how to" of intervention rather than "why" this concept exists in the first place. In fact, the problem of focusing on the methodological principle is also true of partnerships, coalition building, and community health interventions. Raising questions rather than relying on answers therefore means interrogating methodological principles by examining existential and conceptual logics. This means questioning theories and their assumptions rather than accepting them by promoting their product-methodological principles.

It is in the construction and naturalization of the methodological principles that ownership of knowledge production is established, defined, and refined. When identity and culture are erased from the methodological principals, their deployment to other countries and regions is seen as a process of advancing knowledge for improving well-being. Identity as embodied in ownership of values and institutions becomes a central value that must be understood in addressing questions of health and behavior.

In *Hopes and Impediment*, Chinua Achebe (1988) recounts a story of a snake that owns a horse. The snake got on top of the horse and was struggling to situate itself properly on top of the horse while it galloped awkwardly along the path. In the meantime, a toad was watching the snake, got tired of watching the snake struggle, and kindly offered to teach the snake how to ride a horse properly. The snake came down graciously, and the toad got on top of the horse, positioned itself firmly, and proceeded to demonstrate effortlessly how easy and smooth it was to ride a horse. Upon completing his demonstration, the snake thanked the toad, climbed back onto the horse with the same awkwardness as before, and remarked to the toad, "To know is good but to own is better. What is the point of being a good horse rider when you do not own a horse?"

The ownership of ideas and development of new tools for addressing the cultural contexts of health behavior comprise the primary goal of this book. In the final analysis, it may be nice to be a good horse rider, but the identity of the horse, the path on which it must travel, and the knowledge of the contexts for good horse riding remain with the owner.

2

To Think Locally and Act Globally?

The preindependence generation of African intellectuals was mostly concerned with political power and strategies for ideological succession. . . . A new generation prefers to put forward the notion of epistemological vigilance.

—V. Y. Mudimbe (1988:36)

A popular slogan that expresses collaboration across geographic divides is to "think globally and act locally," to which I counterpose, "Who drew the boundaries?" Or, better yet, how has the reverse—"think locally and act globally"— claimed political currency in the United States, particularly following the attacks of September 11, 2001. Of even greater importance is the question of whose local (cultural origin) is the global, since the global cannot produce itself without an original local. Furthermore, who maintains intellectual vigilance over the boundaries that produce the global, on the one hand, and the simultaneous blockage of other locals from becoming global, on the other?

For some time, the word *international* has slowly been replaced with the word *globalization*. *International* suggests moving across boundaries, while *globalization* is represented as a borderless world. In *Health and Culture: Beyond the Western Paradigm*, I argued that globalization is nothing more than a language that grants Western ideologies a license to further marginalize cultures of non-Western countries, such as those in Africa, through ideological and economic domination and strangulation of these countries' resources. Since then, progressive thinkers in Western and non-Western countries have publicly protested the economic violence visited on the poor by the World Bank and International Monetary Fund (IMF). Thandika Mkandawire (2004) notes that "for years monetaries trained by IMF had ensconced themselves in

13

central banks very much like 'sleepers' awaiting instructions from Washington when the time came" (8). Such practices were institutionalized in ways that promoted failed economic policies. It is quite evident that the increased attention to global economic violence has gained momentum as European countries are increasingly "colonized," economically and politically, by American corporate and political entities. More people have begun to realize that repression and inequity are among the outcomes of capitalism even though capitalism is the economic expression of democracy. In understanding democracy and the political economy on which it is anchored, capitalism may be the most effective means of production, but it is clearly a most ineffective means of distribution and indeed the very source of inequity. In *Necessary Illusion: Thought Control in Democratic Societies*, Noam Chomsky (1989) interrogates the naturalization of corporate oligopoly within the U.S. capitalist democracy. According to him, in the U.S. capitalist democracy, "the political class and the cultural managers typically associate themselves with the sectors that dominate the private economy; they are either drawn directly from those sectors or expect to join them" (23).

The dominance of the ruling class in production is even more problematic in knowledge production. Mkandawire (2005) critiques the training of African economists for their dependence on Western theories to frame solutions to African development: "Much of the cream of the new competence in economics is captured by donors themselves, and is often deployed by them. Access by African governments to this competence is often mediated by donors through the donor-dominated consultancy industry" (24). According to Paul Zeleza (2004), African intellectuals found themselves fighting the authoritarian of institutions like the World Bank while at the same time fighting the domineering Western paradigms that have been normalized in academic training and rewards. This institutionalized approach to controlling the intellectual capital on which African development is to be anchored is nothing new. Attempts to redress this have led to the era of capacity building. Capacity building has been more of an exercise in skill development rather than the offering and nurturing of a space where a more relevant theory for African development could be advanced. The outcome of most capacity building leaves neither the experts nor the participant-trainees with any meaningful dialogue that will have true impact in their countries. A capacity-building exercise where a dialogue is meant to ensure knowledge production between the experts (in their Westernized and universalized orthodoxy) and their trainees can only result in what Mkandawire refers to as a "conversation between a ventriloquist and a puppet." Neither's capacity is likely to be built or strengthened. The result is the increasing gap between the very economically and politically privileged and the disenfranchised in the society.

Sadly, the mass media, which have the responsibility for educating the public, have failed the public by helping to perpetuate this system through manufactured consent that anesthetizes public sensibility to the real source of inequity in the society. In the pyramid of a global capitalist democracy, the United States has become the sole hand that gives and maintains its position firmly on top of the pyramid. European intellectuals, politicians, and business leaders have begun to complain about U.S. dominance using the same language and arguments that they heard from former colonies and had trivialized. The United States, in turn, has responded using the same language and discourse once engaged by Europe to justify its imperialism.

Beyond the new realization of capitalism as an engine that fueled increased global inequity, the language of human behavior is enjoying a value in emotionality as a positive human quality. Emotionality rather than rationality has gained a new level of openness in public discourse. It would appear that emotionality is no longer believed to be a weak expression of rational being. Emotionality is a form of catharsis (individual and collective) that precedes and occasions a desire to redress an injustice. The central role of emotionality in group identity gained visible (post-9/11) attention even though it would appear that the newest flag bearers believed and continue to believe in the dominance of rational volition over emotionality. It would appear that William James's (1909) postulate of the late 1800s—that intelligence without emotionality is empty—found renewed validation in the overwhelming majority of Americans and American institutions that raised only the U.S. flag while withdrawing the United Nations and the Red Cross flags. Indeed, the almost unanimous waving of the flag gave reasons for a new form of collective identity to the extent that it was suggested in the media, including the *New York Times* and the major television networks, that September 11 erased hitherto racial division in the United States. *To think locally and act globally* in a most "nationalistic" sense was welcomed and celebrated. The possibility of encouraging a United Nations flag or the International Red Cross flag would have meant to think globally and act locally. Homilies like patriotism (for waving the flag) became commonplace in conference rhetoric and conference presentations by public health scholars and workers. In fact, Michael Eric Dyson (1996) observes that there is a new "PC" in public discourse: political correctness has yielded to "patriotic correctness." The new language of nationalism is marked by the size of your flag and the degree to which one thinks locally and acts globally rather than the reverse. It is as though conservative flag bearers among U.S. politicians and educators finally understand (or so it would seem, although I rather doubt it) and have adopted the language that symbolized the struggle for marginalized groups in the United States. African Americans should no longer be considered as too sensitive for allowing emotionality to unite them in their fight to assert their group identity (don't we wish). In a sense, globalization has found new meaning in the boundaries of the politics of identity. What happens when a nation begins to apply the concept and method of the very group it has oppressed and demonized for so long? What does is mean to think locally and act globally? I will attempt to use this new representation to explicate the meanings of identity and health.

HEALTH IN THE WEST AS HEALTH FOR ALL

William Foege (1997) believes that infectious disease and violence are the two most serious global health problems of our time. He further states that control over infectious diseases has been relatively successful (albeit within a Western analytical frame), while control over violence has not. Although questions remain about the level of success over infectious disease at the global level, clearly very little has been done about violence as a global rather than an individual or regional problem. In the United States, the advent of "White-on-White" crime (e.g., the Columbine high school killing rage and subsequent tragic cases in other suburban schools) and the September 11 attacks have reinscribed war and conflict as functions of ideological divides with global consequences for the health of the public.

A direct parallel can be drawn between political behavior and the health and well-being of a country's people. The multinational corporation and the economic policing agencies such as the World Bank and IMF are complicit in this scenario because of their history of using their stamp of approval to support political leaders who are known to use the money they borrow to enrich themselves and to further impoverish their populace. These economic policing institutions have normalized and enabled kleptocracy in national political leaders, even though such behavior is universally considered to be unacceptable in individual lending practices—lending money to individuals that show no promise of repayment or of using the funds for what is not intended. The practice has been to lend money to or support the lending of money to national political leaders without holding them accountable for producing what is owed.

Moreover, beyond these dubious lending practices, the World Bank as an institution has had a history of advancing development ideologies, usually constructed as a development theory, that are not responsive to the needs of Africans. An adequate theory does exist for African development, and the foundation of these theories has been established in the work of Frantz Fanon, Chiekh Anta Diop, and Kwame Nkrumah, to name just three. As Lasana Keita

(2004) has argued, these theories are constrained between the draconian dictates of the World Bank and IMF, on the one hand, and the internal constraint of some African intellectuals who are in leadership positions but whose theoretical groundings are apolitical, ahistorical, and acultural, on the other hand.

Beyond the control over monetary policies in Africa, the World Bank has repositioned itself as a "knowledge bank." For example, it is the policy of the World Bank, as expressed in the work of John Evans, that countries must go through a three-stage linear path from infectious disease in the first stage, to a mix of infectious disease and chronic disease in the second stage, to chronic disease in the third stage. William McNeil (1976) has long challenged this thesis by arguing that it is social ecology that determines the pattern and occurrence of disease. Historically, the transmission of diseases occurred along trade routes, not unlike the role of truck drivers in spreading HIV. The creation of cities and the resulting housing congestion have led to the rapid spread of communicable diseases. In addition, development projects such as irrigation have led to problems with water-borne diseases.

Transformations in the means of production, such as industrialization, reflect the changes that take place in the broader social environment. These changes are often beyond the influence of how individuals think, what they desire, or how they behave. In nonindustrial nations of much of Africa, Asia, and Latin America, both past and present means of production continue to coexist. Along with the confluence of means of production is the coexistence of diseases of the past (sanitation and poverty) and diseases of the present (lifestyle and affluence). This convergence in contrasts between industrial and nonindustrial nations reflects, in great part, the history of colonization, imperialism, and exploitation that enabled industrial countries to build economies, scientific complexes, and systems of public health and medical education.

In more recent times (i.e., the turn of the twenty-first century), writers and scholars have documented efforts by mostly Western-trained medical and health care practitioners to address health problems around the world (see, e.g., Garrett 1994), only to realize that their medical school training did not prepare them for the challenges they must confront. The last two decades of the twentieth century witnessed the ravage of the HIV/AIDS pandemic at the same time that the prevalence of smoking became epidemic. HIV/AIDS and health problems of consumption such as poor nutrition and tobacco use are among the most devastating public health ills of the twenty-first century. Malaria, even though not a health problem in industrial nations, continues to devastate nonindustrial nations in epidemic proportion. These global health problems have brought into sharper focus the limitations of medical and

health training curricula in dealing with health problems whose manifestations are beyond individual behavior but rather indicate the complexities and
influence of social contexts.

Unfortunately, rather than focusing on these complexities, the emphasis
continues to be on individual-level analysis that isolates and focuses on sexuality, alcohol and drug use practices, nutritional practices, and tobacco consumption, even though these conditions require a broader examination of social and institutional influences. At the social and community levels, there is
the challenge of addressing "social processors of behaviors" such as culture
and identity, the status of women as it relates to health outcomes, inequity (in
value) and inequality (in access to resources), in addition to discrimination
and marginalization in the context of institutional racism. These institutions
have produced the present condition of suspicion and distrust that are becoming increasingly problematic in addressing HIV and AIDS in Africa.

POLITICS OF SUSPICION AND MISTRUST

As I will discuss later when considering race and ethnicity and the question
of double consciousness, the consciousness of Africans and other peoples on
the economic development margin can no longer be viewed without a clearer
understanding of their cultural identity. They must contend with a form of hybridized and multiple consciousnesses that sees a heightened form of global
economic hegemony eroding all forms of agencies they once knew. Indeed,
nations are fighting the battle to maintain their cultural identity, as is evident
in the French government's protectionist policy over what it believes to be the
need to expunge the English language from the French language. Other nations are fighting identity battles even though such battles are commonly
framed within scientific discourse, as demonstrated in the South African government battle against major pharmaceutical companies that manufacture
HIV/AIDS drugs, to protest their stranglehold on the sale and distribution of
antiretroviral therapy. In fact, although much has been written and debated
about the polemics of South African president Mbeki's position on the relationship between HIV and AIDS, very little has been written about the historical context on which the initial question about the context of HIV spread
in Africa has been based.

The work of Didier Fassin has been very instructive on this issue. In the
case of South Africa, the politics of suspicion and distrust must be histori-
cized to understand some of the medical polemics around HIV/AIDS. According to Fassin (2002, 2003), the history of racialized heath politics in
South Africa includes the bubonic plague of 1900 in Cape Town, which was

used to justify the removal of Africans from their homes to create the first "native locations" under the first segregationist law that was passed in 1883. White leaders "publicly rejoiced over the possible elimination of black people by the disease [AIDS], as one member of parliament did in 1992" (496). Fassin (2003) draws a parallel between this debate and a similar polemic around the cause of the cholera epidemic that devastated France in 1829–1830. During this period, there were two schools of thought. The "contagionists" school of thought, based on biological science, accurately concluded that cholera was contagious and therefore the solution should be based on recognition of the bacterial infection and implementation of the appropriate treatment regiment. On the other end of the debate was the "anticontagionists" school of thought, represented by social reformists from multidisciplinary fields, including philosophers and hygienists who argued forcefully that cholera was not contagious but rather that it was caused by poverty and not the scientific explanation that was offered by the contagionists. The public support for the social reformists (even though they were scientifically wrong) galvanized a huge political groundswell and started to mobilize resources to alleviate poverty to reduce cholera. The result of this socioeconomic argument was the transformation of Paris and other urban areas by targeting poverty alleviation, which led to huge success in cholera reduction since the condition that favored the spread of cholera was indeed largely poverty, even though poverty was not a scientifically accurate "causal" explanation for the disease.

One could argue that even though it would be scientifically inaccurate for President Mbeki to question the relationship between HIV and AIDS, had there been a sociopolitical groundswell supported by resources to successfully alleviate poverty by closing the racial economic inequity gap in South Africa, the incidence of HIV and AIDS would be reduced. This is particularly true given scientific reports by David Gilsselquist and colleagues (2003) that health care transmission of HIV/AIDS in Africa has been ignored even though, according to the authors, evidence shows that "general population studies through 1988 suggest that medical exposures were responsible for more African HIV than sexual exposures" (151) at a time when there was an "acceptance by experts of the 1988 consensus that 90% of HIV transmission in Africa was of sexual origin" (156). This article was followed immediately by an expert committee report (World Health Organization [WHO] 2003) that maintains that unsafe sex is the primary mode of transmission of HIV in Africa. At the 2003 international conference on sexually transmitted infections (STIs) and AIDS in Africa (ICASA) in Nairobi, WHO insisted that the nosocomial (hospital-based infection) route of HIV transmission was only about 2 percent. Gilsselquist el al., at the debate, questioned why

WHO, as a matter of policy and practice, provided needles to its senior staff while they were traveling to Africa if in fact they believed this were a low and "insignificant" level of transmission. He and his colleagues reviewed several studies conducted in Africa on the mode of HIV/AIDS transmission and concluded that a significant number of cases of HIV/AIDS infection in Africa should be blamed on transmission through the use of unsterilized needles in hospitals rather than through sexual transmission, as has been reported. A recurring issue that is not openly addressed is the suspicion that focusing on sexual transmission (especially when other modes of transmissions are ignored) serves to promote the Western construction of Africans, particularly African women, as oversexed. An important lesson of this debate is that there are multiple modes of transmission that must gain simultaneous attention rather than focusing on the one that confirms researchers' images of African identity and sexual behavior.

For Fassin (2002, 2003), the debate should be less about questioning HIV as the cause of AIDS and more about understanding the evolution of a new South Africa, particularly in the way in which HIV was hailed by political leaders in South Africa's parliament in 1992 (two years before the postapartheid era) as a welcome scourge that will devastate Black South Africans. The seed of a conspiracy against South African Blacks/Africans was sown out of sight from public discourse.

The position of President Mbeki cannot be completely understood without a thorough excavation of the racism inscribed in South Africa's political legacy. It is important to disaggregate the extent to which the discourse on the question of the relations between HIV and AIDS is a scientific question, an identity question, or a political question. If it is a political question, then to leave the conversation solely at the level of science is to erroneously advance the notion that the formula for thinking locally and acting globally holds true for thinking globally and acting locally. The intent here is not to question the scientific validity of the cause-and-effect relationship between HIV and AIDS, nor is it to support President Mbeki's position, whatever such position is. It is rather to question the arguments that have been raised about how the discourse around the analysis of this relationship has been located outside the historical-political contexts in South Africa. Such historical-political analysis must include housing policies that created "informal settlements'" that are linked to poverty and vulnerability to HIV and AIDS. There is no question about the fact that HIV causes AIDS. However, poverty is a critical risk situation that creates and maintains vulnerability to HIV and AIDS. In a population-based HIV seroprevalence survey led by Dr. Olive Shisana in 2002 and again in 2005, risk environment, such as living in an informal settlement, was shown to be more of a risk factor than any other group category for determining the potential risk of HIV (Shisana et al. 2005). For example, th IIV prevalence rate for South Africans living in urban informal settlements (shantytowns) was 17.9 percent compared with 9.1 percent for those in urban formal housing, 11.6 percent in ethnic/language communities and towns, and 9.9 percent in rural areas. Many scientists who privately agree and accept the role of poverty in the spread of HIV are publicly reluctant to acknowledge it.

Here lies the ethical dilemma of refusing to publicly acknowledge what is known to be empirically valid. HIV causes AIDS. Poverty creates and maintains vulnerability to HIV and AIDS. Identity has always mattered in what lenses are used to report a condition that is highly stigmatized. You cannot address one without the other. However, to address poverty, one must address issues of inequity and social injustice and what roles identity plays in them. To address inequity and social injustice in South Africa is to confront the history of racism. For many scientists, this matter is too complicated and remains outside the realm of their expertise. Moreover, it is safer to remain at the perceived impersonal level of science and relegate the personal level of science to politics, from which social science is supposedly impervious.

Finally, the concern is often raised in the scientific community that to acknowledge the role of poverty is to say to the public that they no longer have to follow preventive messages, because accepting poverty as a fact would mean other behaviors are no longer important. There is an ethical question here that will be addressed in chapter 4. In the final analysis, that a political leader believes that poverty plays a major role in HIV/AIDS is not enough to undermine such a belief simply because the debate has been confounded with the scientifically established causal link between HIV and AIDS. This could only happen when professionals and politicians are all engulfed in an environment of suspicion and distrust, whether it is among scientists or between scientists and political leaders.

The suspicion of conspiracy continues to be a central issue in the debate around the origin of AIDS. Policymakers and AIDS workers have often used the response of "not worrying about how the snake enters the house but figuring out how to get rid of the snake." What is often not understood is that in a world that blames Africans for their depressed economic situation, worsened by some corrupt leaders who are nurtured by Western institutions like the World Bank, the issue may be less of questioning the origin of "the snake" and more of whether a snake as a cultural totem, an identity totem, may have obscured the ability to respond effectively and whether such a response should be a "hamburger-based intervention" (from the point of view of the United States) or a "fufu-based intervention" (from the point of view of Nigeria and some other West African countries). In the first instance, the notion of a single snake focuses our attention on a single invading foreign object rather than examining internal and external factors that may create an enabling environment for a snake to enter the house in the first place and then alter the structure of the house and the cultural arrangements of the household. This may very well be the issue of the exclusive focus on sexual transmission of HIV, when poor medical resources have contributed to the spread of HIV. The longer the snake remains, the greater the desire to blame the house for the snake's origin and sojourn.

The logical reaction, particularly in the face of an overwhelming assault on the cultural identity of the house, is to question the origin of the snake as a way of defending the honor of the household. Hence the desire to dispel any credence to the belief that Africa is the source of this global scourge. In other words, the issue of identity is always a central question when interrogating how a pandemic has devastated one region compared with another. Even more crucial is how the ways of knowing of the affected region has been marginal to the construction of "solutions" to the pandemic, particularly when it is these ways of knowing that are blamed for the pandemic, as will be addressed later.

With the origin of AIDS still in question, suspicion becomes a logical analytical frame that guides the collective response to the presence of the snake. Yes, it makes sense to focus on getting rid of the snake. Where suspicion is the analytical frame, several constructs could evolve. One such construct is in the form of a question that asks, Did the snake actually come into the house, or was there an egg in the house? Perhaps the snake was brought in by a well-intentioned scientist who wanted to breed a nonpoisonous snake with the potential to protect the house from a rodent invasion, but an unintended consequence was that a poisonous snake was hatched instead. Still within the suspicious frame of analysis, another construct may posit that AIDS workers are so focused on killing the snakes in their house, blaming innocent children for leaving the doors open, and forcing parents to reconstruct new doors that no one bothered to look up to realize that someone was throwing snakes into the house through the window. The construct that would be of the most concern to interventionists is the one that links suspicion with stigma. If we have snakes in our houses and the origin is not known, "we" cannot be associated with any disease and death that result from the snake's presence, nor would "we" want to be associated with anyone who does, including AIDS workers. In fact, "we" would rather blame our children's death on a more culturally accepted explanation such as witchcraft than this mystery of a snake. Thus, an unexplainable snake becomes the making of witchcraft and magic.

In the meantime, we have forgotten that people go in and out of the house, and one of them could have been infected while receiving blood in the hospital. In fact, it has been a common practice for nurses and medicine salespeople to go into people's homes in towns and villages to give injection treatments for various illnesses. In the context of the HIV and AIDS crisis, in which suspicion and distrust are engulfed in the politics of African identity, the representation of Africans as an oversexed population in the Western imagination has blunted any analysis that may question the role of medical care in the spread of HIV unless it is thought to occur in traditional healing. Whether the snake is real or not, the perception of its presence is real. Indeed, the perception of reality has been demonstrated to be an important indicator for health outcomes. An experience of suspicion and mistrust could not be subjected to the same analytical framework as an experience that is shared by all. The issue is not to leave this analysis at the level of myth but to invite history and mores to the equation. Even more critical is the need to refocus our solutions from a language of a distrusting victim whose behavior we must change to a language of institutionalized practices whose history of deception has rendered them untrustworthy. Trustworthiness must be a central focus of regaining the support of communities with a history of victimization. By focusing on institutional trustworthiness, we can focus on institutional behaviors to change policies and practices that created the mistrust in the first place rather than focusing on the behavior of the victims.

The 2005 Human Development report from the United Nations Development Programme (UNDP) indicates that extreme inequality and perception of inequity are central indicators of health disparity. The foundation of such a perception does not seem to be important as long as there is such a perception. But what is perception if not the confluence of what is real and what has been experienced? How do we understand what is experienced without an understanding of the acceptability of its interpretation? Of course, the relationship between the West and the Rest of Us is replete with inequity. The hallmark of globalization has been a widening inequity between rich and poor nations. Indeed, one outcome of the intersection of culture and globalization is that some people may begin to consider their culture to be irrelevant to them since for them hamburger is global (read: good) and fufu is local (read: bad). Such inequity is not simply a function of economic differences often expressed in a poverty index. Inequity is more of a function of value, while inequality is a quantifiable difference between or among entities. Thus, the question of inequity is very important in global health because it addresses perception and its intersection with reality. Indeed, studies of inequality commonly expressed in terms of a poverty index often lead to certain inequity values that may be misleading. Leading social scientists studying disenfranchised populations often study the poorest of these populations and extrapolate their findings as a construction of these people's identity. There are many social and behavioral scientists in the United States who cannot and do not articulate an African American identity without a poverty index. The result is that the condition and experience of a quarter to a third of the population (albeit a significant proportion) is represented as the identity of the entire group. Even when one examines global statistics, the question of poverty is important, but actual disease outcomes that produce societal ill health transcend the poverty index. For example, using infant mortality as an important indicator for societal health, D. Gwatkin (2000) showed that more than 50 percent of under-five deaths occur among people who are not in poverty. However, it is almost certain that any success at poverty alleviation will benefit also those above the poverty line in health promotion and disease prevention.

FINAL THOUGHTS

The relationship between the local and the global has always been problematic. The question of identity and culture requires that one think locally and act globally. The notion of thinking globally and acting locally has meant that there is a universal solution that can be transferred to any local situation. As wonderful as it is as an idea, the reality is the construction of global is always the foundation of someone's local, even though the local has been neutralized when the idea travels. The reality is that our knowledge is produced within our local contexts. It is through cross-cultural discourse and experience that we transform and reproduce our knowledge for global benefits. Perhaps a new slogan should be "think locally, share globally."

3

Language Elasticity

The Intersection of the Senses

The effect of a cultural bomb is to annihilate a people's belief in their names, in their languages, in their environment, in their heritage of struggle, in their unity, in their capacities and ultimately in themselves. It makes them see their past as one wasteland of non-achievement and it makes them want to distance themselves from the wasteland.

—Ngugi wa Thiong'O (1993)

The contestation over language and culture is particularly problematic in the ways in which the African experience is represented to the outside world. Faced with the desire to represent all experiences in the same universal code of language, the African experience is often represented as exotic and strange and needing to be overcome. I discuss in chapter 12 that English, French, and many of the Western languages are gendered languages, while Edo, Yoruba, and many African languages are languages of seniority. Moreover, a language of physical environment is not sensitive to gender or seniority, whereas the language of social environment is. A language of physical environment stays rigidly within the five senses. A language of social environment within African tradition transcends senses as expressed in "a seeing voice" or "an audible vision." For example, a Guyanese friend once mused to my wife, "Why are you looking at me in that tone of voice?" The location of language in defining literary discourses is one of the debates in the humanities regarding what constitutes African literature. However, this is not the focus of this chapter. In this chapter, I consider the use of certain terms to normalize relations and thus nurture a hegemonic influence in global relationships.

The linear and rigid rules of language that circumscribe the manifestation of the senses in what Edward T. Hall (1976) refers to as a low-context culture does not apply to a high-context culture. Hall describes a low-context culture as one where the thinking is very linear in the tradition of Socrates. Countries that exemplify low-context cultures are Germany and the nonminority culture in the United States. In high-context cultures, as in African and other Asian cultures, thinking is very robust; hence, expressions would not follow a linear code. Time as an expression of encounter and experience is a function of experience that measures commitment not in precision but in endurance and commitment over a period of time. The value of time in low-context cultures derives from measurement of the physical environment, such as temperature, and physical space, including volume and pressure. The value of time in high-context cultures derives from the social environment such as family and social space, including relationships and spirituality. A clash of linguistic code has often resulted in using measures of physical environment to validate experiences in the social environment. For example, the measure of the relationship between volume and pressure is so constant that it is referred to simply not as a theory but as a law, as in Boyle's law. Unfortunately, researchers of social environments have been attempting to use standards for measuring a relationship that is constant regardless of the language in which the relationship is expressed. Social relations are greatly influenced by the language in which they are expressed. How one feels about one's susceptibility to a given disease and the behavior for reducing susceptibility all depend on several contextual factors often mediated by the language in which they are expressed.

If theories and models are based solely on Western thoughts, it is through language that these thoughts are normalized and universalized in the academy. If we are to recognize knowledge production from Africa, we must first recognize the codes and elasticity of language within the African context before we make any attempt to deconstruct the dominant gaze of the West. But first, we must interrogate certain hegemonic terms that have been normalized in Western identity discourse. For example, the notion of "belonging" has different meanings depending on the cultural context. In the cultural context of individuality, belonging is defined in terms of "ownership" (property, adoption, rights). However, in the cultural context of collectivity, it is defined in terms of relationship and responsibility (e.g., naming a child in the seventh day).

Beyond issues of individuality and collectivity is the notion of belonging as cultures go through necessary transformations. The omnipresence of the Internet and cell phones is one sphere where necessary transformation of cultures must confront questions of belonging and identity. Space for public consumption of the Internet is often referred to as an Internet café or cybercafé (in most Francophone countries). However, café is a social space derived from places where coffee is usually consumed, as in coffeehouses. The consumption of hot drinks has come to symbolize another form of cultural ownership, as in the case of tea in Britain and coffee in France or Ethiopia. However, there are other hot drinks with equal cultural significance that have not been accorded the cultural legitimacy in the definition of pubic spaces for Internet use. For example, *ataya* (meaning tea) is a traditional hot drink drunk in Senegal and some other African countries. Cybercafés are commonplace in Dakar, but I was not able to locate any "cyber ataya"—a name that would have affirmed a Senegalese cultural space as a global participant in web conversations. There is no question that should one say that one were in a cyber ataya, it is clear that the person was in Senegal or one of the contiguous nations that uses the term *ataya* for tea. In what follows, I will examine a few commonly used terminologies and their representation discourses in the African contexts.

EXPLORATION AND DISCOVERIES

The notion of discovery often means that nothing existed before the arrival of the foreigner(s). A history professor from a prestigious liberal arts university was once quoted as saying that he "discovered Kenyan history." The emptiness of such arrogant expression notwithstanding, the professor's view echoes the hollowness of an educational value that a people's experience begins its legitimacy at the point where a Westerner wrote about it. Beyond the obvious arrogance of race and language that punctuate this unspoken value are the ways in which history for the Kenyans, in this case, was thought only to exist at the point when a Westerner started to write about it for Western consumption. In this case, the language of discovering is the language of ownership. This is an example of linguistic hegemony where the language of he who has captured the Kenyan experience is believed to be the liberator and the explorer because he dared to journey to, in this case, a foreign territory. In lamenting the devaluation of African history, Basil Davidson (1969) concludes that the arrogance of Whiteness is in believing that something is of value when he (the White man) says it is. Indeed, neither the Native Americans in the United States nor the Aborigines in Australia were ever acknowledged as being the true explorers and original discoverers of their lands.

The language of discoveries and exploration could gain legitimating values if we begin to examine ways in which common terms and expressions assume different cultural meanings. For example, studies indicating a strong influence of friends over family fail to recognize the importance of the verb *to choose*. Friends are relations of choice, whereas family is not. In fact, in the Edo language, it is said that (*otenghabun-oseaze*) where family is plentiful, one chooses friends among them. Thus the choice you make—friends—will definitely influence your decision more so than the choices you did not make—family. Studies showing a strong influence of friends are thus also showing a strong influence of choice. Moreover, for different decisions made in a normal course of our existence including preventive health behavior, the choiced relationship is more important than blood choice. Although blood may be thicker than water, it is also heavier in responsibility. The situation may be different in addressing crises situations. The fact that there are no terms for different degrees and levels of *cousins* in many languages may also buffer the otherwise emotional closeness that such a term may confer in other cultures. The language of exploration and discoveries continues to underlie present relationships between the Northern institutions and Southern nations in form of technical cooperation and technical assistance.

TECHNICAL COOPERATION AND TECHNICAL ASSISTANCE

The relation between Western nations and poor resource nations is played out in the polemics around the language of the United Nations and established donor agencies. The specialized agencies of the United Nations, such as the WHO and UNDP, have long adopted the principle that the technical relations it establishes with poor resource countries will be considered as cooperation rather than as assistance. It is believed that to call technical linkages "assistance" is to evoke a language of superiority and inferiority, with the poor resource nations as the latter. The term *technical cooperation* is considered to be a more egalitarian term to define the North and South linkage even though the actual relationship is one of Western domination of ideas and rules of poor resource countries.

These relationships operate at several different levels. As I have argued (Airhihenbuwa 1995b), my experience at WHO was one in which programs were developed in Geneva for implementation in African countries. My argument not to develop programs or frameworks outside the experience and knowledge production of Africans addressing these problems was considered to be antithetical to the model of relationship between the UN and African countries. In a study funded by the UNDP to examine how some African leaders experience technical cooperation, Cheikh Niang could not find a single policymaker or scholar who thought that true cooperation existed within technical cooperation. What he found were policymakers, many of whom agreed to speak only on condition of anonymity, who were very clear that technical cooperation has and will continue to be an exemplary mechanism for the West to maintain its hegemony over African countries while assuming an image of egalitarianism.

Many forms of ideological domination have been promoted unquestionably through the UN under the guise of technical cooperation. The most common form is the use of measures of behavior that were developed in the West for implementation in African countries with the argument that such standardized measures allow for international comparative analysis. Not only are African scholars not encouraged to develop measures that are more representative of their contexts and reality, but many are actually threatened with the discontinuation of funding that supports such technical cooperation. In fact, some Western scholars have assumed that African scholars are not capable of producing knowledge but rather could modify knowledge that has been produced elsewhere (in West) for adaptation in Africa. This has become very common in the practice of some Western scholars presenting survey questionnaires to research collaborators in Africa with the expectation that these African researchers should simply translate these questionnaires into local languages and administer them. Those scholars (including some White Western scholars) who resist this unethical practice are often marginalized in the donor community, and, in some cases, attempts are made to discredit their work. In other instances, research studies that conclude with results that place Africa in positive lights are discredited and kept from being published. When Cheikh Anta Diop (for whom the University of Dakar in now named), the famous Egyptologist and anthropologist, first presented his doctoral thesis establishing that Egyptians are Black Africans, it was rejected by the Sorbonne in 1954. It would take Diop over a decade of further research and publications coupled with the findings reported in his second doctoral thesis in sociology before his groundbreaking work would be recognized by the scientific community at an international scientific meeting organized by UNESCO in 1974 (UNESCO 1980).

One of the few attempts to challenge this ideological dominance that is being paraded as goodwill was the development of the UNAIDS communication framework for HIV/AIDS (see chapter 11). As much as the framework has been lauded by scholars and practitioners for its ability to centralize the experience and knowledge production in these regions to guide future intervention efforts, support from UN agencies has been very limited. Indeed, with the exception of the eastern and southern African region of UNI F that has publicly endorsed the framework and uses it for its activities, no.ie of the eight UN agencies that are cosponsors of UNAIDS have promoted the use of the framework. The global affirmation it has received has been due to the promotion of the framework by organization such as the Panos Institute in London. As countries began to express interest in the implementation of the framework, it became evident that technical hegemony advanced through universal solutions by institutions like Johns Hopkins University with an established record of involvement in international development began a campaign to discredit the framework. At the invitation of UNAIDS and the Ghanaian government, I went to Accra in 2001 to begin the process of a country implementation plan. Before my arrival, an international staff from this country program office in Ghana began an underground campaign to discredit the framework. Even though Ghanaians were convinced that this university's program model was not effective and does not have the potential to be effective, and even though the UN-AIDS framework offers the hope and direction they have been seeking, their voices were silenced by the financial leverage that the university program offers to the few nationals who are hired and paid very well (relative to the salary of their counterparts in the country). The experience in Ghana was true of many countries in Africa. The problem has never been the absence of a culture-based solution. It has been one of the policies of Western hegemony implemented under the rubric of technical cooperation.

Another form of technical cooperation has been the policy of donor agencies, including major foundations in the United States, who have developed a program to focus on the exclusive training of lower and middle managers under the auspices of capacity building. In late 2002, I was to receive funding from a well-known family foundation in New York to implement the UNAIDS framework only if I were to focus on the capacity building of people in rural areas. I was to exclude any involvement of researchers from in-country universities. As much as this foundation/donor has been vocal about the importance of promoting communication for social change rather than focusing exclusively on individual behavior, its policy has also been to not strengthen capacity at the top level of scholarship or policy development. Heaven forbid that these Africans were to begin to develop their own knowledge or advance the knowledge they have developed. From institutional support in Kenya that intended on supporting only master's-level training (even though African scholars had recommended training at the doctoral level) to the insistence that capacity building was to take place at the lowest level of communication intervention, there is an ideology of supporting Africans only if they are willing to accept knowledge that has been developed in the United States for implementation in Africa. Any form of cooperation that is sought is predicated on the premise that Africans should be trained to function at the implementation level of intervention. Developing the theory and model for the planning and evaluation of the outcome to determine its fidelity to the theory is the domain of the West. The result is that many progressive organizations, such as the Panos Institute, have been working to promote the application of the UNAIDS framework with no support (as far as I am aware) from donor agencies—not even from foundations/donors that have either hosted or cosponsored several international forums just on this subject.

Given the limited resources and opportunities to produce knowledge in Africa, educators have resorted to "buying used knowledge" wholesale from the United States. Never has the feeling of being a good Samaritan been so commonplace as in this era of "book drives" for African universities. Indeed, the popularity of book drives as a way of supporting African universities is a disturbing form of technical cooperation/assistance in part because both Africans (at home and in the diaspora) and non-Africans equally promote it. The possibility that these books are the source of the intellectual marginalization is hardly ever questioned. This form of socially constructed placebo (Latin for "I will please") has been very pleasing to both donors and recipients even though these books have no sustainable health and development value. For many nongovernmental organizations (NGOs) that are asked by donors to provide matching funds as a form of eligibility for receiving a grant, the book and equipment drive (often old equipment) provide the double benefit of meeting eligibility requirements while at the same time enhancing their public relations image for the unsuspecting Africans as a good Samaritan organization. The fact that these books and equipment provide the foundation on which dependency is nurtured is never questioned. Ask a well-intentioned friend or a colleague why he or she is supporting such a retrogressive project, and you will get the response that something is better than nothing. It is acknowledged that the problem is not the absence of African scholars who can produce knowledge but the lack of resources and limited technology that discourage such scholarly enterprise. Looking within the country for solutions is not considered to be an option. A country like Nigeria, where newspapers and magazines were still producing knowledge and information under the most oppressive conditions, might have something to say about making something from nothing. The solution to producing knowledge may lie in familiar places. In fact, it is almost too familiar not to notice.

Could the ingenuity and knowledge production of newspaper and magazine publishers, such as TELL in Nigeria, that continued to maintain its publication schedule under guns and bullets constitute indigenous knowledge? If the absence of books in Nigeria were the reason that book drives have become a common feature of projects undertaken by Nigerians in the diaspora, why has no one sought the expertise of TELL and other dailies and weekly to understand how books could be produced in Nigeria so that the people's reality is the foundation of learning in Nigerian schools rather than the reality of others? One could even go as far as saying that the failure of the educational system in Nigeria has been due largely to the inability to prepare Nigerians for Nigerian reality but rather the reality of the countries from where the books are produced. If the humanities have made inroads in locating learning experiences in African reality through the work of Chinua Achebe, Mariama Ba, Ngugi wa Thiong'O, Wole Soyinka, Ben Okri, and others, the social and behavioral sciences and public health profession have not even begun. One area has been in the representation of what is often considered to be indigenous knowledge in health and medicine (see chapter 8). In the final analysis, we must understand communities for their possibilities rather than focusing solely on their limitations, as may be conveyed in a language of community diagnosis.

COMMUNITY DIAGNOSIS

Training institutions have conditioned learners to think of communities for what they lack rather than what assets they have and what potential they possess. This problem is more prominent in public health discourse whose professional code has been anchored in disease and medicine. Like cultural voyeurs, public health workers have learned to build relationships with communities only for the problem they see in communities but never for the potential that could be unearthed. They have learned to think of the community as one that needs the help of professionals but not one from which professionals can learn to strengthen their own values. This process may be evident in public health because of the focus on improving health and eliminating diseases, which are easily evident in their impact on society. However the problem of using crude categories to simplify an otherwise complex process is true of the many professionals, including those in the humanities from where I have advocated that public health draw experience. Wole Soyinka (1976) has been critical of literary production that fails to examine the context and the ideology that enriches or truncates a social vision. In *Myth, Literature, and the African World*, he writes:

> Thanks to the tendency of the modern consumer-mind to facilitate digestion by operating in strict categories what are essentially fluid operations of the creative mind upon social and natural phenomena, the formulation of a literary ideology tend to congeal sooner or later into instant capsules which, administered also to the writer, may end by asphyxiating the creative process. Such a methodology of assessment does not permit a non-prejudicial probing of the capsule itself, at least not by the literature which brings it into being or which it later brings into being. (61)

Similarly, in public health, the administration of capsules (theories and models) renders them neutral and acultural, thus leading to the evolution of a methodological process that produces terms like *community diagnoses*. Diagnose a community and one is likely to asphyxiate the positive community lifeline, thus resulting in failure to motivate an organic creative process in the community that can lead to fluid construction of the community reality—positive and negative. A major challenge in transforming the methodological approach to professional training in public health continues to be how to change professional language that has hitherto described "community" as a problem in need of solution. The term *community diagnosis*, a common curriculum dance for training public health students, represents the community as a diseased entity (Airhihenbuwa, Jack, and Webster 2004; Beech and Goodman 2004): one that cannot act but must be acted on by trained professionals. A language of "community assessment" offers opportunity for the professional and the community to collectively develop a fluid process that allows the community to be embraced from various perspectives so community itself affirms its assets (positives), showcases its unique identity (existential), and critiques its liabilities and shortcomings (negatives). This process of engaging the community in a fluid process will be discussed in chapter 12. In the context of addressing community strengths and weaknesses, we often have to interrogate ways of naming knowledge believed to be indigenous to the community.

INDIGENOUS KNOWLEDGE

When is knowledge considered to be indigenous? Is it when one thinks locally and acts globally? Does such knowledge cease to be indigenous when it is represented in a discourse of thinking globally and acting locally? The representation of African identity as one different from Western identity has been the focus of scholars committed to locating African ways of knowing within African cultural spaces and produced through African identity. Contributions include intellectual visionaries who were the forebears of modern African identity construction such as Kwame Nkrumah's (the first president of Ghana; 1970) philosophy of *consciencism*—Africans' value of community, collective action, mass participation, and involvement—and Julius Nyerere's (the former president of Tanzania) concept of *Ujamaa*—Kiswahili for the African value of the centrality of family and the shared sense of oneness. While recognizing the important and pivotal direction these leaders established for African identity, their critique, according to the analysis by Samuel Imbo (1998), believed that these philosophies were centrally located in socialism and other analytical frameworks outside Africa, albeit anchored in global appeals for the universal, rather than the African value of community and collective hard work that gave birth to these reasonings. The Negritude movement, the intellectual brainchild of Leopord Sedar Senghor (2001) of Senegal, Aimer Cesaire of Martinique, and George Gontran Damas of French Guiana, was another philosophical contribution designed to anchor African identity in African ways of knowing. Negritude is commonly represented as focusing almost exclusively on the emotional essence in African identity. Such perceived emphasis on emotion, critics were quick to point out, eschews the rational essence that is the feature of Western identity. In Senghor's response to these criticisms, he emphasizes that both emotion and rational thoughts coexist in African identity; however, emotion was never recognized in Western ideological construction. The primary criticism, however, has been an identity construction that is juxtaposed to Western identity and interpretable as a reaction to Western hegemony.

Rather, negritude is an analysis that considers African identity as the center such that other identities are incidental rather than the point of reference for constructing African identity. It is noteworthy that critics were as concerned about wanting to be thought of as not different from Western identity as supporters were determined to emphasize what separates Africans from Westerners. In the final analysis, the Western notion of identity has inscribed a problematic referent on the discourse on identity even as some scholars attempt to distance themselves from its hegemonic gaze as the identity referent. It is important to historicize these debates on African identity since such theorizing emerged out of a global political epoch, where identity construction and analysis could not be considered to be complete without some form of a response to the dominant Western gaze that sought to demonize African humanity from birth to death.

For Soyinka, therefore, African philosophy, theories, and methods for analyzing knowledge production must be located within African contexts and experience. Imbo (1998) offers a critical analysis on the debate around the definition of African philosophy. Of particular note is the Kenyan's philosopher Henry Odera Oruka's (1990) philosophical sagacity in which Oruka developed a philosophical classification of knowledge production in the African contexts, including nonliterate intellectuals. Imbo summarizes Oruka's philosophical sagacity by stating, "Philosophy is the exercise of subjecting one's cultural world to the standard of reason. Although philosophy is universal, African philosophy originates in African culture in the sense that historical and social realities of the continent provide the experiences upon which the sages and other philosophers theorize" (26).

The word *indigenous* often resonates with an unchanging location where ways of knowing may often be romanticized and maintain certain voyeuristic notions of innocence. The Ghanaian philosopher Kwasi Wiredu (1980) encourages knowledge production that could unearth the philosophical thinking embedded in oral traditions in Africa. African philosophical thinking ought not to be one of valorizing a nonscientific way of knowing but rather one in which the various models and logics of thought are presented. To juxtapose African ways of knowing against the Western tradition (often narrowly represented in scientific enterprises) is to accept a narrowly defined view of African thought often appropriated in the discourse on indigenous knowledge—a code for what some would consider to be an outmoded set of values and beliefs from the perspective of the West.

Indigenous knowledge can be discussed as a theoretical project as well as a cultural one. In the *Indigenous Theories of Contagious Disease*, Edward Green (1999) offers a powerful argument about the analytic framework that informs the ways in which healers in eastern and southern Africa organize their philosophical thinking around diseases. One example, is "pollution belief" as an explanatory category for contagion that is based on environmental dangers. Although *pollution* as an environmental term is shared with other cultures outside eastern and southern Africa, the use of the term *pollution* in this case actually represents the individual form of contagion for which purification may very well be the treatment. According to Green, "polluted persons are considered socially marginal, in part because they are in a dangerous state, one that could contaminate others within range" (66). Examples of a polluted person could be one who touches a dead body of a murderer.

Beyond the challenge of understanding the indigenous theory of diseases, it is even more crucial to question the understanding of healers regarding the language of conventional health. When a well-meaning healer claims that he or she can cure a disease such as AIDS, I often wonder whether the healer uses the term *cure* in the appropriation that is the convention in allopathic medicine. First, the reference to well intentioned is important in this case given the number of healers and physicians who claim to have cures for AIDS. The question at hand is whether the well-intentioned healer actually meant "treatment" when he or she said "cure." The era of chronic condition allows us to make a clear distinction between curable diseases—which means the disease is gone—and treatable disease—which means the signs and symbols may not be in evidence but the disease is still in the body, such as cancer and high blood pressure. The concept of treating a condition that does not impair one's daily functioning may be problematic for healers who deal with conditions that impairs and debilitate. After all, calling a condition a disease is more to affirm the normalcy of a coexistence of health and disease than the impairment of the body to respond to daily demands. In a context where there is no insurance company with which to contend about payment for maintaining certain health conditions, the language of cure and treatment may very well be fused together in the mind of a healer to mean the same outcome. The point here is not to excuse healers who knowingly claim to cure a disease for which there is no cure but to question whether treatment and cure have the same meaning for healers as they do for physicians. One factor that has shaped the practice of the healing modalities has been the nature and value of resources contributed to their healing practice.

INCOME AND WEALTH

M. L. Oliver and T. M. Shapiro (1997) define *income* as "flow of dollars (salaries, wages, and payments periodically received as returns from an occupation, investment, or government transfer, etc.) over a set period, typically one year." *Wealth* is defined as "the total extent, at a given moment, of an individual's accumulated assets and access to resources, and it refers to the net value of assets (e.g. ownership of stocks, money in the bank, real estate, business ownership, etc.) less debt held at one time" (30). For example, when one compares two individuals (one White and the other Black) who have the same income, occupation, and education, their generation level in middle-class status will determine the flow of their income. A first-generation middle-class person could expect to support kin who are probably mostly in the lower class, and this middle-class person will likely need to obtain a bank loan to purchase a house since there is likely to be little wealth to use even for a deposit for the loan. A third- or fourth-generation middle-class person (who has the same income, occupation, and education as the first-generation middle-class person) may not need the bank for a down payment on a new house since he or she may be able to get the money from his or her parents with no interest.

Michael Brown and his colleagues (2003) provide a comprehensive analysis of how one's legacy of accumulation or disaccumulation influences and dictates the directional flow of income to define wealth. This is even reinforced in the tax code in the United States, as outlined by Oliver and Shapiro: "The lower tax rates on capital gains and the deduction for home mortgages and real estate taxes, we argue, flow differentially to Blacks and Whites because of the fact that Blacks generally have fewer and different types of assets than Whites with similar income" (43). In accounting for the historical context of the present financial status of comparable individuals and groups, it makes a difference whether income or wealth is used in such a comparison.

It is generally agreed that one's level of economic power is associated with one's level of general well-being. This has been translated in social and behavioral science literature into SES that is often measured by income, occupation, and education even though these commonly used measures of SES do not account for all the differences in health outcome. The SES debate has often gone as far as to conclude that income, education, and occupation alone are enough to predict health outcomes in a population. It is further asserted that such prediction can be achieved independent of race or culture.

As I have argued in previous publications, the commonly used socioeconomic indicators of income, education, and occupation cannot capture the nature and range of disparity between Blacks and Whites in the United States. Indeed, it is the language of income as the most powerful indicator of disparity and what income represents that has led to low income as a language of disadvantage. Oliver and Shapiro (1997) offer a compelling analysis that shows that it is wealth and not income that allows us to understand the disparity between African American and White populations. According to their analysis, "Whites possess nearly twelve times as much median net worth as Blacks, or $43,800.00 versus $3,700.00. In even starker contrast, perhaps, the average white household controls $6,999.00 in net financial assets while the average Black household retains no net financial assets or nest egg whatsoever" (86). The lack of wealth is the result of accumulation of disadvantages, which is the theme of William Julius Wilson's 1978 book, *The Declining Significance of Race*. In other words, historical experience has a way of transferring liabilities and assets to generations that follow. For Whites, historical privilege leads to accumulation of privileges, whereas for African Americans, historical disadvantages lead to accumulation of disadvantages that cannot be captured by simply comparing the contemporary status of the two groups. While race or racism may be a difficult measure to explain the disadvantaged position of African Americans today, any analysis of the disadvantaged position of African Americans is incomplete without it being situated in the historical racism that is embedded more effectively at the institutional level than at the individual level (Brown et al. 2003).

The notion of accumulation of disadvantage to describe the worsening condition of African Americans locates their status within a historical context that examines how the present was preconditioned by the past. This analysis holds true for wealth. Looking at income only examines the present, but to historicize the present, one has to look at wealth. This is not unlike a study of the status of being disadvantaged in society. In the final analysis, we still use low income as opposed to low wealth as the measure of disparity in society. Such disparity in wealth status affects the location of neighborhood, options for schools for children, and future wealth for children, to name a few. On the issue of schools, the location of one's housing is a factor in the quality of health and quality of schooling for the family in the United States. U.S. school systems are funded through property taxes. If we take two individuals with the same income, education, and occupation but living in two separate neighborhoods, the school system in the neighborhood with the higher property value will have a higher-quality educational system because of its ability to attract the best teachers, since higher salaries can be offered from resources generated from their higher income tax–paying property owners. However, if we were to examine the difference between these two individuals with the same education, income, and occupation, their identity (race and culture) may be the only difference in their status and may have influenced their neighborhood location. Such analysis offers insights into the challenges of development interventions in a global context.

DEVELOPMENT AND GLOBALIZATION

Globalization, as a concept produced within the context of global changes, has tended to focus only on economic production, capital restructuring, and their attendant political implications, with little regard to its role in producing negative cultural changes in many societies. According to Thandika Mkadanwire (2005), it is not that Africa has not been involved in globalization, because it has been—and very heavily so. The problem remains the way in which globalization has led to retrogression in African economic growth through policies such as currency devaluation. Globalization, within health and human development constructs—like its predecessor, development—promises an acultural world, where an individual can be at home anywhere. Unfortunately, for people in Southern nations, who make up two-thirds of the world's population, globalization projects resonate with memories and experiences of themselves as "target groups" with all the disparities that consign them to be consumers and not producers. Development as an instrument of globalization in which Africans are being policed has resulted in many Africans, particularly those in the rural areas, feeling like strangers in their own home (Macamo 2005).

The ideology behind the concept of development has further reinforced Western hegemony by anchoring measures of "progress" on the values and principles of the West. It has been argued that development conceived of as a prepackaged formula that is only manufactured in Northern nations for application in African nations is an outmoded construct (Zeleza, 2003). After more than half a century of exposing the historically surbordinating apparatuses of the concept of development, a new concept is invoked that is equally disempowering since it promises to further marginalize the cultural expressions of Southern nations: globalization. Although globalization, as theorized from political, sociological, economic, environmental, geographic, and even historical perspectives, necessarily advances an inevitability of the new global era, its appropriation and deployment in the areas of health and human development as "a marker for progress" have become increasingly problematic.

Decades after the realization of the failure of development concept, and over a decade after the 1993 UNDP's *Human Development Report* called for the inclusion and emphasis of noneconomic indicators (e.g., food security and status of women) in measuring progress, the implementation of the development concept as informed by the dominant paradigm continues to flourish in African nations. Although the World Bank and the UNDP reports have questioned the validity of equating development/gross national product (GNP) with progress, they have still failed to centralize cultural production and meaning at the core of the measurement of progress.

Globalization has now been echoed and praised in popular discourse as the twenty-first-century language of universal truth. The life support of globalization rests on fulfilling the "needs" of the "wretched of the Earth" and the "faces at the bottom of the well." Like its predecessor, development, globalization is acultural and promises to further medicalize and psychologize, in the Western sense, human behavior such that non-Western cultures are further subordinated in their plights to assert their agencies and identities.

For many African countries, globalization, like development, has come to mean progress and growth in GNP, even though such an equation has been long rejected by those who initiated and promoted it, including the World Bank. Chinweizu and Jemie (1987) have argued that African development is not merely a matter of growth in GNP statistics; it is a matter of shaping certain cultural institutions, of creating and elevating critical consciousness in the African population, so that this consciousness can properly guide the production, distribution, and consumption of the items usually reflected in GNP figure. For Chinweizu and Jemie, the point about Nigerian development ment is not the supervisory transfer to Nigeria of American or European expertise but development based on Nigerian expertise by giving Nigerians the opportunity to try, fail, learn, and succeed. The myriad positive and progressive values and mores that enabled African countries to withstand the emotional, psychological, and physical violence of colonial as well as postcolonial oppression are being forsaken for what is believed to be the path to progress. Progress is believed to be a natural outgrowth of development and, more recently, globalization, which in turn is believed to be concomitant with modernization. Modernization and development are touted as the twin engines of progress to be deployed through globalization, even though the economic policies advanced by modernization have been incapable of addressing the transformation of the productive forces and productive relations that lead to progress. Modernization has been nothing more than an attempt at Westernization and ideological containment of African nations in the name of development. Many African scholars have observed that development in Africa does not mean modernization, particularly given the ways in which modernization has led to environmental decay in major cities. For example, pollution of the environment as a result of the "progress" of modernization and pollution of the body as a result of consumption of fast food due to "progress" in modernized food production continue to lead to increased morbidity and mortality, resulting in societal regression in conditions of living. This reality has become increasingly evident in assessments of the impacts and outcomes of numerous health and education programs intervention in both Northern and Southern nations.

INTERVENTION

The idea of intervening was meant to offer positive direction for people whose context has been disrupted naturally or by design. The notion of intervention has come to represent the injection of ideas into an environment where the inhabitants are often treated as though they have no mind of their own and are thought to be in need of ideas rather than resources. The approach of helping the needy has meant the elimination of humility and decency—two important qualities that often underscore successful intervention in the African context. As Cheikh Niang (1994, 1996) once cautioned, you must provide people, particularly leaders in the community, with the opportunity to save face. Community interventionists often behave as though saving face is a quality that should be reserved for themselves and their funding agencies but never for people in the community, since "experts" believe that community members have no ideas of their own—hence the presence of the expert in the community. It is the absence of humility and decency in public health interventions that often leads to the belief that Africans do not talk about sex because the Western discourse on learning dictates that learning takes place when the subject has verbalized what he or she learned.

To come to voice does not mean to be vocal. To have agency does not mean verbal declaration of one's power. Silence can be a very powerful declaration of voice and agency. What is important is to understand voice and agency as affirmation of one's humanity and decency. Senegal has been hailed (and rightly so) as the most successful country in the world in its strategy toward HIV and AIDS prevention and care. However, the reality that condoms are never mentioned on radio or television in Senegal, even though they are widely used, is never acknowledged. It is as though the situation in Senegal was simply incidental. Moreover, culture is not represented to have a role in the success in Senegal. Religion (specifically Islam, which is shared with many other countries without similar success) is represented as the primary reason (and sometimes the only) indicator for success. Even when sexuality is discussed in the African context, sensuality is never addressed. It is believed to be a foreign concept, one that will be too developmentally modern and progressive for the Africans. Yet many African cultures have and continue to engage in cultural practices of teaching young girls about eroticism and sensuality in relationships particularly in preparation for marriage. Since sensuality is often constructed as a modern Western cultural practice for which credit is never given to Africans, the focus of intervention is on the sexual acts or misbehaviors that produce diseases. Thus, interventions are mostly about sexual diseases or the deviance of sexuality. When sensuality is addressed in the African contexts, it is often not within the contexts of health and culture.

SENSUALITY AND SEXUALITY

It is generally assumed that Africans do not talk about or do not want to talk about sex. There is a major difference between talking about sex and talking about sex openly. A former minister of health from Zambia was quoted as saying that she cannot talk to young girls about sexuality. What is often misunderstood is the fact that Africans *do* talk about sex given the proper context and circumstances. The refusal to understand language elasticity about sexuality has led to this misunderstanding. The Dimba of Senegal discuss sex in the proper contexts. The Laobe nurture the production of eroticism in Senegalese culture to the point of educating young women about the production of sexual pleasure. Indeed, many African cultures address sexuality and eroticism within their gender space. The value of sensuality and behavior about sexuality is often the hallmark of rites of passage, particularly presented by older women for young girls. The process through which sex is discussed is totally gendered and cultural. An example is the use of beads in the African discourse on sexuality. The use of beads as an instrument and symbol of eroticism transcends many African cultures. It is so important that there is a cultural name for the particular bead a woman wears around her waist. In Senegal, it is called *ferr*. Among the Edos of Nigeria, it is called *akpolo*. There was a popular Edo song in the 1950s and 1960s that exalted the romantic essence of akpolo by encouraging the "old woman" to wear akpolo so that she might attract a man who could become her husband. Through the enhancement of the erotic essence of waist bead with a traditional perfume (the *thuray* or *curaay* in Wolof), the Senegalese have further centralized and to some extent mystified the significance of the waist bead in sensuality and eroticism. Indeed, certain practices are believed to have been driven underground. In some instances, these practices continued within the cultural context within which they were always practiced. What is different is that some African modern state apparatus denied legitimacy to these practices in the modern westernized public spaces until they were later found to be relevant to improving the general well-being of the people.

FINAL THOUGHTS

We should not analyze African cultural logics and thoughts based on non-African linguistic codes. Beyond the limits of using Western cultural logic to explain African cultural productions, we must understand the problem of cultural dominance often hidden in the language of health intervention. These hidden languages and codes are responsible for the negative outcomes and conclusions reached in many health interventions. Although some of these interventionists may mean well and be sincere in their commitments to African issues, the use of language that has become central to their intervention efforts often will betray such commitment and dedication. The language of social and behavioral sciences and public health interventions must be transformed to effectively respond to the values of Africans in communicating about health behavior.

4

Ethics and the Politics of Professionalism

Human rights activism likes to portray itself as an anti-politics. . . . In practice, impartiality and neutrality are just as impossible as universal and
equal concern for everyone's human rights.

—Michael Ignatieff (2001:9)

The challenge facing the human rights paradigm . . . is how to ensure that
people enjoy the same rights within their communities, while respecting
the cultural autonomy of those communities.

—Abdullahi A. An-Na'im (2002:1)

Like some human right activists, many social and behavioral scientists like
to believe that any true scientific and intellectual project is neutral and im-
partial to politics. Individuating knowledge and the resulting behavior are
represented as neutral process that are never shaped or influenced by the social political contexts. That a funding priority of government, such as bioter-
rorism, influences the scientific priority of social scientists is quietly accepted
as incidental to the research topics and choices made by scholars. Like the
chameleon that blends effortlessly with its environment, believing that it is
the environment that changes to accommodate him, the social scientist has
mastered the skill of a polemical disconnection from historical-political
events that have shaped and continue to shape his or her intellectual landscape. In social science research, focusing on behavior is privileged over a focus on the contexts of behavior and hence the predominance of research is on
behavior compared to research on social contexts of behavior. In an editorial
of the *CODESRIA* (Council for the Development of Social Science Research
in Africa) *Bulletin*, Adebayo Olukoshi and Francis Nyamnjoh (2003) express

concern over the ways in which HIV and AIDS research that focuses on health behavior, particularly in Africa, "has been tilted excessively in favor of narrowly conceived and articulated behavioral change issues" (1). Their concern resonates with that of many African social science scholars addressing African health issues in the way in which the exclusive focuses on behavior "sometimes obscure as much as they reveal" (1), thereby leading to conclusions that deflect attention away from the critical contextual and political economic questions that must be the focus of scholarship on health behavior.

Joseph Ki-Zerbo (2005) has argued that no discipline can claim to produce meaningful scientific results without taking into account the inter-African dimensions. The reality is that social science is political and partial to the ideology that nurtures the context of its intellectual project. That this is so does not weaken its epistemological location in the academy. But the realization of the role of politics is important to the meaning of professionalism in social science. In health education in the United States, some scholars do recognize and address the political aspects of research and practice by employing multilevel analysis in their work. They operationalize their work in social ecological and cultural approaches to health intervention. They are, however, in the minority compared with the majority of their colleagues whose training and practice are firmly anchored in individual health behavioral outcomes. In the United States, these scholars' work includes Kathleen Roe's approach to community-based intervention with multicultural populations; Meredith Minkler's approach to social change in the community; Nina Wallenstein and Bonnie Duran's application of Freire's notion of raising critical consciousness, particularly in projects that focus on Native American Indian populations; Leandris Liburd's approach to context-based analysis of diabetes rather than one narrowly focused on symptomatology; Lawrence W. Green and Marshall Kreuter's advancement of the PRECEDE/PROCEDE framework and its ecological implications; Robert Goodman's combining process evaluation with community-based participatory action research; Eugenia Eng's advancing the lay health adviser approach; and Kenneth McLeroy's ecological approach to analyzing the problems rather than beginning with a theory. Others' work has focused on social cultural analysis of health among people of African descent. They include Thomas Laveist's interrogation of the question of race in approaches to eliminating health disparities; Lee Green's analysis of historical events like the Tuskegee syphilis study to inform health actions of African Americans; and emerging scholars and practitioners like DeWitt Webster's work with community members as their own change agents, Titi Okoror's research on how one successfully engaged the so-called hard-to-reach African American population in addressing HIV and AIDS issues, Stella Nyanzi's research on the role of tradition and healing in Africa, Aranthan Jones's addressing the role of policy and politics in health disparity, Lenora Johnson's focus on health practices that informs theorizing of research, and Titi Okoror's focus on successful research strategies to ensure African American participation in HIV testing. They all represent different levels of engagement with community in the health education profession. Beyond health education, health communication scholars like Mohan Dutta-Bergman invite a culture-centered approach to interrogating and framing strategies to achieving equity in global health using experiences from India as a point of departure. Others, like Shiriki Kumanyika and Vanessa N. Gamble, have extended our understanding of the importance of the social context in individual actions. In fact, some scholars hyphenate their traditional discipline with the term *social* to signify their commitment to the social even as they operate within their disciplinary epistem. Examples include social demography and social epidemiology. These scholars have helped to focus our attention on questions surrounding the politics of identity that is inscribed in the crisis of global public health.

Professionalism is one of the outcomes of higher education/training that is differentially shaped according to one's disciplinary orientation. Professionalism operates within social political reality. There seems to be a willingness to acknowledge the influence of politics and partiality in professionalism insofar as they relate to the practice of the profession. For Stuart Hall (1991), to try to expunge politics out of professional practice (as opposed to the theoretical aspects) is a form of what he refers to as "an arbitrary closure." Hall wonders how a practice can hope to make a difference in the world without a political stake for such difference. The American Medical Association's special interest lobby is reported to be one of the most visible and influential in American legislative cycles. However, the training process that leads to professionalism is designed to have the appearance of being neutral to politics and partiality. In other words, a social psychological theory may be represented as apolitical and acultural in its abstract articulation; however, the application of such theory for behavior may be acknowledged to be influenced by politics. I argue that both the development of the theory, its location (central or margin) in the academy, and the language that exalts or silences it is very political, partial, and cultural. A common code used to disguise the political and cultural shell of a theory or model is the language of objectivity as juxtaposed with subjectivity.

Objectivity as an academic dogma of cultural and political neutrality is a site of debate in community and public health discourses. John McKinlay and Lisa Marceau (2000) argue that the very insistence that public health discourse is objective is in itself very subjective. The subjectivity in a seemingly objective way of knowing does not render it irrelevant (albeit perhaps limited in its utility in every context) but rather offers an opportunity to acknowledge the cultural space from which its subjectivity has meaning and the possibilities it offers for other spaces. While the academy prides itself in policing policymakers to ensure that what is preached is consistent with what is practiced, the same policing appears to be missing in the academy. Thandika Mkandawire (2004), one of the foremost African political economists, admonished African economists for not policing themselves as do others through economic policies and recommendations for governments. Several public health and communication scholars agree that the theories and models that are commonly believed to be the foundation on which intervention programs must be based are flawed and inadequate to improve health conditions, particularly among people of African descent (more on this in part 3).

I would argue that an interventionist or a funding agency that knows that changing individual behaviors is a flawed approach but continues to promote it is violating professionalism, ethics, and human rights. One reason that knowledge of the limitations and/or inadequacy of theory does not lead to practice is the fear of being on the margin of donors' political and cultural interests. Indeed, some funding agencies are now concerned with what they consider to be a "funder-induced pathology." This refers partly to the consistent tilting of the funding scale toward medical intervention at the cellular level at the expense of a community-based participatory approach to health promotion and disease prevention. Funder-induced pathology also refers to researchers' worshipping of funders' priorities even when they (researchers) do not agree with these priorities. It should be recognized, however, that a person's freedom to choose to challenge the traditional funding norm often comes with a price of possibly not being funded for one's research. It could also mean not having one's article accepted for publication in mainstream journals or even having one's book published by mainstream (within the profession) publishers. Thus, the politics of professionalism must extend the debate around a global cultural representation both at the level of funding and the level of professional practice in the academy. One of the terrains of this debate is around the focus on individuality for which much professional capital is invested as opposed to a community/group-based approach, which is proven to be more relevant in improving the health of the disadvantaged population in health disparity.

INDIVIDUAL VERSUS GROUP RIGHTS

The debate around issues of the absence of a global cultural representation in the development of the UN Human Rights covenants remains a sensitive issue in human rights discourse. At issue have always been how to balance the rights of the individual with the rights of the group and whose rights come first. Individuals representing cultures that promoted group rights were, at times, individuals who were schooled to reject group rights even when their culture of origin, which they were to represent, believes in group rights over individual rights. This was clearly the case, according to Abdullahi Ahmed An-Na'im, with Chang Peng-Chung representing China (Taiwan) and Charles Habib Malik representing Lebanon, the only two non-Westerners who participated in the UN debate on the 1948 Declaration of Human Rights. The issue of representation has always been problematic given that the views advanced by each representative were shaped by their Westernized experiences. For representatives from non-Western regions such as Africa, promoting individual rights over group rights would be contrary to the collective sense of identity that is promoted within their communal cultures. Of the fifty-one original members of the United Nations, only three countries represented Africa: Ethiopia, Egypt, and Liberia. Of the eight countries represented in the drafting committee of the Universal Declaration of Human Right in 1948 (Australia, Chile, China, France, Lebanon, the U.K., the United States, and the Soviet Union), no African country was represented. It was the case that African cultural mores and history were not central to the development of global rights as they were designed by the colonizers and are still maintained today. Such absence of African values may not suggest that human rights instruments and covenants are wrong, but it does suggest that we contextualize the application of the instruments in African countries.

The tension between individual versus group as the point of departure in public health interventions operates through the prisms of theories and models that are advanced to explain health behaviors and how to change them for improved health outcomes. Public health professionals have become proficient at bemoaning the limitation of these theories and models while continuing to initiate research investigations that are anchored in them or their constructs. Calls abound for the need to focus on root causes of health problems rather than on their behavioral attributes that center narrowly on individual risk factors and individual behavior changes. Central to this contradiction between what is believed to be effective for the people and what is actually practiced is a violation of professional ethics and the human rights of those on whom ineffective approaches are imposed, particularly in communities of people of African descent.

As AIDS continues to ravage countries and destroy lives, issues of institutional responsibility have become apparent. Examining the concept of institutional behavior change has gained increased attention as more scholars document the roles of policy in promoting or impeding effective strategies to

HIV and AIDS prevention and treatment. Institutional behavior change must be based on institutional trustworthiness. Closely tied to the question of trustworthiness is the question of professional behavior change. To the extent that the strategy for effecting a change needs to be changed, professionals and scholars would need to change their professional behavior if they are to become effective in promoting the new strategy for change. An example of professional behavior change is a careful examination of relations of power in the discourse on White privilege. For example, Laura Garrett in both *The Coming Plague* (1994) and *Betrayer of Trust* (2000) does a superb job in recounting the history of disease investigation and the deservedly s/heroism of Western epidemiologists, nuns, and lab assistants engaged in improving health of the population under conditions of uncertainty. However, any contribution that was made at the local or country level was visibly absent. There are ways in which professionals report on diseases in Africa that leave the reader with the impression that the Africans did nothing but sat and waited for help from the West. In *The Coming Plague*, Lassa fever is reported as an endemic disease, but the fact that it may be treated, even if with only a limited outcome—in Sierra Leone, perhaps with herbal remedies—is not addressed. At the height of the child survival revolution, a homemade salt and sugar solution used by people in the African communities was found to be most effective and to have a better chance for sustainability. However, the sale of oral rehydration sachets was often promoted as a measure of program effectiveness. These sachets were mostly manufactured in the West (some built factories in African countries to manufacture them) for sale and distribution in African and other countries. The resulting dependence meant that several programs failed because they could not be sustained. The coming of the sachets was often promoted more than the use of the homemade solution. The latter was also sustainable.

Thus, most reports of success are still credited to Western discoveries, a factor that has been used as an excuse to maintain secrecy by those who claim falsely to have cures for AIDS. Since knowledge production in Africa is almost never recognized, some practitioners (physicians and traditional healers) claim that their ideas are likely to be stolen if revealed. Instead of exploring the potential in traditional healing for this dreaded condition, we get reports of physicians and healers who claim to have cures or those who frightened their clients into believing that there is nothing to be done for people living with HIV because they are practically dead. In all these debates, a central issue is the question of the most appropriate professional training that would prepare the future generation to adequately address the gulf between health crisis and the solutions that must be anchored in cultural identity. Unfortunately, most of the professions, including social work and health education, that trained people in health to address root causes of health problems are systematically being downsized, and their programs have been phased out in many universities.

ETHICS OF TRANSLATING SCIENTIFIC MESSAGES TO THE PUBLIC

There is a problem of professional indifference to concern that research might lead to negative preventive public health behavior. This is a major ethical problem in public health. The issue of the comparative risk of smokeless tobacco and smoking is a case in point. In an attempt to discourage smokers from switching to smokeless tobacco use, the U.S. Centers for Disease Control (CDC) had a message on its website (revised in 2002) that claims that smokeless tobacco is not safer than cigarettes. This message was challenged as deceptive, misleading, and unethically presenting research data that show otherwise (Kozlowski & O'Connor, 2003). However, the issue is less of the CDC scientists not being aware of the misrepresentation of their information and more of their fear that staying true to science, in this case, could lead smokers to switch to smokeless tobacco rather than staying away from tobacco use altogether. The issue for debate surrounds profe onal ethics and accuracy in translating scientific information into public ealth messages. The concern for CDC and public health agencies is public interpretation of messages and the resulting potential negative preventive health behavior.

A similar issue about professional ethics and the fear of message interpretation has led to questions about the acceptability of the published HIV/AIDS study result by the Nelson Mandela Foundation and the Human Science Research Council in South Africa mentioned earlier. Under the leadership of Olive Shisana, this first "Population Based HIV/AIDS Sero-Prevalence and Mass Media Impact Survey in South Africa" was conducted in 2002 and repeated in 2005 (Shisana et al. 2005). The results of this study, which include HIV tests of participants, show that HIV rate in South Africa is 11 percent compared with 16 percent, estimated using mathematical modeling based on HIV/AIDS rates among women who visit antenatal clinics. As in almost all African countries, what we know about the rate of HIV/AIDS in these countries is based on antenatal clinic projection. It is very surprising that sampling a national population and actually going to people's homes to collect information and conduct HIV test nationally has never been done until Shisana undertook this project. Those who have invested their professional careers in disease projection have been questioning the methodological accuracy of this new study primarily because it reports a seroprevalence that is less than what they had projected.

What is even more astounding is that scholars who have no clue about how antenatal clinic projections are calculated but have consented to its believed accuracy are questioning the accuracy of a more logical and rational population-based study. In fact, those invested in disease projection for Africa have become very emotional in defense of their long-established method even though it is least understood by scientists and the public. It would appear that the controversy is more about whether it makes sense to believe what household people tell us (as it is done in the United States and other industrial nations) and what their HIV tests reveal than what has been projected from a sample of pregnant women in the clinic. However, the central ethical issue is this: some public health professionals are afraid that if the seroprevalence rate is actually as low as this study reports, then the public might become too complacent to engage in positive health behavior because they would assume that the problem is not as serious as once thought. Moreover, policy-makers might consider a budget reduction for HIV/AIDS given the new lower reported rate.

Once again, we use the argument of questionable scientific accuracy to mask concern over public interpretation of messages and a resulting believed potential negative behavior. In short, we ignore science on the basis of how scientific results might alter public behavior, thus producing a different form of professional suspicion and conspiracy. This should clearly be a concern for future training in public health and, indeed, for higher education.

Scholars and educators commonly believe that the future of higher education will focus on issues of legitimation of identities (domestic and international) in our multicultural world. They also believe in environmental and ecological frugality in our personal, economic, and political spaces. This leads to a conviction that we must rupture traditional disciplinary walls to promote multidisciplinary and transdisciplinary approaches to producing knowledge, valuing acquisition of knowledge over the acquisition of material resources. Knowledge will be increasingly potentiated by technology as the primary tool for generating, exchanging, and controlling information. When the outcome is positive, it could result in learning that is emancipatory and empowering whereby individuals are able to successfully navigate their sociopolitical contexts in ways that would otherwise have been impossible. Applied negatively, technology can become a knowledge tool that is used to control and in some instances subordinate and disempower some individuals and groups. Technology, however, is now a mainstay in our training process.

A major component of population-based education is distance education, which has a model for implementation quite different from campus-based learning. Distance education has gained the interest of many traditional academic programs. Unfortunately, much of distance learning now focuses on use of the Internet and video teleconferencing as a method of teaching and learning. Very little attention is paid to the way in which video teleconferencing, despite its highly positive potential, could actually compromise the demonstrated effectiveness of person-to-person and small-group process needed to adequately debate and collectively develop solutions to transforming the contexts that create and nurture vulnerability to diseases. The area that suffers the most is knowledge production that is quantitative by design.

The battle over what is considered to be outstanding scholarship that is worthy of recognition in the academy is particularly fierce in the dualism of quantitative versus qualitative ways of knowing. Although those who embrace qualitative methods see the complementarity of both methods of inquiry, quite often those with a quantitative mindset deride those with a qualitative orientation. When recognition is given for qualitative work, it is usually for being a part of or a precursor to the development of an associated quantitative methodology. Unmoved by the apparent failure of the exclusive reliance on quantitative methods to provide meaningful solutions to the myriad of global health problems (e.g., the failure of the millions of dollars spent on quantitative research to have a meaningful human impact on smoking cessation and/or failure to initiate smoking), the leading advocates of quantitative methods are continuing to inscribe and reinscribe their perceived dominance of cells (i.e., genetics, biology) over society (i.e., cultural and environmental/ecological contexts) in the academy. It is this war of paradigm where the academy does not favor the coexistence and simultaneous validation of different ways of knowing that has in part devalued the practical component of academic training. Yet the limited role of practice in public health training is one of the concerns schools of public health are asked to address in the Institute of Medicine's (2003) report entitled "Who Will Keep the Public Healthy? Educating Public Health Professionals for the 21st Century."

DEFINING IMPACT AND EXCELLENCE

The newest form of academic reproduction of its dominant tradition, which privileges quantitative over qualitative methodology, for example, is the introduction of what is being referred to as the "impact factor" in scholarly contributions. The impact factor supposedly measures the impact that a scholar's contribution has had in his or her professional field by enumerating the frequency of references to a particular publication, on the one hand, and the ranking of the journal based on certain criteria for hierarchical value and importance, on the other. An attempt to understand the impact of a scholar in his or her profession is important. However, basing such an impact on the factor of frequency of references and/or publication in celebrated traditional journals is problematic. For example, the celebrated traditional journals in social and behavioral science, although they continue to offer important contributions to knowledge production, are the same journals that have excluded new ways of knowledge production about other cultures in the academy, thereby leading to the establishment of many journals that now give voice to those who were disenfranchised. The current formula for determining the impact of a professional journal privileges scholars who are making contributions in traditional fields, particularly those that address conventional research agenda.

When I first started writing about the centrality of culture in health behavior in the early 1980s, none of the traditional, mainstream journals were receptive to the idea of culture as important in health outcomes. What these journals were interested in was representation of a culture in which the research participants were seen as exotic Others, whose health problems (life) were represented through the researcher's own voyeuristic gaze. In fact, most of my colleagues, within and outside the academy, were at best indifferent to the notion of culture and health. Most of them dismissed it. One reason often advanced for the refusal of culture in health behavior is its implication in the politics of identity. Derrick Bell (1992) notes that in the United States, ethnic minority educators whose research is focused on the political subtext of their scholarship are often dismissed as having introduced ideological concerns into scholarship leading to a selection process that favors minorities who reject or minimize their identity. Francis Nyamnjoh (2005) concludes that given the high rejection rate for African scholarship in Western scholarly publications, African scholars have had to chose between compromising the theoretical relevance of their intellectual enquiry or seeking, creating, and sustaining alternative outlets that will offer them the intellectual space to engage and be engaged for their scholarship to advance the diverse expectations and aspirations of Africans. Today, several institutes and centers of the U.S. National Institutes of Health are supporting research projects on culture and health even though questions remain as to the true commitment of some. The journals that provided an opportunity for the initial introduction of health and culture were journals that would not be ranked very high for impact factor using the current formula. Yet, were it not for these journals, many scholars who insisted that culture and politics must be engaged in public health scholarship would never have had the opportunity to grow and mature their ideas before eventually using the celebrated journals as outlets for their research publications.

Several professional journals that focus on a particular marginalized population have and continued to play these critical roles. The *Western Journal of Black Studies* is an important example of a journal that has provided scholarly space for important new ideas to come to voice where they can be critiqued and their contributors can then have the opportunity to mature these ideas. *AIDS Education and Prevention* is a better-known journal today than it was in 1989 when it first published my cultural model—PEN-3 (discussed in chapter 12). *Ethnicity and Disease* went into hiatus for some several months not for lack of significant contributions but for lack of funding that would have allowed it to continue uninterrupted. In 1995, its editorial board had to send some manuscripts (one of them ours) that it had accepted for publication to another journal in Europe for publication. As important as *Ethnicity and Disease* has been to advancing the science of public health and to offering important insights into ways to eliminate health disparities, the decision of the editorial board to go beyond the American shores in search of other credible and culture-sensitive outlets echoes the politics of identity inscribed in the crisis of global health—even more so since the editorial team were seasoned scholars who are members of the editorial boards in celebrated public health journals. A journal is only as influential, in identity discourse, as the resources it has to promote its vision and the degree to which the social context nurtures the identity consciousness of its editorial team and reviewers. *Ethnicity and Disease*, the *Western Journal of Black Studies*, and a host of others exemplify a declaration of the lack of confidence in celebrated conventional journals to adequately and/or accurately represent scholarship that has the highest impact factor for African Americans and other marginalized groups. Yet, it is these groups that the U.S. public health goal of eliminating health disparity was meant to benefit by removing excess disease and death burdens.

In the final analysis, many of the celebrated journals are complicit in the violation of professional ethics addressed in this chapter because it is these journals that continue to promote and nurture the imposition of flawed theories on African and African American communities. The impact factor has focused on accumulation of privileges for certain scholars rather than an examination of the institutional biases that privileges certain scholarship at the expense of others. These institutional biases continue to influence how the question of race is addressed in public health.

Camara Jones (2000) offers an analysis of the context of privilege and how instead of examining the institution and ideological of race-centered discourse, we often seek ways to feel sorry for those who must shoulder the burden of having been marginalized. Jones uses an allegory of a gardener to establish three levels of racism: institutionalized, personalized, and internalized. The allegory is about a gardener who had two flower boxes. One of the boxes had a rich soil, whereas the other box had a poor soil. The gardener planted the red flowers in the rich soil and the pink flowers in the poor soil. A contextual examination should show that the outcome is predictable because the red flower will blossom whereas the pink flower will struggle. However, generations later, the flowers themselves, which either were not taught about their history or were taught but rejected the lesson of their history and started to believe the history of the offspring of the other box, began to exhibit behavioral manifestations that reflect their accumulation of privileges or accumulation of disadvantages. The institutionalized racism manifests at the level of the context of the differential status of the soil in which their future was established. However, social and behavioral science will focus on the personally mediated racism in which the flowers all believe that individual rational volition determines their future, and faith and history and experience have very little value in current health status and behavior. Indeed, this view will become well established in society as deployed through the academy. It could become so naturalized that the pink flowers may begin to question their own worth and value. They would do this not in any directly self-deprecating manner but in actually believing the red flowers do offer a more secure future than pink flowers, and they begin to encourage bees to bring some of the red seed from red flowers to pollinate their pink flowers for a future they believe would be better for pink's progeny—internalized racism. Those pink flowers that point out the differential historical richness of the soil are quickly told by the red flowers, and some of pink flowers, that they should stop complaining because a rose is a rose regardless of the color. Indeed, the journals have gained maturity and domination by red flowers with their accumulation of privileges even though such privileges are believed to be earned on merit. Some pink flowers may begin to establish their own spaces to examine the context of the flower boxes and their relations to current conditions not simply to complain but to provide effective strategies for eliminating the differences that create the disparities in their comparable conditions. This may result in establishing journals such as *Phylon* and *Ethnicity and Disease*, to name two.

The rest is, of course, history. Ordinarily, this story is often told within a discourse on race and identity (see chapter 5). I present the story to raise the most important question of Jones's (2000) allegory: who is (not was) the gardener?

FINAL THOUGHTS

Professionalism should reflect the ability to connect history, politics, and public health such that the connection should enable us to interrogate theories and models that are used to guide the implementation of health projects. A critique of one's profession and one's theoretical and methodological tools allows one to actively call for a transformation of the terrain and parameters of scholarly inquiries in one's own field. In the final analysis, professionalism rests on the ethical principles of being able to reconcile the identity of the population that has a problem with the theory and models advanced to frame solutions.

We are at a philosophical and practical crossroads in public health and health education/promotion. In 2005, as the president of the Society for Public Health Education (SOPHE), I launched an inaugural summit to eliminate racial and ethnic health disparities in the United States. The goal was a reexamination of health education's professional future to frame a research agenda for the profession. A key recommendation at the end of the summit was an unequivocal focus on social cultural contexts of health rather than focusing only on diseases. This means a focus on the historical, political, and racial forces that create and maintain vulnerability to diseases rather than the diseases themselves.

5

Ethnicity and Race

A New Double Consciousness?

I wonder sometimes whether school inspectors and government functionaries are aware of the role they play in the colonies. For twenty years they poured every effort into programs that would make the Negro a white man. In the end, they dropped him and told him, "You have an indisputable complex of dependence on the White man."

—Fanon (1958:216)

In analyzing the casualties of colonization that consign Africans to being the wretched of the earth, Fanon (1958) exposed the colonizers' educational agenda as the classical project of blaming the victim. Using the example in this quote to illustrate the flaws in the social science approach to behavioral health particularly among African Americans, one could conclude that training institutions have spent resources in trying to convince the African American child that his or her behavior in general, and health in particular, is based solely on his or her individuality. With persistent disparities in health outcomes, these same academic and political institutions have started to dump these children while accusing them of too much dependency on government and health professionals for their personal survival. It is on this premise that I address the debate on whether race or ethnicity should be the identity marker for health status.

I want to state at the outset that it is not a question of race or ethnicity. It is as much the issue of race as it is the issue of ethnicity played out in the politics of cultural identity. In the United States, race allows us to define the problem within a historical context, whereas ethnicity provides us with the cultural identity framework for affirming meanings of positive health and generating solutions to health problems. Defining the problem under the prism of race also allows us to disentangle historical experiences that are conveniently labeled as cultural because of their negative appropriation. For example, slavery is not a part of African American culture but a part of the African American experience born of the history of American and European racism. Such racism may no longer exist in its seismic destruction, but its periodic tremors and accumulation of developmental sediments have generations of its victims' offspring in social quicksand that manifests in developmental unevenness such as health disparities between African Americans and Whites. Institutional responses to health disparity and health inequity have tended to focus on pulling survivors out of desperate situations by focusing on clinical interventions to prevent death with little attention to the historical experience that created and continues to nurture the social contexts that promote vulnerability. Some efforts at institutional response have tended to focus on whether the relatively poorer health of African Americans can be blamed on environment. Such thinking has given rise to episodic interventions to offer remedial curriculum and programs in schools and communities.

For many years, violence was constructed as part of the Black experience, particularly if one lived in the inner city. Scientists and educators started to develop a research agenda to examine what they considered to be the genetic basis of violence in the Black community. The rate of violence is considered a public health problem because of its comparatively higher numbers among African Americans compared with those of the White population. What is curious about this reasoning and the attendant research enterprise it produced is that on a global level, violence among White American males is comparatively higher than the rates in Canada, Britain, or Sweden. Yet, no similar research project has been proposed to examine what might be considered to be the American White males' genetic predisposition to violence compared with White males in Canada, Britain, or Sweden. The politics of race, a fact that is often unacknowledged in behavioral research, meant that Blacks are constructed to have an innate problem with violence by virtue of their race (however scientifically inaccurate racial categorization may be) rather than violence as an environmental and systemic production whose victims in the United States happens to be predominantly people of African descent in America.

Indeed, the debate about whether to reject race and replace it with ethnicity has been circumscribed by the "all or nothing" epistemology of the academy, particularly in the United States. The issue is not whether it should be one or the other but recognizing that they both have roles to play. What is often ignored is that race, as an identity, was never concerned with solutions but rather focused on defining Blacks as "the problem." It is for this reason that W. E. B. DuBois (1903) posed the question "How does it feel to be a problem?"

The use of ethnicity or culture is not about defining the problem as Black or White but rather about examining the past and present contexts so that effective strategies for solutions could be developed, with a focus on solutions that are derived from within the group. Race may be used to categorize; it is not adequate for developing an intervention because its historical, legal, and social appropriation was designed to diagnose rather than heal. Ethnicity and culture may be used for categorization, but their most important function in public health intervention may very well be in healing our differences. Ethnicity and culture offer an opportunity to develop health strategies in ways that those for whom interventions are intended to benefit are able to articulate "who they are" rather than how they are defined.

The politics of identity debate in social science research around the question of race or ethnicity suffers, unfortunately, from the problem of attempting to challenge notions of universality while still under its influence. Indeed, the convention of reinscribing race in the public health professional imagination as the identity that matters remains very strong, even though institutional roles in representing race as the only identity that matters in conventional scholarship are often muted, frequently resulting in underestimating the role of institutions to effect change. The debate of race versus ethnicity is often engaged within the context of its value for social science as if social and behavioral sciences and their values are not products of crisis of health and the politics of identity. In fact, it begs the question, Is race and ethnicity/culture the new production of double consciousness?

Tommy Lott (2001) uses an anthropological analysis to reexamine the biological bases of DuBois's definition of race in his speech "The Conservation of Races." For Lott, the definition of race was anchored in biological sciences as a pragmatic project designed to challenge the basis for this definition given the broader political implications of "vindicating Black people and their cultural heritage" (59). For DuBois, to the extent that racism was the effect of race, the issue was never one of exclusive marker of identity on biological ground but one of acknowledging the prevailing definition, while engaging in a scientific and political project to challenge the racist and unscientific notion of such definition. For Lucius Outlaw (1996), Du Bois's conservation of races was a political project. In analyzing Anthony Appiah's criticism of Du Bois's speech as a biological essentialism, Outlaw, like Lott, makes a compelling argument that DuBois's definition of race was a political project. Beyond the tendency to fossilize DuBois's thinking at the time, it was also the case, as Bernard Bell (1996) notes, that "The Conservation of Races" was a speech delivered during a historical period when the biologization of identity was at the height of usage, on the one hand, and racialized politics sought to separate and marginalize Blacks, on the other. For Bell, DuBois's speech must be situated in the historical and political debates of the time. For example, two major historical events occurred in the two years leading to DuBois's speech in March 1897. The first was the Booker T. Washington's Atlanta Cotton Exposition speech in 1895, in which Washington advocated for separate-but-equal status between Blacks and Whites in the United States. The second event was the nefarious 1896 Supreme Court decision *Plessy v. Ferguson*, which supported separate-but-equal between Blacks and Whites. For Bell, DuBois's definition of race could not be reduced to a belief that African American identity should be based only on biological determinism. DuBois's definition of race was social, cultural, and above all political. Indeed the tension between the DuBois school of thought and the Washington school of thought is the debate between existential and conceptual principle that were challenged by DuBois, on the one hand, and the acceptance of the methodological principle that was championed by Washington, on the other.

RACE AND THE HEALTH PROBLEM

Race is often never thought of as an identity marker but only as a problem. Indeed, the desire to expunge race from identity discourses is due primarily to the ways in which race was used historically to demonize Blackness because race was constructed to mean Blackness and all that was considered to be wrong in America. Under such demonization, a subtext of racism has remained within the definition of race. An understanding of race is critical to contextualizing the many variants of racism that manifest in the United States today.

The criminalization of the Black body is one example of this variant. From Rodney King (an African American) being wrongfully attacked and beaten by White police officers to Susan Smith (a White woman) knowingly accusing a Black man of the murder she herself committed when she killed her two sons, the criminalization of the Black body has become one variant of what Michael Eric Dyson (1995) refers to as racial mystification. The different transformations that racism assume have led to recoding race in American society. Another variant of racism manifest in academic research has been evident in certain research enterprises designed to bridge the health disparity gap between Black and White. For example, as was indicated earlier, race is justified in conducting studies to examine a hypothesized genetic predisposition of Blacks to violence compared with White Americans without a comparable study that might examine the predisposition of White American men (if violence is indeed believed to be the result of of gene) to violence compared to White British or Canadian men. The subtext in these studies is less of the need to address disparity in health outcomes but more of a scientifically sanctioned political and social project that criminalizes the Black body because of a believed genetic deviation from the norm (read: the White body). It is under this racial subtext that Richard Hernstein and Charles Murray's (1994) bell curve was constructed. Indeed, whiteness as a racial identity, and as a believed dominant identity, has slowly become less favorable as an identifier than Caucasian has become for some. *Caucasian* is seen more to be descriptive and less hegemonic in its identity representation than *White*. Where *White* is power and domination, *Caucasian* is race and classification, a more palatable marker than *White*.

There is not a clearer representation of the notion of double consciousness advanced by DuBois than in the debate around the use of race and/or ethnicity in public health and social science research. Double consciousness is appropriated as the experience of African Americans living simultaneously in a "black" and "white" world. The notion of double consciousness is often addressed as a function of the inescapable prison of conscience that tugs one's concept of one's identity against that which has been imposed by state power and institutional authorities. Double consciousness, however, also serves as an apparatus for not only a means for African Americans to survive but also a process for ability to thrive. The power of DuBois's sage in naming this dualized consciousness is in its potential to transform those who have been objectified. To name an experience is to help to understand it and perhaps transform its negative apparatus into a positive one. To deny either one of a dualized consciousness is to underestimate its potentiating coupling force in defining the identity of the thriving subject. The power of the thriving subject rests with the ability or desire of, for example, African American agency to balance this dualized experience with the possibility of shifting the balance (an example is code switching in languages) to maximize the opportunity to fully understand the context. Such balance does not mean that each consciousness has equal space in the agency's identity but that each consciousness is present with the relative distribution having the tendency to shift. What appears to be the point of contention is whether the ethnic consciousness that has always maintained vigilance of the movement of the racial consciousness should remain silent. The ethnic consciousness was always relegated to the margins even though it has always nurtured agencies that transform the margins. These margins sometimes become powerful sites from which to maintain not only vigilance over race consciousness, at the center, but in fact redefine the center in ways that may very well shift the focus from the center to the margin. As scholars like bell hooks (1992) have noted, the margin is a powerful site of struggle and analysis about the conditions on the margin as well as the condition at the center.

As was briefly discussed in the introduction of this book, Charles Mills offers a critical analysis of the sociopolitical arrangements, both nationally and globally, that centralizes race as a political construction that dates back to early nineteenth-century European history. In *The Racial Contract*, Mills (1997) offers a critical analysis of the ways in which racism has been inscribed in the politics and institutional arrangements of the Western political systems since the beginning of nation-states. It is this political arrangement that produces the two worlds of superior and inferior beings. It is no wonder, therefore, that scholars from these two worlds are preoccupied with one side of a two-phased issue. According to Mills, the White scholars are preoccupied with issues of political philosophy, ethics, rights, and justice, whereas African scholars, for example, are preoccupied with issues of colonization, imperialism, land rights, race and racism, reparations, and so forth. For Emmanuel Eze (2001), the academic foundation of the racial contract or the racial state can be traced to the work of Immanuel Kant, a German philosopher. Kant (2001/1775) propounded the first academic concept of race by arguing, in 1775, that all races have a common origin. Although he was opposed to the notion of polygenesis, he did not believe in race mixing and would further expand his race theory into a racial theory that would promulgate White supremacy (see Eze 2001).

Understanding the foundation of the construction of race and racism is critical to the debate around the social construction of racial identity. Even more critical, according to Eze, is the exposure of the silence around the philosophical construction and nurturance of race and racism. This unearthing of the collective mutedness around the racial contract is gaining currency in social science discourses and particularly in public health and health promotion. Giving voice to this silence is the foundation of building a new way of knowing so as to achieve the very best of humanity. First we have to examine the coded language that has maintained this silence about race and identity. Central to this is the language of objectivity.

OBJECTIVITY AND THE MYTH OF THE RESEARCHER'S NEUTRALITY

It is true that many African cultures believe that "to know who you are is the beginning of wisdom," as Mazrui (1986) reflected in his work. In the first instance, if you are an American or a South African, to know who you are is the beginning of racialism. For educators and researchers engaged in the study of human behavior, to know who you are is the foundation of any serious cultural project. Knowing who you are is knowing your own cultural identity as separate from professional identity.

Most social scientists whose research focuses on human populations often begin by focusing on populations who look like themselves with an occasional inclusion of "others" in their population of interest. Indeed, scholarship begins at home. This is why the seeming dominance of White scholars' research interrogates as much about the affirmation of their identity as the affirmation of their profession. This is also why scholars like Morrison and Fanon have challenged the misrepresentation of African agency (compared with, e.g., African Americans) in the discourse on identity. The question is less of the commitment of the scholars themselves to accurate representations of African identity but more of the depth of cultural representation in capturing the wholeness and fullness of African identity without resorting into a discourse of Otherness. To have a depth of understanding of a culture requires a certain emotional investment. Indeed, the process of researching issues related to identity such as health behavior may be likened to the difference between participation and involvement.

Participation and involvement are better illustrated by the story of the hen and the pig that were out for a morning stroll. They walked by a restaurant advertising bacon and eggs. Pointing out her identity link to the advertisement, the hen noted that the egg will not be possible without her participation. Amused by what sounds like a partial appreciation in commitment, the pig counterpoised by educating the hen that participation was easy when compared with the pig's experience of not just participating in producing the outcome but affecting the outcome such that it would not be possible without her "involvement"—literally sacrificing her life (or rather that of her agency) to produce the bacon. The contestation between participation and involvement is not a simple one of engaging in scholarly enquiring across identity divide but one of having a profound understanding of one's identity and where this places one on the participation and involvement rubric. In d, this process is even more complex because sharing the same identity between a population being researched does not make one involved any more than being different from the population of interest makes one a mere participant. The issue often is whether the researcher knows and understands his or her cultural identity outside of his or her professional identity. Stated differently, how sincere and committed is a researcher who studies "others'" identity without a clear understanding and articulation of his or her own identity?

A most fundamental problem with many scholars and educators is that they don't know "who they are" without "what they do." They cannot or refuse to identify with their culture in the same way they expect from community members who participate in their research. The casual engagement and disengagement of Henry Louis Gates's (1999) *Wonders of the African World* on the subject of African identity and the politics of hybridity comprise one example of the uncertainty that often occasioned the discourse on identity research. Gates produced a travelogue in which he visited some African countries and interviewed persons in the community to elicit their views on chiefs and other African leaders who were complicit in the kidnapping of Africans who were sold into slavery. The theme of the project was an important one. The subject matter is very significant in the history of Africans in the continent and the diaspora. However, Gates's approach to engaging both community members and leaders (including his interview with the Holy Patriarch of the Ethiopia Orthodox Church) indicate one who has little reverence and humility for others' value, whether cultural or spiritual. It was apparent that Gates would not or could not articulate who he is without what he does. His identity expressed in this project was anchored fully in his professional status at Harvard. Although some argue that it is not necessary to separate one's professional identity from one's cultural/ethnic identity, Gates was effectively asking his interviewees in Africa to do just that. He was less interested in the professional/career identity of his objects/subjects but more in their identity, particularly as progeny of shameful legacy of certain African chiefs' complicity in the kidnapping of Africans into slavery in America.

Many researchers involved in studying communities (particularly those that are disenfranchised) expect persons whom they interview as research participants to express their views based on who they are rather than what they do. This problem is even more pronounced when researchers in the United States and Europe attempt to examine the views of Africans by using questions that have been structured from the perspective of the researchers out of Africa. Whatever the researcher's experience and cultural space, a serious historical analysis should be undertaken as an important first step to understanding the issues of identity and health. This is particularly critical in researching African American populations.

RACE AND THE HISTORY OF PUBLIC HEALTH

The U.S. racial policy on identity has its foundation in the U.S. census. The racist politics and science of Josiah Clark Knott sowed the seed for the racial classification of Whites, Blacks, and mulattoes. Knott not only believed in White supremacy but also advanced the "mulatto inferiority theory" in an 1843 article published in the *American Journal of the Medical Sciences*. For Knott, mulattoes (those with hybrid identity) were considered to be inferior to anyone of so-called pure White or Black stock. Knott's writings were very influential in the racial politics of the 1850s, a politics and science anchored in what was considered to be evidence of polygenesis—the belief that different races originate from different species, hence their believed endowed superiority or inferiority. The fact that the U.S. census has four racial categories and one ethnic (Hispanic) category attests to the fallacy of race as a valid category. What Hispanic represents in race is hybridity that refused to be accepted by scholars who believe in race-only politics. Thus, the insistence on racial categorization embraces the notion of racial purity.

The debate on identity categorization also owes its existence to the history of medical atrocities committed against Blacks in the United States. The result of this distrust is very much current. The impact of the Tuskegee experiment is often cited as the reason for persistent distrust of the medical system by people of African descent. Vanessa Northington Gamble (1997) has unveiled evidence that locates the roots of medical distrust to a century before the Tuskegee medical experimentation. According to Gamble, Georgia physician Thomas Hamilton conducted studies to test the duration of prolonged exposure to sun as the cause for heatstroke by burying Black men up to their neck in the ground and watching them until they fainted. In a second example offered by Gamble, between 1845 and 1849, "Dr J. Marion Sims, the so-called father of modern gynecology, used three Alabama slave women to develop an operation to repair vesicovaginal fistulas" (1774) by subjecting these three women to thirty painful operations without anesthesia. Such history of medical atrocity may not be easily articulated or known by all persons of African descent, but it is evident that there is still a level of fear. There is a tendency to believe that simply educating the populace about the facts of current health system will eliminate distrust of medical institutions.

I have had personal experience with trying to reconcile the desire to engage in health promotion through personal involvement with the question of racism in the heath system. I had to renew my driver's license, and one of the two questions asked during the renewal was the option to register for the organ donor program. The question was simple enough, but it took me several minutes to question the question. I had apparently spent too much time in front of the computer monitor, which prompted one of the attendants to ask me whether I needed any help. "Not really," I responded. I have always known that knowledge does not translate into action or behavior. It is one's experience that produces knowledge. Experiences, in the first instance, are shaped by our social cultural context. Culture teaches us to cope with life experiences. Yet a group's experience does not necessarily mean that it is their culture. As indicated earlier, slavery is a part of African American experience, but it is not a part of African Americans culture. Culture is often mislabeled and misused in constructing people's identity where experiences are more appropriate and vice versa. It is accumulation of experience that shapes culture and helps it to evolve.

The case with my difficulty in responding to a very simple question was the clash of historical experience with a professional commitment to public health. I was determined to maintain a consistency of who I am with what I do and believe. The cliché "I am what I do" does not apply in this instance. It was not an easy process. I did make a decision. I also decided to share my experience with African American scholars at a consultative meeting of the National Institutes of Health where I was invited as one of three scholars to speak on the issue of cultural approach to eating and exercise among African Americans. No sooner had I reached the point of my story where I was standing in front of the computer monitor than my African American sisters (they happen to be leading experts in public health) opined quickly that they hoped I did not mark yes. Like me, the experience and currency of medical racism necessitates an intervention that says, in effect, "First do no harm to yourself" or make no decision that may bring harm to yourself. Many educators wonder and debate whether Tuskegee continues to be a factor in question of distrust of the health system. The question is moot because African Americans with higher education and income are distrustful of the medical system whether they directly link such distrusts to the Tuskegee syphilis study. As Gamble reflected, the study should be called the U.S. Public Health Syphilis Study, because Tuskegee did not own the study in the first instance. The study was visited on them. Moreover, the tendency to focus on distrust means the focus on the behavior of the victims. If a system perpetuates fraud on its victims, it is the system that must be changed. This is why scholars are asking that we should focus on the lack of institutional trustworthiness in medical institutions.

I would argue that one of the most important measures of medical distrust should be the reluctance and refusal of people of African descent to participate in organ donor programs. There is a hidden fear that should the medical establishment be aware that one has signed up as an organ donor, a life-threatening accident or injury may quickly lead to death if White medical practitioners want the organ to save a "preferred" White client. The point is not whether it is true because it is not a function of knowledge. The point is whether it is perceived as knowledge based on collective experience. When leading public health scholars are afraid of translating what they believe into personal action, it should not be difficult to understand the true meaning of DuBois's double consciousness. In this case, it is not a matter of one's social economic status; it is a matter of being Black, and culture provides the resolve to transcend the otherwise disadvantaged position. Indeed, cultural resources can be empowering in coping with otherwise difficult conditions. How well one copes is also a function of one's resource advantage, which cannot be measured solely by income and education.

IDENTITY AND ACCULTURATION

Earlier empirical studies on cultural identity of African Americans were limited to exploring degrees of acculturation to the White mainstream culture. Indeed, cross-cultural research often locates the White/Western culture as the point of reference, with other cultures judged only in relation to how close to (read: good) or distant (read: bad) they are from the referent. Indeed, an acceptance of a White identity symbol coupled with a simultaneous rejection of representational symbols of Black identities was commonly concluded to be indicative of self-hatred. The research of Kenneth Clark and Mamie Clark (1939) that concluded that Black children's preference for White dolls over Black dolls was indicative of Black self-rejection was influential in earlier policies that blamed African American culture for African Americans' disadvantaged conditions. In challenging the serious limitations of this and other similar earlier studies, Bill Cross (1991) concludes that a perspective on "the actuality of race as a debilitating factor in the lives of a fraction, albeit a significant fraction, was confused with the potentiality of race damaging the lives of the majority" (29). The limitations of these earlier findings have become evident in recent studies, conducted by Margaret Spencer and colleagues, that question, among other things, the wisdom of basing adult or youth behavior on the choices of preschool children and that group identity can be inferred from self-concept measures. Spencer (1995) revisited the study of Clark and Clark and concluded that although the Clarks' study provided a useful link between children's identity and their social contexts, it was limited in its omission of children's cognitive development. Such omission suggests, for example, contrary to the conclusion reached by the Clarks, that a preference for White dolls could not be indicative of Black self-hatred. Beyond the nature/nurture complexity of identity formation and reinforcement is the intragroup variation that is often omitted in the construction of African American identity. Indeed, Spencer's findings are more consistent with the notion of double or multiple, positive consciousness among Blacks. Moreover, a broader understanding of the power of the social and physical environment is critical in understanding identity and the relations to health. It is for this reason that Spencer and her colleagues developed a model of understanding the complex interaction of environmental factors that conflate to shape health behavior in what they refer to as the Phenomenological Variant of Ecological Systems Theory (PVEST) (Spencer 1999).

Shiriki Kumanyika (2001) at the University of Pennsylvania has also made compelling cases for promoting a complex analysis that accounts for environmental factors in research on obesity rather than focusing singularly on the biological manifestation of the disease. In addressing the problem of obesity, Kumanyika advocates that public health scholars partner with farmers, the food industry, and policymakers to collectively develop strategies that allow us to analyze the chain of food from production to consumption. Central to such analysis is the need to focus on cultural identity issues relative to health behavior.

Mohan Dutta-Bergman (2004) has advanced the notion of a culture-centered approach to health communication. For public health and communication, Dutta-Bergman's culture-centered approach offers the opportunity to engage people in the community in the production of knowledge rather than simply disseminate or translate to them what is believed in the academy to be the solution for the community. Although the work of these scholars has helped to advance the centrality of culture in health, unfortunately, many other scholars who focus on culture tend to focus on acculturation as a solution to improved health.

Regarding the bias in acculturation studies, the challenge of conceptualizing and measuring is in the ability to recognize that the culture of origin remains active in the individual and group. Indeed, acculturation in the form of cultural homogeneity should not be mistaken for abandonment of culture of origin. Hybrid socialization processes occur in all kinds of neighborhoods. Such a socialization results from network interaction that sustains the legitimacy of subcultural perspectives against any form of dominant identity control. In one respect, there is a sense of unique cultural homogeneity in American cultural diversity. The emphasis on the acquisition of mainstream cultural values by minorities may lead to the erroneous conclusion that such acquisition necessarily deactivates the culture of origin. It does not. The culture of origin often remains salient in shaping values and behaviors. The constant exposure to the dominant culture through the media may appear to reduce the salience of the culture of origin. The resulting hybridized cultural experience may be very positive. However, any form of threat to the identity of the person often bubbles up the cultural salience to provide a protective net for the person who may consider themselves to be vulnerable to the threat.

RESEARCHING THE POLITICS OF AFRICAN AMERICAN IDENTITY

The project of legitimating and affirming the voices of African Americans' cultural spaces has been a focus of research and practice by scholars of African American culture. One example of this cultural project is Afrocentric theory, which is anchored in a belief in the centrality of Africanity in any analysis involving African culture and behavior. For instance, as Molefe Asante (1987) notes, "The communicationist who defines a speech as an uninterrupted spoken discourse demonstrates either a disregard or ignorance of the African tradition of speech, much as Leslie Fiedler showed a purely European conception of fiction when he contended that romance was a central theme in literature" (6). According to James Stewart (1992) Afrocentric theory tends to fall into two basic categories. The first is the

> "strong claim"—the assertion that the liberation of peoples of African descent requires a psychological reorientation that focuses on reconstructing selected aspects of traditional African psychology, values and behaviors in the present. The second is the "weak claim"—the position that liberation requires that top priority be assigned to the interests of peoples of African descent in social and political intercourse with other collectives. (35)

African American cultural scholars have consistently challenged the application of traditional models based on White culture for recommending treatment and/or behavior change targeted at health promotion and disease prevention among African Americans.

Stewart (1989) has called for the development and prioritizing of a grand theory of Africology based on a full understanding of the nature of history, time, space, and technology in Afrocentric terms. He argues that our political and intellectual efforts should be devoted to restructuring community ties and translating the language of African American intellectual elites into the language of African American popular culture. Such a framework will capture the beliefs of Africans and African Americans in postmodern history. However, some scholars, such as Manning Marable (1993), have questioned the wisdom of analyzing African American culture and behavior based solely on African culture: "African, in effect, represents only one-half of the dialectical consciousness of African American people. Blacks are also legitimately Americans and, by our suffering, struggle and culture, we have a destiny within this geographical and political space equal to or stronger than that of any white American" (121). In the words of Angela Davis (1992), "There is no simple or unitary way to look at expressions of Black nationalism or essentialism in contemporary cultural forms" (320).

It is not my intent here to debate what constitutes the production of African American culture in the early twenty-first century, but it is worth noting that even after African Americans' many years of lived experience in the United States, many compelling similarities still remain between African Americans and Africans with regard to certain cultural codes and meanings in actions and behaviors. Such behaviors can be found in choices and values assigned to foods, the importance of orature and oracy in communication, and the use of traditional healing, all of which are important in the development of health promotion and disease prevention programs. In this context, this chapter focuses on the degree to which African Americans' health conditions can benefit from culturally appropriate paradigms that are grounded in historical correctness rather than mere political correctness.

In spite of efforts to understand cultural values as they relate to personal behaviors, little attention has been given to the development of a culturally appropriate paradigm for health promotion in the African American community. Currently, culturally sensitive educational and behavioral change models for health promotion in African American communities tend to be based primarily on the Caucasian experience. Attempts to make these programs culturally appropriate tend to rely on the individual and family psychology of African Americans. A major shortcoming of these models is the failure to ground personal crises in the social political context within which the individual has to function. It is critical to establish a balance between behavior the individual is capable of changing and the social-political factors in the environment that must be managed before those changes are made and sustained. The outcome is that these approaches offer no models for translating known cultural and institutional realities into a working framework that could guide the development of culturally appropriate health promotion and disease prevention programs in African American communities.

There is no doubt that the failure to recognize the cultural inadequacies of traditional models, so as to promote and educate people to use alternative models, has contributed significantly to the profound disparity in health status between African Americans and the White population. Although efforts seem to be commonly focused on the health of *poor* African Americans, as if they should be held responsible for their economic status and hence a focus on their behavior, much needs to be done about addressing the contextual environment that breeds disparity. Although SES influences health outcomes, racial and cultural oppression are mostly responsible for the low health status of African Americans. Segregation and poor housing have long been established as root causes for poor health of African Americans. In the words of Derrick Bell (1992), the inner city is the American equivalent of South African homelands. Low economic status is linked with poor health status, and other factors, such as structural discrimination and institutional racism, favor the disproportionate representation of African Americans in low-income groups, which ultimately results in their poor health status. A focus on individual income fails to address the social context and environment in which a disproportionate number of African Americans find themselves. Even among African Americans whose income levels are the same as those of the majority White population, many other factors—such as total assets, housing, prior SES, and social mobility—influence health status (Williams and Collins 2004).

Indeed, there are persistent inconsistencies in the way in which the question of economic status is addressed by social scientists. Robin Kelly (1997), for example, questions the victimization and stigmatization of African American women in social and behavioral health research. Behavior only seems to matter when the health problem is about the lower or underclass. Where there is a problem with the middle or upper class, there is an urgent call for societal and institutional changes rather than the behavior of the individuals. However, the story is different for lower-class individuals. For them, the focus is on their individual behavior that must be changed, as Kelly illustrates. Most interpreters of the underclass focus on the behavior of the group and treat such behaviors as cultural. For Kelly, behavior seems to be important only when social scientists are conducting studies with the underclass. It is as though they are poor because of their behaviors. The focus on behavior for the underclass, lower class, and inner city is commonly a coded language for African Americans whose behavior must be a focus for change. Rarely is the racism inscribed in such language.

The need to examine the personal or cultural health beliefs of African Americans is increasingly critical. For example, teenage pregnancy is an issue that has received increasing public attention in the past decade. In the development of health interventions targeting teen pregnancies, the assumption is usually made that all such pregnancies are unwanted. Consequently, interventions tend to concentrate on recommendations of birth control methods for all teenagers. Such recommendations, however, are totally irrelevant for teenagers whose pregnancies are planned, an increasing number of whom are African American. Programs aimed at preventing pregnancies among teenagers who want to become pregnant need to examine and deal with societal failures that condition these children to want to have children. Children having children is one concern, but children *wanting* to have children is another. There is no worse evidence that a society has failed its youth.

Dealing head-on with the truth of this individual construction of reality is not to suggest an endorsement of such reality but to focus on the manifestations of human growth and transformation. In other words, accepting the truth of wanted pregnancies among teenagers can allow interventionists to explore why these teenagers want to have children. Both wanted and unwanted teenage pregnancies have important policy implications. Health and social practices are usually manifestations of several forces that collectively shape individuals' cultural beliefs and individual life experiences. In the case of children wanting to have and having children, the interventions that may be

most successful in the long run may be those that concentrate on the factors—
such as failed government policies, high rates of unemployment, and various
forms of marginalization and discrimination—that have contributed to
teenagers' feeling that they have no future.

THE ENVIRONMENTAL CONTEXTS OF DISEASE

A critical point often not addressed in studies of cultural identity and health
is the different meaning and labeling of studied variables when projected on
other populations. For example, SES in minorities is often used as a proxy of
low income and acculturation, but it stresses only one part of the minority experience, missing active components of multiculturality or double consciousness. David Williams (2002) has reported that African Americans are more
likely to be exposed to occupational hazards and carcinogens, even after controlling for job experience and education; receive lower returns on education
than Whites; and have less purchasing power compared with their White
counterparts of the same income level, due to such factors as higher payments
for rent, food, and higher lending rates for mortgages.

Interestingly, the perception of African American food patterns as responsive to environmental circumstances emerged in a way that suggested a high
potential for dietary change in the African American community. In my study
with Kumanyika (see Airhihenbuwa et al. 1996) on the context and meaning
of lifestyle behaviors, responsiveness to context was a recurring theme
throughout the discussion of food practices. Thus, in the same sense that certain foods (e.g., soul food) represented adaptations during slavery, the need to
respond to new conditions and new health problems was seen as likely to result in changes in soul food. On the other hand, there was no indication in the
discussion that food patterns would necessarily change if environmental circumstances continued to favor current consumption patterns. However, recent studies are showing that the availability of grocery stores in a neighborhood directly influences the intake of fruits and vegetables by African
Americans. The more grocery stores there are in the neighborhood, the more
the increase in fruit and vegetable intake (Morland, Wing, and Roux 2002).
Indeed, it has been known that institutional "supersizing" has had a devastating impact on African American eating habits before it became evident in
fast-food restaurants. As an undergraduate student in Nashville, Tennessee, I
quickly learned that the single-family grocers in our predominantly African
American neighborhood could not compete with the supermarket food chains
for lower prices and fresher produce. This reality was not evident for most
White Americans until the supersized Wal-Mart squeezed small family stores

out of the market. Institutional supersizing was a health hazard for Blacks' food well before McDonald's and Burger King made it a visible consumption threat. If only society would listen to the sounding trumpet of Blacks' social crises as it does to their music.

Although the importance of relaxation in the form of yoga and medication has gained increased attention as an important ingredient for a healthy life in today's stressful world, the importance of relaxation has always been recognized among African Americans. It is surprising that this has not been represented in the past as an African American health behavior, particularly given that most of the studies about African Americans were focused on the working poor. In my study with Kumanyika and other colleagues (see Airhihenbuwa et al. 1995), the importance of *rest* as a cultural value was one of the major findings. A second major finding was the possibility that exercise could be a stressor depending on the circumstances. Indeed, the label "exercise" also needed to be examined, as has been reported by other researchers, because many participants in our study believed, and rightly so, that one could expend energy during one's daily job such as loading a delivery truck. Thus, most studies on exercise are actually interested in leisure-time physical activity. This assumes, of course, that one has leisure time. The person who has two full-time jobs and family may not have leisure time to engage in physical activity. For such individuals, depending on the demands of their job, rest should be recommended to become a part of their daily life even though this may be unattainable for them.

The meaning of health-related identity is constructed at the level of exteriority or interiority. Other researchers have addressed the notion of internal and external voices. Identity exteriority is how I classify the desire for perfection that typifies American culture. In dental health, for example, the obsession with symmetrical and white and whiter teeth is based on identity exteriority. When studying weight management and body image, analysis is often conducted at the exterior level. However, African American women tend to address identity at the interior level. Indeed, the notion of resiliency in general and Black superwomanhood in particular are factors of interiority and identity. *Resiliency*, in fact, is a problematic term because it normalizes a problem condition for Blacks in a way that suggests that normal behavior is an exception. Moreover, resiliency is an individual-based diagnostic code that places the onus of change on the individual rather than addressing the institutional and structural forces that produce and maintain the weight on the individual. This (resiliency) is one of the factors that has given rise to the notion of the superwoman image. For Black women, identity is who you are inside and not on what people think of you on the outside. It is for this reason that spirituality serves a central role in Black identity.

FINAL THOUGHTS

According to Stuart Hall, you must position yourself somewhere in order to say something at all. It is that sense of our own positioning that is connoted by the term *ethnicity*. Our relationships to what peoples of the world have to their own past are part of the discovery of their own ethnicity. They must honor the hidden histories about which they have never been taught or been taught not to speak. The foundation of eliminating health disparities nationally and globally rest in the resoluteness with which we examine the ways in which the politics of identity have been distanced from the behavioral construction and the resulting crisis of health. Race and ethnicity provide both historical and contemporary lenses from which to better understand the framing of African American identity and health behavior around it.

2

THE LOCATION OF IDENTITY

6

Omon

The Cultural Meanings of Childhood and Youth Identity

Omonkaro—A child is the leader.
Omonsigho—A child is more valuable than money.
Omonsefe—A child is more valuable than wealth.
Omonrotionmwan—A child is one's kin.
Omonragbon—A child is the world.

—Common names in Edo (Benin, Nigeria)

The naming of a child among the Edos of Nigeria, as well as many other groups in Africa, marks important cultural rituals within the family. Whether or not the naming of a child is marked by a ceremony, the selection of the name itself within the cultural context is never random. The name is designed to establish a specific historical trajectory as mediated by culture in the life of the family. The naming of children is symbolic of how families and the broader kinships try to reproduce themselves within their cultural codes and meaning.

In this chapter, I define *youth* broadly as that period in a person's life between childhood and adulthood. This period may include preteen, teen, and some postteen years. In many African cultures, persons at these ages are often referred to as young adults, because there is no term equivalent to *adolescent* or *youth* in many languages. In fact, the term *adolescent* is a modern construction with connotations that are rather problematic, as I will discuss later. A teenaged person is usually referred to as "the young male child" or "the young female child."

Children and youth foreground the constitution and meaning of the family in Africa. I refer to family here in the context of what is often referred to as extended family. Therefore, an understanding of the role of children within

77

African culture would be incomplete without an adequate contextualizing of the construction and functions of the family as a cultural institution. Many reasons have been offered in the literature to explain why Africans have many children, principal among which are that children provide a cheap labor pool in agrarian societies and that high infant mortality rates lead to the naturalizing of multiparous desire. Explanatory models that problematize high birthrates and attempt to offer solutions often focus only on economic outcomes. Although it is important to consider income levels when addressing family size and structure, it is more important to go beyond economic interpretations and understand the psychosocial, cultural, and spiritual dimensions of family formation. Although high infant mortality rates are undeniable in many parts of Africa, the desire to have many children is equally evident among nonagrarians who live in a first-world environment within third-world societies. In other words, living in the city, away from agrarian economic base, does not completely change the expectation or the reality of the number of children in the family. Thus, it is customarily understood that children form the core of what constitutes a family in most African contexts. It is for this reason that motherhood has a central meaning in women's identity in African (see the next chapter).

THE CONTEXT OF FAMILY

In Nigeria, most "professionals" (e.g., university professors) have larger families than do their counterparts in the United States or France. It would appear that not even "enlightened" professionals are impervious to the cultural and social expectations of what is considered an acceptable family size. Surveys that constantly show the desire for fewer children among youths in secondary schools are quick to credit family planning programs for such reported expectations. Those who conduct the surveys, however, fail to recognize that similar expectations were expressed by many of today's parents who now have relatively large families. Expectations may be individually constructed on the basis of institutional and social formations as understood (and learned in school) at a particular point in time, but reality is collectively produced on the basis of many factors that are not always within the person's immediate control yet actively engaged by the person consciously and subconsciously.

The survival of the child is very much dependent on the survival of the family, particularly of the mother. It is said in Africa that an orphan is "a motherless child." To the extent that African mothers are the primary caretakers of children, mothers' well-being is inextricably bound to the well-being of children. Attempts to address children's well-being have led to such international health projects as child survival programs instituted under the strong support of international donor agencies. Some international health experts question the rationale for such vertical programs—vertical in the sense that they tend to stand alone and be unconnected to other interventions and they tend to be a product of the mandate of an international donor agency. These programs tend to overlook the myriad factors affecting the health of children. Furthermore, the factors that influence the desired number of children, how the wife and mother in the family negotiates her decisions, the role that family support has on the financial responsibilities assumed by the husband, and the average number of children found in one's community all affect the number of children planned and whether those children will survive and have economic, cultural, and social support.

NAMING AND IDENTITY IN LEARNING

If the importance of a cultural domain affects the lexical complexity of that domain, then the absence of words to delineate family kinship along biological lines in many African cultures is of lexical significance. As I have indicated, the youth's identity and humanity are central to the family cultural identity. Such identity formation begins with the naming of the child at birth. According to W. Kamau (personal communication, 1993), among the Kikuyus of Kenya, the first male child (I do not say "first son" because the terms *son* and *daughter* resonate with parent–child closure that does not allow for the inclusion of other members of the extended family in the rearing of the child) bears the name of his paternal grandfather, and the first female child bears the name of the paternal grandmother. The second male child bears the name of the maternal grandfather, and the second female child bears the name of the maternal grandmother. The relationships between children and grandparents in this context are rooted in a strong belief that the future (our children) is an extension of the past (our parents). A grandparent becomes closely bonded with his or her rebirth (the grandchild) and assumes unflinching and unwavering personal responsibility toward the child. The child is often referred to in the name and designation of his or her grandparent, whose life the child is on earth to relive. The child soon begins to internalize the role, persona, and values of the grandparent in a psychologically preordained role-modeling relationship. In most cases, according to Kamau, the child begins to manifest certain physical and behavioral traits of the grandparent—a powerful form of family and cultural production and reproduction.

Among the Kikuyus, these cultural codes and meanings are critical for couples' decisions regarding the number of children they desire (a goal for family planning programs) and the number of children they have in the process of seeking to balance the gender representations of the children as a fulfillment of their cultural expressions. Such cultural fulfillment may result in undue pressure on a couple, especially the wife, to have at least two boys and two girls. However, the bonding, psychogenealogical extension, and family and cultural reproductions are values and nurturing that symbiotically benefit the children and parents in their nurturance of their identity and the protection of progeny. These collective experiences, which are not always quantifiable—nor should they be—are the hallmark of the sustenance of the family in Africa. Unfortunately, the use of Western cultural logic to understand African identity has resulted in the impoverished interpretation of African identity. This is even more problematic in defining and naming relations among members of family.

The fact that many relatives are referred to as brothers and sisters (even though these include those who would be considered nephews, nieces, and cousins in Western cultures) is often believed to be an example of the limitation of languages in African cultures. The possibility that this way of speaking is deliberately constructed to capture the closeness and bonding that typifies the sibling relationship is rarely entertained. To learn that there is a difference between one's brothers or sisters and one's cousins and other so-called distant relations is to learn about developing psychological and behavioral distance in the way one relates to those relatives. Among the Edos of Nigeria, where children are familiar only with the concept of brothers and sisters, there is a type of closeness and reciprocal responsibility peculiar to the culture that is theirs to value. In fact, the concept of brothers and sisters in the African context is one of the most important factors in the maintenance and sustenance of extended family in Africa in its broadest extension.

Moreover, the term *extended family* suggests that the Westernized nuclear family is the referent. When the African family is the norm, situating it at the center instead of the margin, the Western family becomes the alternative type of family, the "constricted family." As a child growing up in Nigeria, I always knew that my nephew was my brother. Upon coming to the United States for "training," I began to refer to my brother by the Western designation (my nephew). As time progressed, I started to experience some level of inexplicable mental distance that was never the case in Nigeria—even more so given that we live farther away than we had in Nigeria. It was as though I suddenly discovered that my brother was adopted by my parents or I by his. But, unfortunately, my parents were not with me to buffer the shock and confusion that followed this discovery. It was up to me alone to overcome the irrelevance of the Western cultural and linguistic and Kartesian demarcation, as it were, and hold on to the wisdom of my parents and my culture. I had to make a conscious effort to revert to referring to my brother as my brother.

I would argue that our forebears intentionally left out words and delineators that could potentially distance relatives. Such affirmative vision speaks to a cultural sophistication that is promoted through its linguistic codes in the production of knowledge, with its carefully constructed relationships and meanings. Of course, for Eurocentrists, to affirm this is to subscribe to an episteme that is not consistent with their preferred pedestrian interpretation of African culture. One does not have to understand or logically follow cultural codes or expressions to affirm and respect their legitimating values. After all, everyday language usage that defies logic has always influenced the interpretive meanings and visual imagery given to life experience. For example, we speak of *sunrise* and *sunset*, although these terms tend to suggest that the world is flat rather than that the Earth spins in its orbit around the sun. This has never stopped people from using these expressions or led them to change their value and meaning, even though perhaps more accurate terms would be *earthrise* and *earthset*. What is clear is that as much as education is critical to advancement of a people, the miseducation of the youths in African schools (in the ways youths are being taught to devalue their language and culture) has contributed to the marginalization of African cultures.

GLOBALIZATION AND LEARNING IN SCHOOLS

Cultural imperialism is manifested in school curricula that hold up Western and European experiences as the only experiences of value. Even when other histories, languages, and cultures are taught, the images and the instruments of learning are often presented in such a way that they are rooted in the past. It seems that the achievements of other cultures are to be glorified only for their nostalgic value because they are represented as not holding future possibilities. There is often no attempt to connect any information about African cultures with current political realities, power, and education. In *Cultural Imperialism*, Edward Said (1993) argues that individuals who are the products of colonial and postcolonial realities are conditioned to believe that everything good about themselves and their cultures existed only in the past and should remain there. This has long been true for many people of African descent all over the world, particularly in matters relating to health beliefs and practices.

The success of health promotion programs in Africa rests with the degree to which they are based on the sociocultural realities of Africans. According to Ngugi wa Thiong'O (1986), economic and political control of a people is commonly institutionalized and complete with cultural control. In this way, literary traditions and scholarly discourses, regardless of whether they are Africans or Westerners, reproduce the marginal representation of the logic of the system as a whole without ever questioning how such a system was produced in the first instance. The most effective institution for cultural control has been the school, with its Western-based curriculum as its instrument. Some of these measures of control have been analyzed by scholars who have examined the root causes of the miseducation of African American youths in the United States. Eurocentric approaches to global educational processes should be deconstructed and transformed to reflect varied cultural expressions. Attempts to affirm cultural differences in schools and communities often result in calls for program and curriculum integration, although program and curriculum reformation and transformation hold more promise for centralizing diversity in the learning process.

In a culture-centered approach to health and education, the experiences of the Others must be centralized in the mainstream school curriculum for the benefit of students from both the center and the margin. As Paulo Freire (1993) notes, "To open up to the culture's soul is to allow one to become wet, to become soaked in the cultural and historical waters of those individuals who are involved in the experience" (103). Such involvement and total commitment are transformative for both the teachers and the learners. The resulting reformation of the curriculum and programmatic paradigm includes affirmation and encouragement of different languages of expression, health beliefs, and cultural values. For example, binary opposition is unnecessarily constructed between modern information channels that are based on the Western construct and traditional information channels (oral communication). Both systems of communication are effectively functional within their contexts; in some cases, the two are quite complementary. Unfortunately, many health communication programs in the past have negated a form of cultural production by ignoring oral communication. This has been true particularly in the planning, implementation, and evaluation of programs in many African cultures. Thiong'O (1993) notes that the biggest weapon wielded and unleashed daily by imperialism against the oppressed and the exploited of the Earth is the cultural bomb: "The effect of a cultural bomb is to annihilate a people's belief in their names, in their languages, in their environment, in their heritage of struggle, in their unity, in their capacities and ultimately in themselves. It makes them see their past as one wasteland of non-achievement and it makes them want to distance themselves from the wasteland" (3).

Ultimately, a broader discourse on the politics of representation in global health calls for the decolonization of the minds of the members of the marginalized group. Africans, the Caribbeans, and African Americans must insist on appropriate representation in the production of knowledge and cultural identity, particularly concerning learning opportunities in health and development. Although some interventionists understand and respect the value of oral tradition, the programmatic response to this form of cultural expression tends to focus only on the storyteller. This is consistent with classical pedagogy, which positions the teacher/educator as the ultimate dispenser of knowledge and relegates students to the status of objects that cannot produce knowledge but can only acquire it. Ultimately, the teacher/educator's opportunity to learn is truncated by the failure to engage the learner in the production of knowledge such that the terrain of learning is multiaccented and mutually enriching. In an attempt to construct what they believe to be a terrain of learning for the voiceless, interventionists assume the role of the storyteller by constructing stories under the guise of responding to cultural sensitivity to achieve cultural competency. Such an approach fails to understand the dynamic of the story listener, which is as equally important as, if not more important than, that of the storyteller.

Cultural dynamics such as communication codes, meanings, and context between the storyteller and listener promote knowledge production and acquisition. Thus, oral tradition generally is not only the heritage of the spoken or sung word, according to M. Faseke (1990), it is also the heritage of the ear. Stated differently, people in oral traditional cultures (as in many African countries) are accustomed to learning by listening. Learning by seeing is important to the extent that what is seen is congruent with what is heard. Critical aspects of learning by listening include *who* was speaking, the way the words were expressed, and in what context. This issue raises questions about the ethical and cultural incongruence of assuming the role of storyteller without experience, or education for that role, and without a thorough understanding of the cultural implications of storytelling for learning. I do not mean to generalize here about all African cultures as cultures of the ear; rather, I want to emphasize the importance of taking this form of cultural expression into account in health intervention projects as a valued form and sometimes the primary form of cultural production. In *Toward the Decolonization of African Literature*, Chinweizu and colleagues (1983) conclude that storytelling requires that one immerse oneself in the storytelling tradition, undergo appropriate apprenticeship, master the verbal arts, and be able to write one's own re-creations of traditional stories. For Trihn Mihn-ha (1991), the storyteller, through whom truth is summoned to unwind itself to the audience, is a creator, a delighter, and a teacher.

When listening is the cultural logic for learning, health professionals involved in developing, implementing, and evaluating programs in such cultures should be required to develop the requisite skills for effective and meaningful program implementation. Institutions of higher learning, there-fore, that have claimed the citadel of knowledge in the training of future teachers should reform their health curricula to reflect the cultural realities of the global population.

CULTURAL CONSTRUCTION OF YOUTH

Youth connotes vigor and energy, whereas *adolescent* connotes conflicts and problems. An adult who is thought to be youthful accepts such a remark as a compliment. Yet the same adult if referred to as an adolescent resents the im-plied deficit in his or her personhood—a connoted interpretation of a kind of an arrested development. *Adolescent* is a term that is anchored in the med-icalization of human growth and transformation. As this term is a signifier that foregrounds such negative characteristics as out-of-control behavior, ir-responsibility, indecisiveness, and unpredictability, it is not surprising that many programmatic efforts directed at adolescents are designed to address a "natural deficit" that is believed to be inevitably present in this group. Thus, the word *adolescent* has several meanings and representations that include medical, cultural, political, legal, social, and historical.

The years that mark the bridge between childhood and adulthood are a very important evolutionary experience in a person's growth and transformation. With so much negativity about the term *adolescent*, given its medicalized ori-gin, perhaps a better term is *youth*. The youth of Africa today face more so-cial and developmental challenges than do their parents. The often conflict-ing value systems of their culture and of Western culture have complicated their decision making and their ability to withstand environmental pressures to make healthy decisions. The confluence of the African top-down hierarchy of information flow and the top-down information flow within the school sys-tems, which are borrowed from the West, has prestructured the youth only to receive information, never to produce it.

Youth may not be independent of family and societal institutions, such as schools, but they do function under the changing traditional values and cus-tomary practices of their environment. When tradition is wrongly viewed as a static state, with the necessary knowledge for its function stored in the minds of the elderly men and women in the society, the youth of Africa are often seen as divorced from traditional values and hence are assumed to be the products of modern values. Contemporary African youth do represent a confluence of traditional African culture and Western modern values, but al-though they are constantly exposed to Western values through the media, their interpretations of these values are often based on their interactions with, and their relationships with, their families, and family relationships are often characterized by experiences that are based in traditional culture. Furthermore, young people may not fully understand or acknowledge the degree to which certain of their behaviors manifest their cultural experiences. Thus, the extent to which a young person acknowledges that his or her behaviors are grounded in traditional culture may be dependent on many factors, such as the opportunity for exposure to other cultural values, with whom the youth is communicating and what the youth perceives such a person to represent, and the culture of reference the youth believes such a person represents.

In some societies, for example, a close relationship between a father and his son is believed to be optimal for the psychosocial well-being of the adolescent or youth. Such a relationship is commonly typified in the West by statements such as "My son is my best friend," and vice versa. Although close relationships between parents and children are also a goal in many African countries, such relationships translate to healthy and mutually enriching interactions and yet do not typify the notion of "friendship" as understood in the West. When I was growing up in Nigeria, the idea of throwing a ball around with my father would have been as strange to me as it would have been to him. Yet I had the closest of relationships with my father at the same time that I had good friends among my peers. The need to engage in leisure activities with one's child, such as playing ball, is a Western concept that partly results from having fewer children so the parents becomes proxy playmates. Such family arrangements have no social value within the cultural milieu in which I was nurtured. Now that I am a father and have a young son still living at home, I do play ball with him even though the amount of time I spend with him is qualitatively similar to the time I spent with my father at my son's age. One major difference, however, is a qualitative difference in the level of security in the environment in which I was raised in Nigeria compared with a relatively more untrusting environment in which our son is being raised in the United States. Indeed, family size and concern for children's security in an unsafe environment are important factors that condition the nature of the relationship between parents and their children. In society with small family size (one or two children in a family), parents do assume the role of children's playmates, which also offers parents the opportunity to monitor the child's security. In societies of large family size and relatively safer environment, parents do remain parents, and children are expected to find their friends within their peer group. This culturally based family interaction pattern is particularly salient given the average number of children in African families and the centrality of children in these families. As we recognize the economic benefit of having fewer children, we should also recognize the sociopsychological and cultural benefits of having many children within this context. Such contextualization of family size is vital if we are to debate and make recommendations about "appropriate" family size.

It should be noted here that there are certain disadvantages to having few children, even in the West. Increasing numbers of individuals in cultures in which small family size is the norm are tending to engage in professionalization of the extended family in the form of group therapy or support groups. Having no elders in one's family to advise one can also lead to professionalization of friendship in the form of counselors and/or therapists. A concept know as the elders' circle has begun in the United States as an attempt to celebrate the elderly and also to tap into their wisdom to offer American youth the benefit of their elders. Such social alliances are necessary in cultures of small family size where elders are not always available in the family to help shape the minds and future of youths. The economic disadvantage (economic status being the core of Western notions of living) notwithstanding, there are notable social, psychological, and cultural benefits of having many children that we must not overlook in addressing the issue of family size in African cultural groups. The goal in deciding appropriate family size is to maintain a balance in all the important forces that shape the culture at a particular time.

CULTURE, LEARNING, AND HEALTH

Attempts to promote cultural differences in schools and communities often manifest themselves in calls for program and/or curriculum integration, although program and curriculum reformation is a more progressive approach to centralizing diversity in the learning process. Such reduction, for example, of inequity in class structure based on income totally undermines the incongruence between the construction of learning opportunity in the schools and the cultural expressions of the Others, whose experiences are not central to the model of learning in the schools.

> Neither sociologists nor journalists have shown much interest in depicting poor whites as a "class." In large measure, the reason is racial. For whites, poverty tends to be viewed as atypical or accidental. Among Blacks, it comes close to being seen as a natural outgrowth of their history and culture. At times, it almost appears as if white poverty must be covered up, lest it blemish the reputation of the dominant race. (Hacker 1992:100)

In some cases, special programs are developed to redress the grievances of the marginalized. In the United States, Henry Giroux (1992a) notes, attempts are often made to atone for racism through measures aimed at reducing and eliminating racist institutional barriers such as compensatory programs to enhance the cultural capital and skills of African Americans, as are evident in various remedial programs in education and the workplace.

Although the elimination of institutional barriers ought to be considered in programmatic efforts, the primary tool for exclusion often lies in the Eurocentric model of learning employed in schools. For example, in contrast to the Eurocentric model, Barbara Christian (1987) observes that African American people have always theorized in narrative forms, "in the stories we create, in riddles and proverbs, in the play with language, since dynamic rather than fixed ideas seem more to our liking" (52; quoted in Giroux 1992a:131). I do not mean to assert here that all African Americans are alike in their production and acquisition of knowledge, but rather to argue for the legitimation of one valued form of cultural production found among African Americans. The differences in production and acquisition of knowledge and values of many African American children are not central to school curricula. Jacqueline Jordan Irvine (1990) writes:

> White middle-class parents and white middle-class teachers used "known-answer" questions, which solicited responses to names, shapes, and colors of objects. On the other hand, the Black children and their parents engaged in more sophisticated verbal storytelling involving the uses of metaphors and analogies. In school, Black children asked questions such as "What's that like?" or "Who's he acting like?" rather than the more middle-class attributional "What's that?" (23)

Asa Hilliard has found that White children tend to tell stories in a "linear" fashion, whereas African American children are more apt to employ a "spiral" style, similar to learning styles found in many African cultures. When given an assignment, they frequently skip around to other obviously unrelated topics before they refocus on the theme (cited in Hacker 1992:172). Such a spiral process of knowledge production is customary in storytelling.

Educational reforms that focus on legitimating cultural differences have important implications for research methods. For James B. Stewart (1992), the general method of oral history research should be applied more commonly in Black and Africana studies because of the importance of oral communication in the historical experiences of peoples of African descent. Such a focus on the significance of orature in research methods does not compromise the value of other hitherto exalted research methods; rather, it deepens and extends the possibilities for understanding cultural productions among people of African descent. The multiple forces that African Americans experience demand an opportunity to advance meaningful solutions that are multidimensional and that can be articulated in response to the complexity and diversity of these experiences in today's global reality (West 1990). If diversity is not central to the construction of learning opportunities in U.S. schools, the reality for African countries is even more troubling. I have argued that the fixation on seeking so-called universal truths (the melting pot mentality) has negatively influenced the learning possibilities that legitimate and celebrate differences in cultures (the salad bowl paradigm). The result has been the development and implementation of health programs that fail to recognize and centralize culture in health practices and behavior.

FINAL THOUGHTS

Youth are products of their environments, and they can be expected to behave in positive ways only as far as the support of adult guidance and their society makes possible. In this context, concern for their behavior must be examined within the contexts of such social mediators as unemployment and the relevance of the education and skills training youth receive to function in their society. Beyond these social concerns, there are social and cultural expectations that affect girl and boys differently. Young girls are faced with the pressure to experiment sexually just as boys are, but with the added burden of having to bear the brunt of the responsibility should unwanted pregnancy result. Unwanted pregnancy is perhaps the single most important event that can take place in a young woman's life, which, if it occurs unprepared, is certain to limit and can sometimes completely derail her future prospects.

The pressure on young women to engage in sexual activity comes not only from young men but in many cases from older men who take advantage of the disadvantaged economic conditions of young women in their society to lure those women into sex. These men, often referred to as sugar daddies (*sour daddies* would be a more appropriate term), are responsible for significant numbers of teenage pregnancies in many African societies. The scenario is usually played out thus: A young woman is enticed with money to engage in sex with an older man and becomes pregnant; the man leaves, looking for other prey; the young woman withdraws from school or other activities that would have prepared her for a good future and has her baby. Any policy designed to address the problems of youth in Africa must seek to criminalize the role these sugar daddies play in truncating the life possibilities of the women they exploit.

If, as the American Indian adage says, "we have not inherited the land from our ancestors, we are borrowing it from our children," then we owe our children a great debt. Children and youth represent our future possibilities. To the extent that we fail them, we have failed ourselves. With so much emphasis on child survival, we must remember that it is also critical that we prepare our youth to make the smooth transition to adulthood.

The social and cultural production of youth in Africa places youth within the context of family with certain responsibilities. Any discussion of the issue of youth is incomplete without special attention to the differential concerns of female youth and the role older men play in perpetuating their marginal status. This concern is one that transcends geographic and regional boundaries.

7

Listening to Her Eyes

Where Motherhood Meets Sisterhood

The true worth of a race must be measured by the character of its womanhood.

—Mary McLeod Bethune (1933)

THE LOCATION OF AFRICAN WOMEN'S IDENTITY

The intersection of gender and culture is a critical entry point to interrogate
questions of identity and behavior and to consider how notions of identities
such as femaleness or womanhood are deeply culturalized to produce different
meanings and agencies. The debate about female identity has revolved around
the points of departure in framing and constructing what constitutes an African
woman's identity and whether the question of sexuality (read: chastity) and
wifehood (read: oppression) around which much feminist discourse is engaged
is relevant for Africa. One manifestation of a universalized and acultural gender identity is that sexism in Africa is blamed on culture, whereas sexism in the
United States is constructed as a discourse of gender. "There continues to be a
fair amount of myth—making about African women, African femininity and, of
course, African feminism" (Mama 2005:105). The very notion of a universal female subordination is not only of limited relevance in Africa but also never
gives credit to the history of women's struggles against colonial domination, on
the one hand, and challenging traditional rules that support women's oppression, on the other (Arnfred 2004a, 2004b). Oyeronke Oyewumi (1997) and
many leading African feminist scholars (e.g., Nkiru Nzegwu and Obioma
Nnaemeka) not only reject the notion of sexuality and wifehood as the site of
contestation for gender identity but have instead advanced motherhood as a

91

more appropriate status by which African women's identity is better represented and understood. The critical issue here is the way in which an identity
that has promoted a purported universal logo echoed in "sisterhood is global"
often obscures the very nature of difference, specifically cultural difference,
that ultimately defines the meaning of womanhood. And for Africans, as
Oyewumi has argued, the defining anchor on which identity is framed is neither sexuality nor wifehood but motherhood.

Whereas in one culture, a person's opportunities to make decisions that ultimately shape her destiny may rest with the person's level of independence in
both the family and society, in other cultures, it is a person's level of autonomy
that determines such decision-making ability. Autonomy is often confused
with independence, especially when discussion focuses, cross-culturally, on
the issue of social and economic freedom for women. Autonomy does not
necessarily require that one be independent of one's family or partner, as long
as one's role and contribution in society are duly recognized and valued economically, culturally, and socially. The issues of autonomy and independence
underlie one of the differences in how Western women and African women
view society, on the one hand, and the qualities that define her agency as a
cultural subject, on the other.

Women in general experience different levels and degrees of marginalization in a male-constructed world. However, African women suffer additional
marginalization when their agency and identity is being subsumed under a
universal code of sisterhood as framed by White women. Based on analysis of
women agency offered by several African feminists, sisterhood is not global.
Indeed, sisterhood is often transmuted into a form of race and gender hierarchy to produce a "sisterarchy" that privileges White women. Most Western
analyses of gender inequity in Africa have tended to focus on women's status
in opposition to men, thereby producing a patriarchal analysis with a focus on
the institution of marriage. In this contexts of analysis, the woman is seen
only in the role of wife—the notion that wifehood is a proxy for womanhood.
The moral lenses of chastity and oppression are confluenced to construct the
status of wifehood in Western gender discourse. As Valerie Amos and P. Parmar (1984) argue, Western feminists, for the most part, do not engage in a dialogue on the hybrid identities that constitute and shape the status of African
women in a family context, as sisters, aunts, or daughters. African women's
agency is invoked as "mothers," "daughters," and "sisters," yet these multiple
agencies tend to be missing when some Western analysts attempt to offer explanations for the location of women's rights in African countries. Often highlighted are non-Western practices that may be unique to or common in Africa
as long as they are centered on the question of sexual chastity. Thus, a common site for the contestation over African women's oppression has become

the practice of female circumcision that is biopolitically constructed as genital mutilation. Female circumcision is a practice that is opposed by many Africans, particularly feminists/womanists, as they are better able to situate such opposition within the cultural framework under which this practice is promoted and nurtured. S. Dawit and S. Mekuria (1993) conclude that a media campaign alone will not stop genital mutilation unless Westerners and those of us living in the West who wish to work on this issue should forge partnerships with the hundreds of African women on the continent who are working to eradicate the practice. Liselott Dellenborg (2004) found in her study in Casamance, Senegal, that women not only defend the practice of female circumcision but have actually played an active role in its promotion even when their men were against it. In this case, female circumcision is seen as an important female rite of passage, a form of sustaining female identity.

As a counterargument to the imposition of Western feminist agenda on what should constitute African women's agency, some observers have pointed out that African feminists have dismissed the use of facial surgery (or is it facial mutilation?) in defining women's agency in the United States, for example. Cosmetic surgery for beauty enhancement is tied to Western normative standards of beauty. This standard, to a large extent, is dictated by male preferences and expectations of beauty even though it is increasingly promoted and normalized by American women (even when their men are opposed to it) as an acceptable form of Western female identity. All forms of surgical alteration of women's body for beauty enhancement often begin with women making choices to respond to men's desire. Whether such a choice is an individual one or a group one, it is nonetheless a choice. These choices are often made by women with the support and encouragement of other women. For example, breast augmentation is clearly a glaring case of female internalization of the male gaze. "We must not be distracted by the arrogance that names one procedure breast reduction and the other sexual *mutilation*, with all the attached connotations of barbarism. In both instances, some part of the female body is excised" (Nnaemeka 2004:61). Breast augmentation and facial alteration are products of cultural expectations, founded on men's desire but realized in the individual or collective choices made by women.

Identity and agencies are often affirmed in the choices made by individuals to fulfill societal expectations, whether such expectations are metaphysically enforced by the individual or directly promoted and implemented by the community. To understand and appreciate facial (eye or nose) alteration as an individual choice is to understand female circumcision as a group choice, particularly in the context of how cultures (whether American, European, or African) shape human behavior. One can only imagine the number of people who would undergo facial, breast, or other bodily transformation/mutilation if such services were free or inexpensive. Awa Thiam (1986) notes that excision and infibulation are deeply rooted in the societies in which they are practiced, which is why protests against these practices by young women are often met with strong resistance on the part of older women.

ECONOMIC BASIS OF WOMEN'S IDENTITY

Measures of judging the status of women versus men is often in the comparative economic valuation in society. Differential salary and compensation between men and women performing similar tasks has been a rallying point for advocating for gender equality. Thus, equal pay for equal work has been a goal for all who seek a just and equitable society, particularly given a history of women's economic marginalization in societies. Beyond the concern for inequality in salary earned for equal work is also the realization of the degree to which being economically and equitably rewarded for work performed does affirm a woman's agency. Indeed, economic independence as a goal in the equality struggle has often been used to frame what constitutes an emancipated woman. When asked whether women had overcome sexism and discrimination in France, Françoise Giroux, the late French writer and feminist scholar, responded that one could claim that women have overcome sexism and patriarchal domination at a point in history when mediocre women begin to assume positions of leadership. Indeed, progress for women is still measured by the number of extraordinary women who achieve success in the economic leadership ladder in geopolitical spaces dominated by men. "Extraordinary" does not offer us a frame to measure equity and equality in the marketplace; "ordinary" does. The true worth of a nation could be said to be measured by the degree to which ordinary women assume political and economic leadership not as an exception but as a rule. Africans and, indeed, the world celebrated when E. Sirleaf-Johnson of Liberia was elected to become the first female president of an African nation. We celebrated when the Kenyan Wangari Maathai became the first female recipient of the Nobel Prize for Peace for her tireless efforts in teaching us all to not only respect but to become committed to nurturing and regenerating our environment. Achievements by extraordinary women even when within the realm of economic advancement is always a welcome change in a global system that has managed to consign women to less visible leadership positions in their nations. However, the politics of identity are less of what extraordinary people have accomplished but rather how the identity of "ordinary" women is framed and their agency affirmed.

On the question of economic reward for contributions made, African women are no different from Western women in terms of working long hours and receiving less equitable remunerative value and rewards commensurate with her labor. Like men, women naturally seek efficient and effective ways to use available human and material resources to reduce their workload, if only to have some leisure time during the day. The differences between African and Western women in general lie in what is used to frame women's identity and what different stages of life means in their agency. Elsewhere I have lamented that gender inequity in Africa is manifested through limited access to resources such as domestic appliances that may help them manage their daily tasks in a more efficient manner (Airhihenbuwa 1995b). This is still the case. What I did not address, however, was the question of their agencies as mothers and the role of nurturance in affirming their identity not as victims of oppression, even though gender inequity exists, but as cultural subjects. Indeed, motherhood as a more appropriate status on which to locate African women's agency has some relevance for understanding the status of African American women.

RACIAL AND GENDER HYBRIDITY

In the intersection of race with patriarchy, people of African descents have multiple identities and experiences that locate their agencies outside the Western construction of American white feminists. Where the Western woman complains of being doubly oppressed, Thiam (1986) argues that African women suffer threefold oppression: patriarchal domination by virtue of her sex, capitalist exploitation by virtue of her class, and a negative appropriation of her country by colonial or neocolonial powers by virtue of her race. In assessing the totalizing of female identity as a copy of male identity, the historian Darlene Clark Hine (1993) asks, in counterposition to DuBois's notion of double consciousness, rather than whether "o'-ne ever feels his twoness," whether he would have mused about how a Black woman ever feels her "fiveness": Negro, American, woman, poor, and Black woman. The notion of African American twoness of identity as a function of race has always been acknowledged. However, such identity intersection as a confluence of race and patriarchy has not always been recognized, in part because much of the earlier work on identity has focused almost exclusively on race as framed by leaders of the civil rights movement, on the one hand, whereas, on the other hand, the universalization of African American women's agency is subsumed within notions of "sisterhood is global" as framed by white feminists. Moreover, there is the belief that the Black male is exposed to much more hostility in the wider environment. This is also coupled with the fact that the more visible form of violence and hostility visited on the Black male body has led to a singular focus on male identity as representative of all identity. In fact, that African American males are believed to have faced and continue to face a more hostile environment may also be misleading if one considers the hostility and violence faced by African American females. Engaging an analysis of African American women's social cultural infrastructure offers some insights into better ways to understand the totality of the Black woman's experience. It is well established that women have better social support networks that men. Their success in buffering the impact of multiple sources of domination should not neutralize any measure of impact these dominations have on women. It is the case that African American women have been more successful at navigating the many obstacles they must confront through their support networks for coping with multiple oppressive gazes. In the words of Michael Eric Dyson (1996b), "I just think black women have learned, more successfully than black men, to absorb the pain of their predicament and to keep stepping. They've learned to take the kind of mess that black men won't take, or feel they can't take, perhaps never will take, and to turn it into something useful, something productive, something roughly beautiful after all" (4). After all, the same women slaves who were raped by the master were expected to also care for the master's wife and children. Moreover, I have observed in my research in communities affected by HIV and AIDS (although not exclusively) that women living with HIV and AIDS tended to be involved in support groups that focus on emotional healing through sharing and support with others, whereas men (although not exclusively) living with HIV and AIDS tended to be in support groups that have a political mission and are engaged more in political activism. A central distinction in the themes of the nature of the support groups to which women are drawn compared with men has been the affirmation of motherhood in the women's support group. Such affirmation is often expressed in sharing and learning strategies to navigate the competing terrains of expectations as a woman whose role as the nurturer of her family often overshadows her personal self-interest to care for her personal health and well-being.

CULTURE AND THE MEANINGS OF WOMANHOOD

Gender inequity was exacerbated in Africa through educational institutions that reinforced separate and unequal values and beliefs throughout society. Because educational institutions offer the same opportunity for men and women, men were privileged for training by the colonial masters so these men could cater for the needs of the colonizers. The result is that the father who has three sons and three daughters but only enough resources to provide a solid foundation for the future well-being and social and economic independence (e.g., education) for four of his children may choose to do so for all three sons, no matter their birth order, and then choose one "lucky" daughter. Already the boys are ahead, thus marking the beginning of their privileged position. To understand the resulting inequity thus requires an understanding of this foundation that has been established (mostly unwittingly) in the family. Today's generation of some African men has been making efforts to redress gender inequity in their own family formations. Such redress, however, is in the context of economic production and educational opportunities that create such inequity. J. Njoku (1980) observes that in today's African philosophy, knowledge obtained through Western formal education is a power that is believed to be reserved only for males, who will inherit the land, thus placing women at a great disadvantage. A clear exception will be in a matrilineal family where inheritance right is through the mother, as is the case in Ghana. Beyond the devaluation of femaleness that was promoted by colonies is the reformation of authority and assets based on ownership of land. Men were to own land and women to nurture it. Men were to get training for the benefit of colonial service sector, whereas women were to remain at home to care for their family and, in some cases, the families of the colonizers as well. Indeed, when unequal foundations are established for both men and women, land-ownership issues may remain a measure of inequity between them. The point here is not to demonize maleness and romanticize femaleness but to illustrate one example of gender inequity that has been interpreted as a form of female oppression in pre- and postcolonial times.

Motherhood does offer a framework within which one can examine women's agency outside oppression. Motherhood thus becomes a form of social cultural infrastructure whose analysis is useful to understand not only the role and expectation of women but also the roles and expectations of men. "Fundamentally, motherhood is not usually constructed in relations to or in opposition to fatherhood; it is conceived in its own right. Mothers are perceived as especially powerful—literally and mystically, in regard to the well being of the child. They are therefore the pivot around which family life is structured and the child's life rotates" (Oyewumi 2003a:13). Motherhood also extends beyond having children even though having children is a gold standard for being a mother. In the tradition of comothering, one's aunt is also one's mother. Motherhood also provides an analytical frame in the promotion of equity through the role of males, and men's expectations can be examined not as an oppressor but as a part of the culture. It is for the involvement of men that the issue of gender inequity should focus on the relationship between men and women and thus the collective efforts of men and women. This is one reason some African American feminists differ from White feminists in the nature of women's emancipatory projects. As bell hooks (1993) has stated, "I believe that men must be part of the feminist movement, and they must feel that they have a major role to play in the eradication of sexism. The term 'women's movement' reproduces the notion that somehow feminism is this plantation that only women should labor on" (20).

As indicated earlier, motherhood as a defining frame for African women's agency has relevance to African Americans. Motherhood among poor African Americans had often been represented as a proxy for motherhood in the African American culture. Yet, according to Felice Jones-Lee (2005), motherhood among African American poor has often been subjected to public scrutiny. The necessity for poor women to seek state support for her children's health and general well-being has also meant an invitation to government to define her motherhood status as wanting and thus substandard. A motherhood that is seen to be a deviation from the middle-class mothering, which typically occurs in private spaces, is demonized as needy. Motherhood in a private space as experienced by most White middle-class mothers is often used as the gold standard to frame motherhood in the United States. Thus, at the intersection of race and class, motherhood among African Americans does not enjoy similar affirming agency as motherhood among White middle-class women in America. Even as motherhood is an acknowledged status for affirming agency, African American mothers' agency, even framed in public spaces, is silenced through the combined oppression of their identity by the state that defines them by the needs that present them for support, and the universalizing of their experiences subsumed under the middle-class White women's mothering that typically occurs in private spaces.

Even in case of noted oppression of women, analysis designed to subvert such oppression against women must historicize such oppression within the context of culture and then affirm the efforts of feminists/womanists in that culture to contextualize such oppression and subvert it, so that these women are represented as legitimate voices and representation for the oppressed. Some of the ways that women have transformed oppression have been in the form of passive resistance. It is important to note that passive resistance is a recognized and legitimate strategy that has been used effectively by the oppressed to subvert oppression. In other words, the oppressed have always lived the true meaning of what Chinua Achebe (1987) meant when he said, "When one thing stands, another thing must stand beside it." The oppressed are not always powerless in the grassroots enterprise, as the notion of development participation would suggest. As M. Rahnema (1992) notes, theirs is a different power that is represented in the thousands of centers and informal networks of resistance that are developed against the prevailing power apparatuses.

SPEAKING FOR OTHERS IN GENDER DISCOURSE

It is not that American and European feminists cannot represent a voice for women in other societies. The problem is that they tend to do so commonly, without affirming the scholarship of the women in these cultures, nor is their identity theorizing based on identity frames that best represent women's agency in these cultures. What commonly results is a form of White female hegemony as well as cultural chauvinism. Such cultural chauvinism is the basis of the economic reductionism of third-world women as found in the literature on women in development. According to Chandra Mohanty (1991), "The best examples of universalization on the basis of economic reductionism can be found in the liberal 'Women in Development' literature. Proponents of this school seek to examine the effect of development on third world women, sometimes from self-designated feminist perspectives" (63). One avenue where African women are constantly spoken for by their Western counterparts is through the ubiquitous NGOs. The everyday, fluid, historical expressions in the lives of African women is commonly collapsed into a few frozen descriptors such as *poor, oppressed, powerless,* and so forth.

A number of the Western-based NGOs that are involved in health and development projects in African countries regularly deliberate over the most effective and efficient methods of promoting economic independence among women. One recommendation has been to train more women in income-generating activities for the sustainability of such projects as the child survival programs. "Gardening" is an occupation often recommended as suitable for women, but the nature of work suggests that what is actually being recommended is farming. *Gardening* seems to be a more acceptable term because it romanticizes the labor involved. It suggests that the work is pleasurable and not as rigorous as farming. On the other hand, one cannot help but wonder whether middle-class professionals, particularly women, are weary of being accused of encouraging their "sisters" to engage in farming. Whatever the reasons for recommending gardening, it is clear that if the same intensity of labor in agricultural production were being recommended for men, it would be called farming.

Breastfeeding is another example of a practice that can be learned and promoted from within the culture, yet many NGOs now believe they have the requisite knowledge to train African women in how to breastfeed. In a feminist framework that is indifferent to motherhood at best and rejects it at worst,

African mothers are being rendered strangers in their own domain. Young Western women now position themselves to teach African mothers how to breastfeed using illustrated posters. They promote themselves to be superior to African mothers, on the one hand, and are mute over institutional forces, such as infant formula manufacturers that compromise motherhood, on the other. Even though they have opportunity to learn about the infant formula industry's assault on breastfeeding, they do very little or nothing to challenge infant formula industries in these countries. These Western-based corporations have contributed to the practice that has led to the abandonment of breastfeeding (long before HIV and AIDS offered a rationale for such a decision) by some women for what is unfortunately believed to be a superior form of infant feeding. The NGOs that engage in teaching breastfeeding have made the assumption that if African women do not breastfeed their babies, it is because they do not know how. Even if younger generations of women do not know how to breastfeed, learning has always been within the cultural contexts that positions older mothers within the community to teach younger ones. The fact that financial privileging of NGOs has produced American women as educators of African women many times has disempowered African female elders in nurturing their agencies through a task that has been their cultural domain as mothers.

The education about breastfeeding in the traditional context occurs within other vital lessons for which elder mothers take leadership roles in educating other women. Nkiru Nzegwu (1996) recalls a similar experience that was recounted by Ifi Amadiume about a young White woman who went to Zimbabwe to teach the local women how to organize. This woman was so intoxicated with her first-world affluence that she neglected to study Zimbabwean history to learn that these women were at the center of the fifteen-year liberation struggle to gain independence from the repressive and racist White minority regime of Ian Smith. This could only have been possible through these women's "incredible fortitude, organizational skills, and participatory role in the liberation struggle" (114). There is no shortage of examples and experiences of African women educating men and women in organizing and effecting change.

African women educating women is a cultural production that affirms a space within which women speak and are heard. Such affirmation confirms that a woman's agency is not measured by the degree to which she expresses her humanity, identity, and femininity in relations to men. This also means that sexuality is only one form of understanding women's agency in Africa. Because gender discourse almost invariably interrogates questions of sexuality, whether it is in relations to men or to other women, the inability to engage a gender discourse that examines the totality of women's agency particularly in nonsexual spheres has led to contestations over which culture is needed to offer insights. As long as the analysis of women's agency is ultimately subjected to a framework of sexuality, an understanding of African women's agency is incomplete. When an older Kikuyu woman "marries" a younger woman with children as a legitimate cultural reproduction, the point of interest for most analysts seems to always be in defining the location of sexuality in such a "marriage." Such a cultural practice that affirms these women's agency in ways that are independent from men or sexuality is totally ignored. Instead, the question is often asked whether such relationships are lesbian. "The 'female wife' is a wife to the female husband in that she (the husband) has jural rights to her and the children produced within the marriage despite the fact that they do not engage in sexual intercourse. A male recruited by the husband (female) impregnates the wife" (Oyewumi 2003a:15). Only if one understands the practice of women educating women, women nurturing women, and women indoctrinating women into womanhood could the Kikuyu practice be understood as a cultural production.

The paradox of some Western feminist discourse, often challenged by African feminists/womanists, is the demand for women-centered discourse to eliminate inequity and inequality, conflicting with a simultaneous desire to have such discourse be engaged and accepted by men as a prerequisite for women's agency. Indeed, the conflict often manifests in uncertainty about whether to retain gendered social titles such as *chairman* or neutralize them, as in *chair*. In other instances, a professional title such as *actor* is retained to signify a neutral title, while *actress* is slowly disfavored. For African women, such questions of identity in social and professional spaces are secondary to the importance of the identity that is produced in a fully nurtured space where women affirm a difference that makes healthy differences, such as retaining titles like *chairwoman*. Having and promoting such spaces is critical and important for subsequent relations with other women and men.

This reality of cultivating and nurturing women's agency has always been a part of African women's cultural production. It is represented in the cultural space of the Mbang of Cameroon in which the agency of my wife, Angele Kingue, was affirmed. Like the Mbang, the Edos of Nigeria, and the Loebe of Senegal, many cultures in Africa have the practice of nurturing a space where women's agency is groomed and nurtured into maturity not for male gaze but for a woman's own identity and personhood. It is in these spaces that sensuality is often engaged and expressed, not for male consumption but as an important aspect of a female and feminine identity. Indeed, dances and other forms of sensual expression are taught and celebrated in these affirming spaces in ways that would have responded in the affirmative to bell hooks'

(1981) book title question "Ain't I a woman?" It is in these spaces that agency is solidified and becomes critical in navigating assaults that include the medicalization of women's bodies.

MEDICINE, SEXUALITY, AND WOMANHOOD

Physiological events that occur only in womanhood (i.e., menstruation and menopause) have become the site of contestation over the medication of a woman's body. Most cultures now embrace the medicalization of menstruation and menopause, such that the onsets of these natural events are marked by negativity. Both physical and emotional isolation and ostracism are commonly associated with the experiences of menstruating or menopausal women. Both of these events may be viewed as part of natural aging processes, but societal (particularly Western medical) responses tend to suggest that many still believe they are pathologic. Very little emphasis is placed on preparing young girls for menarche, and because of the negativity associated with and the medicalization of menopause, there is little interest in understanding how women in African cultures experience this life stage. W. Kamau (personal communication, 1993) interviewed some elderly Kenyan women and found that these Kenyan women never experienced any of the typically expected psychomedical manifestations, such as hot flashes, irritability, and depression. Whether this is representative of the experiences of most women in Kenya and other African countries, it is clear that we are overlooking strategies employed by older women in African nations to live comfortably with the beginning phases of menopause. Rather than exploring the degree to which holistic traditional foods may buffer the so-called menopause syndrome, we place undue emphasis on medical interventions, such as hormone replacement therapy (HRT). Indeed, new studies published in the past two years have shown that HRT have many negative outcomes, leading to the outcry that these medications should be discontinued. Needless to say, many scholars have questioned the reliance on HRT to address this transition process for women. Instead of learning from African cultures about how women can positively experience these events, we have forsaken the cultural richness of human experiences in many African nations and are looking to the West for answers.

In a culture constructed on the complicity between the confluence of silence and submission, on the one hand, and philosophical misogyny, on the other, Rey Chow (1991) argues that Chinese and other non-Western women not only are oppressed but also support their own oppression through the feelings of spiritual resignation that are dispersed throughout their societies. Western culture contributes to the defining of womanhood only through the man's world in various ways that are often not interrogated. For example, Ali Mazrui (1986) indicates that a wife's adoption of her husband's name upon marriage is an alien custom that has been perpetuated by Western cultures in most traditional African societies. Traditionally, Edo women, my mother among them, retain their own names upon marriage. This is a legacy of the traditional African custom that nurtures the establishment of personhood within her family lineage. Indeed, Oyewumi (1997) has argued that one cannot understand fully the status of Yoruba women by examining her role in her marital home at the exclusion of her continued position in her natal home. In a televised program in Cameroon in which my wife, a scholar and writer, was being interviewed to discuss her new novel that had just been published, a caller wanted to know why she had kept her natal name, Kingue, instead of adopting mine upon marriage. Was this a kind of feminist positioning, the caller queried? Asking the caller to recall his grandmother's last name, he and the television audience soon realized that their grandmothers did use their natal, rather than their husband's, name. In my case, my mother always used her natal last name, Asemota. This practice, indigenous to many African cultures, is now considered a revolution in the West as women keep their natal last name or hyphenate it with their husband's. As we challenge the problem of patriarchy that leads to some form of women's oppression, we must acknowledge and celebrate the very positive aspects of culture that have nurtured women's agency in Africa. With such acknowledgment, we must also examine aspects of culture that offer an analytical framework for understanding forms of relationship and role expectation in Africa. A key example is the role of age and seniority.

The Edo and Yoruba languages are gender free and are based on seniority, unlike French or English. According to Oyewumi (1997), it is on seniority that role responsibilities, policies, and the economy are structured. As a result, power relations are better understood along lines of seniority than of gender. Seniority does not necessarily translate to a birth order, nor is it confined to natal bloodline. Moreover, in the traditional Edo and Yoruba, inheritance rights did not privilege children over the parents' siblings. In determining the focus of an intervention project among the Edos and Yorubas, therefore, the focus on the person should begin with the position and seniority of persons and their role in the family. A critical element is the ways of knowing that are grounded in qualitative reasoning, given the cyclical nature of the value system and the resulting relationships. For example, it would be inappropriate, in this case, to employ an individual-based psychological measure to predict individual behavior. If the family comes before the person, then a strategy based on group efficacy is more appropriate. Within such a group, we ought to understand the role of age in forging and maintaining relationships.

One aspect of the dimensions of health-seeking behavior that we have yet to explore concerns how the age gap between couples in Africa affects decision making in the household. In cultures that place emphasis on seniority and aging in decision making, a wife who is much younger than her husband does not necessarily have much decision-making power in the household. Such hierarchy of authority is usually a function of cultural values and reality, albeit to the disadvantage of the younger of the couple, typically the wife. The promotion of gender equity and independence in this context may not prove as practical as an exploration of strategies to bridge the spousal age gap while refocusing on the agency that a woman could assume in a marriage to elevate and enrich her status in the family, such as when she becomes a mother.

SEX, HEALTH, AND WOMANHOOD

In *The History of Sexuality*, Michel Foucault (1978) historicizes the masculinized construction of blame and sexual being that privileged maleness and heterosexuality. Today, such blame has placed the responsibility of controlling the spread of STIs on women. Strategies designed to control STIs such as HIV must take cognizance of the social contexts in which they are operating and must fully appreciate the weight of cultural tradition in structuring the social/sexual relationships between men and women. For example, women have been (and still are, in some cultures) held responsible for the sexes of their babies. Therefore, women's humanity is affirmed admittedly not only by their ability to have children but by their ability to have male children.

A discussion of the issue of sexuality in the African context is incomplete without addressing the role of men in reaching a collective solution. For instance, the issue of stigma has reignited the many facets of blame for which women are held responsible for HIV and AIDS. In the absence of unequal access to education, which leads to inequity in skills development, which further leads to disproportionate level of joblessness in an already depressed economy, a woman may have no choice but to resort to using sex as barter for the financial support from a male partner. Under such circumstances, a woman may rationally place more value on securing food and shelter for herself and her children than on practicing safer sex. Moreover, negotiating condom use with a sexual partner, for example, sometimes creates the perception of distrust and the fear that she may be accused of being promiscuous. If a woman asks her male partner to use a condom, she is thought of as implying either that he has morally transgressed or that she is herself engaged in sexual relations with multiple partners, a status that is believed to be a violation of the status of motherhood. Indeed, motherhood is a defining frame for women's agency in Africa. However, it is not without its challenges and expectations that women must navigate.

In a study conducted among women living with HIV and AIDS in South Africa, Thabang Mosala found that women have to negotiate and balance their cultural expectation to breastfeed with their medical condition and the need to bottle feed their infants to prevent transmitting HIV to their children. These women devise ways of explaining to inquisitive friends and family members about why they chose to bottle feed instead of breastfeed. Their stories ranged from "I have small breasts, and I cannot breastfeed" to "My friend who works in the health clinic gave me free formula, and I am preparing my child for weaning." Clearly, like any form of cultural affirmation, motherhood has its challenges. Women have had to negotiate the cultural terrain of motherhood expectations to provide health and security needed for their children while attempting to live with a condition that is highly stigmatized and makes disclosure a very challenging and sometimes very risky undertaking. Indeed, effective intervention to reduce women's vulnerability to HIV requires strategies to enable her to affirm her agency rather than educating her about her sexual behavior.

As in conventional prevention messages, it is often assumed that educating women about proper ways to prevent a disease will automatically translate to behavior change. The reasons many women do not use condoms or do not negotiate condom use are related to sex role socialization and devaluation of their status as women. In the United States, although it might seem that the inability of women to use or negotiate the use of condoms contributes to the maintenance of the imbalance in the male-female relationship, this female powerlessness is better understood in the larger context of the economic security, the sex-ratio imbalance, and the meaning of sex. Indeed, language of multiple sex partners blunts college students' experience with serial monogamy. *Serial monogamy* refers to having one sex partner at a given time but for only a short period of time because the college campus context does not favor longtime commitment. What often happens is that the average college student will have multiple sex partners over the four- to six-year duration of the college experience. Because multiple partnerships are often constructed as having multiple simultaneous sex partners, many women in college involved in serial monogamy have a false sense of security.

MOTHERHOOD AND PREVENTION STRATEGIES

When health programs are developed for mothers, it is more likely for the protection of their children or the children they are expecting to have rather than a program for mothers because of their agency as African women. A focus on motherhood is not a priority as a cultural project even when there is a need to protect their children and the family. The problem is when it is done only for the children at the exclusion of an interest in mothers' status as the cultural womb of the family. Oyewumi (2003b) explains that motherhood is so central to identity in Yoruba that in *Ogboni* (a Yoruba political organization), member refer to each other as *omoya* (mother's child), regardless of gender. Indeed, among the Edos, "motherhood" is *iye* and "my mother's child" is *omwiyemwen*. Omwiyemwen can be an expression of fondness for a friend but not *omwieramwen* (my father's child). At a conference on the social aspects of HIV and AIDS in Africa in Dakar in 2005, Cheikh Niang explained the limitation of using terms like *brother* and *sister* to express the depth of closeness one feels for a friend. The most appropriate term to use in such an occasion is *doomu ndey*, which means, in Wolof, "my mother's child." This position of motherhood in African society, according to Oyewumi (2003a), could not be gendered in the discourse on patriarchy but rather should be recognized particularly for the spiritual and material power that only a mother can represent to her child and her family. Unfortunately, the context that nurtures womanhood status in African countries has been seriously compromised given the medicalization of mothers' identity. The spiritual growth and what Oyewumi refers to as a mother's godlike power over her child has slowly been taken away from her in an era when her body and fertility have become medicalized. Some of the programs designed to ensure the maintenance of her motherhood status actually serve the interest of pharmaceutical industries that gain more from appearing to prevent her "potential contamination" of her child with "her disease," as we see in preventing mother-to-child transmission of HIV and AIDS. Indeed, female condoms (a primary prevention) for women have not gained the same level of support as has Nevarapin (a medical and secondary prevention) for preventing mother-to-child transmission. Women are targeted in health intervention programs to take responsibility for the improved health conditions of their children, not because women as mothers are considered worthy of such focus but because their survival is inextricably tied to the survival of their children. Yet J. DeWitt Webster (2003), in his study, found female condoms to be well accepted by both women and men if only the cost would be lowered to make them as affordable and accessible as male condoms. Although the focus on prevention of mother to child is laudable, it would appear that a focus on preventing HIV among women in the first instance is more crucial, because the health of the woman often means the health of the family because women are often the caretakers of their families.

A superior location of women, as unveiled in Oyewumi's work, has been hijacked and used as a reason for a woman's weakness primarily because of the same reproductive power for which a cultural analysis locates her in a superior position in her African culture. An example with the role of mothers-in-law is useful here. At this same conference in Dakar, a scholar presented a paper on the role of mothers-in-law in discouraging their daughters-in-law from going to the hospital to deliver their babies. This was viewed as another reason to demonize mothers-in-law. Such demonization clearly reinforces the construction of the evil mother-in-law within the cultural logic of the West. Following the presentation, Niang offered a Senegalese insight as a way to lay bare the social cultural infrastructure that frames the role and expectation of the mother-in-law in Senegalese society. In his study, he explains, he found the same result in mothers'-in-law making decisions about where the daughter-in-law is to have her baby. Upon further exploration and through participant observation, Niang and his team came to understand that the mother-in-law assumes total and complete responsibility for the welfare of her daughter (here referred to as daughter-in-law). This became more evident when the mother-in-law walks and paces with the young mother, asking God to protect the young mother, and if there was any misfortune to befall the young mother, she prays that such misfortune befalls her, the mother-in-law, instead. Further in-depth interview reveals that given the cultural expectation, which the mother-in-law proudly assumes, that she is singularly responsible for the total care of the young daughter, the decision to place her in an environment where she, the mother, has total control is paramount. The hospital setting does not include such a location for which she has control. Thus, rather than seeing the mother-in-law as an enemy, through the Western construction of her identity, these Senegalese mothers-in-law represent the expecting mother's guardian angel. Such cultural analysis is commonly lost in the public health assessment of African response to conditions that typically call for a clinical-based medical intervention.

The same misunderstanding has been true of giving birth. The birthing chair was used by traditional birth attendants for three primary reasons: (1) the force of gravity helps the birthing process when the mother is sitting on a chair rather than lying on her back, (2) the mother is expected to exercise her independence in the birthing process rather than being dependent on a medical provider, and (3) sitting on a birthing chair allows the mother's feet to be firmly connected to the earth. This connection is considered to be very crucial for the mother and baby. Finally, the birthing process has always been a cultural space where women mentor women and support each other in African societies before the notion of sisterhood was ever promoted to be global. In Africa, motherhood matters.

FINAL THOUGHTS

Motherhood in Africa is the agency that matters to a woman's identity. Such agency can only be understood at the intersection of gender, age, and culture. The full context of African women's agency cannot be fully understood without problematizing the intersection of nurturing, on the one hand, and centering women's motherhood status, on the other. Motherhood is an African woman's agency that offers her an opportunity to celebrate her identity. Programs aimed at improving women's health should commence with issues of what the different statuses of women actually represent in society from birth to motherhood and beyond. Seemingly, we should engage the question of inequity and inequality at various levels of society with particular attention to the status of young girls and their opportunity to participate fully in the educational system. Women's health status in society should be understood to reflect how society has constructed and nurtured the character of its "ordinary" women. In Africa, it could be said that the true worth of a race must be measured by the character of its motherhood.

8

Healing Illness and Affirming Health in Africa

> Until the lions produce their own historian, the story of the hunt will glorify only the hunter.
>
> —Chinua Achebe (2001:73)

Traditional healing is perhaps the only health system that is accessible to everyone in Africa. It is estimated that some 80 percent of Africans use traditional healing methods. Traditional healing has been sustained over the years partly because it is based in cultural values and norms of the people and partly because it is available, acceptable, accessible, and, in many communities, affordable.

Africans' use of traditional remedies to prevent, treat, and cure illness dates back several centuries. In examining health services in Africa, as well as in other parts of the world, health educators and designers of health promotion programs must consider the cultural framework carefully to understand how African people view sickness, disease, and appropriate treatment methods.

Scholars of traditional healing like Mthobeli Guma (2002), who study health practices and beliefs among Africans, have argued that patients and clients who seek prevention or cure for illness or disease do so on the basis of their cultural logics. Robert Hahn (1995) provides evidence to support the established knowledge that the sources of prevention and cure of particular problems are determined to a great extent by the clients' sociocultural and religious backgrounds. It is for this reason, and the fact that majority of Zimbabweans use traditional healing, that Guma (1997) recommends that traditional healing be considered the mainstream health care service whereas allopathic (Western) medicine be considered complementary. Because Africa's cultural evolution has often been misrepresented, it is not surprising that its healing modalities have been victims of allopathic hegemony. In Africa, the harsh experiences and upheavals of the slave trade, colonialism, and neocolonialism precluded the pattern of development experienced in the West. Similarly, the evolution of traditional medicine in African countries is different from that of countries that were not colonized, such as China and Thailand.

In all forms of traditional healing, religion and shared cultural values and beliefs are at the core of preventive and curative health practices. Religion, myth, magic, and superstition and their physical and psychological manifestations are all based on rationality. Such rationality is best understood in its traditional (emic) context rather than through a Western (etic) paradigm, hence the popular utilization of traditional medicine in African countries. An *etic* approach is one that focuses on universal traits regardless of culture, whereas an *emic* approach focuses on cultural meanings. However, it is useful for health workers to understand the possibilities offered by both systems of medicine, so that Africans can utilize the most effective health care services for different conditions and under differing circumstances. Edward Green (1999) offers an explanation model for health and illness in eastern and southern Africa based on the cultural logic of people on the region. For example, the concept of pollution as disease causation represents a form of contamination in which the balance of the body as a system has been violated. Pollution in this sense does not refer to industrial emission of poisonous gas, for example, but to physical illness that results from the body being subjected to forces that alter its state of balance.

REAPPRAISAL OF TRADITIONAL HEALTH CARE

It is a commonly and easily observed fact that even the most "cosmopolitized" Christians, scholars, scientists, and entrepreneurs among the African bourgeoisie today still consult African divinities, diviners, and healers when their health or other affairs are in serious trouble. Many have been known to sneak away from their church pews, discard their three-piece suits, steal away by night to some healer either in the heart of the city or at the healers' village shrine, and carry out all manner of ritual sacrifices when these are demanded. Chinweizu and Jemie (1987) note that even among those with Ph.D.s, D.Sc.s, LL.D.s, and other assorted strings of Western bourgeois academic degrees, the going attitude is still that Western medicines and the Western Christian God are fine in their place, but when things get tough, one runs back to one's roots and ancestral ways.

The existence or absence of a corpus of literature that historicizes a country's traditional medical practice tends to depend on whether the country is colonized and the extent to which the colonizers have outlawed the practice and consequently the documentation of traditional medicine. In the nineteenth century and most of the twentieth, Europeans were concerned with colonization, exploitation, and commerce. J. Janzen (1974–1975), in a discussion of Belgian colonial policy in the Congo, states that "indigenous therapeutic practices were never mentioned within colonial manuals or laws. These laws sought only to establish European-modeled institutions regardless of what may have pre- or co-existed in African society" (109). Ira Harrison (1984) notes that Ralph Schram's *A History of Nigerian Health Services*, published in 1971, never mentioned the traditional healers who were serving the people prior to the colonizing exercises of the British.

During the early part of the twentieth century, there was a shift of emphasis from conquest of Africans, Asians, Latin Americans, and Oceanic peoples to control and co-optation of them. This shift in emphasis was aimed at the maintenance of law, order, and economic growth. Thus, non-Western cultural productions were ignored at best and criminalized at worst. The devaluation of Edo language in the classroom was already institutionalized in the 1970s when the school charged us (elementary school students) a monetary penalty for speaking the Edo language on school premises. Such practice continues today in some schools over different part of Africa. Like the devaluation of Edo language, the medical beliefs and practices of most non-European peoples were considered invalid and unsuitable for advancement and progress. As a result, laws were promulgated by the colonizers to criminalize the practice of traditional medicine.

A few decades later, Bronislaw Malinowski (1954) and A. R. Radcliffe-Brown (1952) observed that religious rites, beliefs, and practices served to maintain order in society and to regulate individual and group sentiment and behavior. Religious and spiritual rites have a specific social function—namely, to regulate, maintain, and transmit from one generation to another the sentiments on which the constitution of the society depends. Spirituality (to be discussed in chapter 10) is critical to an understanding of the social and cultural dimension of health, which in turn is pivotal to the maintenance of the relationships we have with the physical environment. In other words, there is more to health care than medical care. Health care delivery systems do not exist in and of themselves, but as parts of larger sociocultural wholes. Health care systems comprise a set of resources that serve both nonmedical as well as medical function and social values.

A reassessment of the disease-focused approach to health care has led some social and behavioral scientists to adopt a social action approach to health care delivery, particularly in addressing the question of health inequity. This means that the views of the community (the emic perspective) should be considered to be central to how scientific (etic perspectives) conclusions are reached. Medical and health beliefs and practices that had in the past been deemed superstitions are being reassessed and given fresh interpretations. These beliefs constitute symbolic representations of various realities, many of which are non-Western. Maladies resulting from hot-cold imbalance, the dislocation of internal organs, impure blood, unclean air, moral transgression, interpersonal struggle, and humans' relation to the spirit world are now seen as different manifestations of some general reality. When people define physical or emotional symptoms within a traditional taxonomy, they are likely to seek help in the traditional health care system. Thus, as Z. A. Ademuwagun (1974–1975) indicates, Nigerians in the Ibarapa district of Oyo state use traditional healers for excessive worry, sleeplessness, malaria, yellow fever, and snakebite. The late T. A. Lambo (1978), former deputy director general of WHO, faults the Western medical practitioner as being too preoccupied with immediate natural causes, with little attention paid to the causal relations between conflicts and irregularities as understood in studies on social relations on the one hand and disease or misfortune on the other. Traditional healers have gained increased attention because of their proven effectiveness in responding not only to diseases that are endemic in the healers' community but to the HIV/AIDS pandemic. In South Africa today, healers have gained new attention with the discovery of a treatment called *ubeja* for the treatment of HIV. Ubeja was developed by healers from a combination of several plant extracts.

TRADITIONAL HEALING CONCEPTS

The belief that a state of balance exists within the individual, on the one hand, and between the individual and the environment, on the other, is a concept that is true for all traditional healing modalities worldwide. How this concept is operationalized varies among cultures and hence among different traditional healing systems. African traditional medicine seeks to secure and maintain a balance among the individual, elements of nature, and the heavenly bodies. Within the individual, a balance is maintained among organic disorders, physiological disorders, and social conflicts. This balanced state is, in turn, balanced with elements of nature—earth, fire, water, air, and metal. Finally, balance is sought with the heavenly bodies—the sun, moon, and stars.

Organic and physiological disorders are concepts that are familiar to allopathic medicine. Social conflict is also a familiar allopathic concept in understanding psychological disorders. Expressions such as "He gets under my skin" and "She makes me sick" are examples of manifestations of social conflicts. In the African traditional healing context, an understanding of social conflict is pivotal to caring for a person who has become ill. This is where the healer deals with the *ultimate* cause of an illness: who or what caused it, and why. The *proximate* cause, or specific etiology, tells only how it happened, not why it happened. For people who believe in this concept of disease nosology, knowledge of germ theory is considered one of the many factors for explaining the medium through which health problems manifest themselves. Thus, the notion of pollution as a causation of diseases serves to offer insights into a form of social contamination of the body that is distinct from pollution as a form of poison resulting from physical pollution of the environment.

Ultimately, the origin of the disease or malady must be explained and dealt with. The body, mind, and environment must function in harmony for the individual to experience optimum health. The closest some allopaths have come to understanding traditional medicine has been in their understanding of homeopathy. In homeopathy, disease symptoms are considered good indications of the body's attempt to heal itself. For example, shivering in cold weather is the body's attempt to generate more heat to increase the core temperature of the body, and one should potentiate the shivering process rather than stop it; high fever is the body's attempt to make the environment uncomfortable for germs; and the cold and clammy skin of a person in shock is the result of the smaller blood vessels' diverting blood to the vital organs for the person's survival. The human body's ability to regulate itself naturally, as well as to synchronize the functions of its various parts to maintain a state of balance and harmony, is a basic principle of traditional medicine. It is this natural mechanism for dealing with states of balance and imbalance that traditional healers have always understood and attempted to maintain.

Traditional medicine is a desirable part of a nation's formal health care system, particularly in rural areas. The majority of physicians in a country like Nigeria live in major cities, and most of the country's rural population relies solely on traditional practitioners. Therefore, it behooves health professionals to examine the strengths and weaknesses of traditional medicine, so that they can promote its strengths and discourage its weaknesses. First, we must historicize traditional healing in relations to modern allopathic care.

Traditional medicine has paralleled the practice of Western allopathic medicine in a number of ways. In 1879, Robert Felkin, a British medical missionary traveling in Baganda (modern-day Uganda), reported a high level of medical and health practice. He saw the successful performance of cesarean sections, with antiseptic techniques, by a Baganda surgical team. Felkin also saw experiments devised to discover a cure for a local epidemic (Davis 1959). Although Felkin witnessed this only two years after Joseph Lister advocated antisepsis use in surgery in London, it was clear to him that the team's "surgical technique" and "public health experiments" were a part of the tradition of the Baganda. This suggests that the use of antisepsis by the traditional healers of Baganda predates its use by allopathic surgeons.

Other contributions made by traditional healers to health care delivery as documented by WHO and others (e.g., Foster 1963; Teller 1968) include the discovery of many herbal remedies, including *Rauwolfia serpentina*, a medicinal plant known as snakeroot, whose active ingredient, reserpine, is used today as a tranquilizer and hypotensive agent; *Erythropleum guineense*, identified from the bark of the sasswood tree, a powerful laxative substance; and *Periwinkle vinca rosea*, an herb containing insulin, which is used in the treatment of diabetes mellitus. Today, healers continue to contribute to development of treatment regimens for AIDS in Senegal and South Africa.

In addition to their contributions in the use of medicinal plants, traditional healers have been very successful in treating psychosomatic disorders. According to Lambo (1961), the Babalawos, in their ingenuity of care, would tie a toad to the penis of the bed wetter. When the child urinates, the heat from the urine wakes up the toad, which then begins to croak, which then wakes up the child. The similarity of this device to the modern anuretic devices is evident. The old anuretic machine delivers a shock to the bed wetter on urinating. The modern anuretic devices give off a buzzing sound to wake up the child with the intent to condition the child to wake up on his or her own. Behaviorally speaking, the old electric shock, the croaking of the toad, and the modern buzzing should function as behavior modification.

Another example was shared by a British-trained physician from Mauritius who attended a lecture I gave on traditional medicine in 1991 at the Boston University School of Public Health. He recounted the story of a Nigerian soccer player who had suffered a compound leg fracture in the 1970s and was healed by a traditional bonesetter. When the limb healed, however, it was shorter than the uninjured limb, such that the patient was left with a limp. The patient went back to the traditional healer to seek a solution and was instructed as follows: He was to ask a friend or relative to go to the river with him and tie him up in the part of the river with the heaviest wave for one hour every day. At the end of six months, the patient's broken leg was back to its normal length—the strength of the river's current had realigned the bone properly. This approach was, of course, very different from the one that would have been taken in an allopathic system, in which the bone would have been rebroken in a hospital and reset. Although it would be naive to suggest that traditional medicine is a panacea for the health problems of Africans, it certainly has the proven potential to improve the health care delivery system significantly for many people.

An understanding of the function of traditional medicine in any culture must begin with an understanding of the culture and its history. This is a challenge for behavioral and social scientists who have an interest in addressing global health problems. As a result of the renewed interest in traditional medicine, partly because of the primary health care movement, the child survival revolution of the 1970s and 1980s, and, more recently, HIV/AIDS, the integration of traditional healers into the country's allopathic health care institutions remains the model of choice for many governments. Unfortunately, governments and international donor agencies interested in funding these efforts often view the potential contributions of traditional medicine as very limited. On the strength of donors' economic resources, Judith Justice (1987) observes that these donors have dominated health policy and practices in the third world since World War II. Along with their influence and funding resources have come policy guidelines and priorities that have always privileged and promoted allopathic hegemony.

Major difficulties with government policy arise from perceptions and definitions of traditional medicine. Murray Last (1986) observes:

> Though within most nations there are usually a large number of medical subcultures, each with its own characteristics and structure, policy-makers often have in mind apparently a single, paradigmatic culture from which they generalize about "traditional medicine." Inevitably such stereotypes are likely to reflect political conditions as of course happened under colonial rule when traditional healers were categorized as "witches." (204)

ISSUES OF INTEGRATION

Failure to historicize traditional healing has resulted in misguided efforts by allopaths, albeit with sometimes sincere intentions, to address the formalization of traditional healing within the health care system. Historically, traditional healers were specialists at a time when allopaths were generalists. Healers specialized in diagnostics, maternal and child care, bone setting, and so on. The earliest attempts by governments to legitimate and confirm traditional healers encountered difficulties when physicians, who were generalists, proposed to traditional healers, who were specialists, that they should all come together under one umbrella as traditional healers. The impetus for such unification was to standardize traditional practice rather than for political and social leverage, as in the case of allopaths. Because the bone setters could never understand the wisdom of a forced marriage with maternal and child health specialists (even though a few might specialize in both), unification never materialized. In cases in which unification has occurred today, it is for the same reason as Western allopathic unification—political leverage within a society. It should be noted, however, that approaches to specialization have changed for both traditional healers and allopaths. Whereas physicians now train to become specialists, traditional healers train to become generalists. Both healing transitions have been fueled by the desire to maximize economic leverage.

Physicians continue to be suspicious of traditional healers because, they assert, healers blame their patients when the patients fail to recover. In their defense of standardization, physicians claim to assume responsibility for the deaths of patients by coming together with their colleagues (in professional standards reviews) and discussing how to learn from mistakes so as to not repeat them. Physicians see this not as professional secrecy, but simply as professionalism. However, when asked whether physicians would be satisfied with traditional healers' "professionalism" if healers were to meet regularly to discuss the outcome of fatal cases, physicians respond with a resounding *no*.

Thus, as perceived by physicians, professional responsibility comprises differing values, expectations, and interpretations for physicians and traditional healers. Few, if any, physicians will actually go to the family of a deceased patient to take responsibility for the death, even though that is what they expect of traditional healers. Moreover, many physicians fail to see that suggesting to the family of a patient who has just undergone an operation that "it is now up to the patient" or that "the patient's will to live is very important at this time" is a form of holding the patient personally responsible for his or her recovery and thus blaming the patient if he or she dies.

Physicians who insist that allopathic medicine is purely scientific, objective, and measurable are strongly opposed to keeping score cards that might compare their professional skills with those of their peers, on the grounds that there are other factors that make medicine less objective and measurable, and perhaps less scientific. Yet physicians accuse healers of being unscientific and insist that healers be subject to individual objective and scientific evaluation—the very measures of professional performance to which they are strongly opposed for themselves.

It seems quite apparent that in medicine there are certain levels of nonscientific, subjective, and perhaps even "magical" practices. The "scientific" aspects and the "human aspects" jointly potentiate the possibilities of healing. Ivan Illich (1976) aptly notes this invoking of magic in allopathic practices in the following:

> To distinguish the doctor's professional exercise of white magic from his function as engineer (and to spare him the charge of being a quack), the term "placebo" was created. Whenever a sugar pill works because it is given by the

doctor, the sugar pill acts as a placebo. A placebo (Latin for "I will please") pleases not only the patient but the administering physician as well. (108)

The belief in magic within the Western "scientific framework" is not exclusive to medicine. According to Chinweizu, Jemie, and Madubuike (1983), perhaps the most revealing of Western superstitions is the fact that many modern, shiny, glass-and-steel skyscrapers, financed, built, owned, managed, and occupied by the cream of Western bourgeoisie, have no thirteenth floors even though this practice has been changing slowly. Of course, the thirteenth floors are simply numbered fourteen to deceive the witches, ghosts, and other evil spirits.

In 1977, the Thirtieth World Health Assembly adopted a resolution (WHA 30.49) urging governments to give traditional systems of medicine the recognition they richly deserve. This became the stimulus that galvanized the WHO to launch the global promotion of trac onal medicine. Three major recommendations were made: (1) evaluation of traditional healing practices, (2) incorporation of traditional medicine as part of national health care systems, and (3) provision of training for traditional healers. To accomplish these goals, attempts have been made in different countries to find common ground for traditional medicine and allopathic medicine. The struggle to locate this common ground has led many to advocate for the integration of these two kinds of care systems. Such integration has been promoted by many respected international organizations, including WHO and UNICEF. Unfortunately, the implementation of integration has been based on a "donor-deficit model" for the traditional healers. The guiding belief is that traditional healers can be trained to "modernize" their healing practices by having allopathic professionals teach them what they do not know; that is, healers are assessed from a deficit model. In the process, allopaths could find out what traditional healers know, so that their knowledge can be improved when applied to allopathic practice (healers become donors). A further and more problematic assumption is that the healer, who supposedly needs some training, can make little or no contribution to improving the knowledge and practice of the allopath.

In discussions about the integration of traditional and allopathic health services, seldom has the traditional healer been viewed as a health provider with adequate or superior knowledge in certain aspects of health care that will be of benefit to the allopathic provider (physician) in a training session. The sources of traditional healers' concoctions and pharmacopoeia, however, are eagerly, even exploitatively, sought. Though deficient in some areas, traditional healers could be donors in other areas. Instead of receiving proper and due recognition for the areas in which they are known to be efficient and effective, healers are encouraged to surrender their herbal lore for the advancement of science.

Such patriarchy in professional devaluation of traditional healers is not exclusive to allopathic physicians. Some behavioral and social scientists who believe in aspirin yet cannot explain how it relieves pain have demanded that traditional healers explain their medications before these scientists consider the medications valid, even though they are used for the same reason as aspirin—a strong belief in its healing power. This kind of inconsistent and one-sided judgment has led to reluctance and suspicion on the part of traditional health care providers. Instead of integration or cooperation based on mutual trust, respect, and collaboration, in most cases the outcomes are distrust and suspicion.

As one explores the concept of integration further, three problems become evident. First, as stated earlier, the healer is seen as one who needs to be trained but who has nothing to contribute to training the allopath. Second, a conflict exists between perceived superiority of didactic learning over experiential learning. Indeed, both professions use both learning methods even though didactic is legitimated because of its allopathic institutional identity. Third, there is a lack of systematic protection of ownership of orally transmitted information, which is a vital form of intellectual and creative property in traditional medicine.

Integration has been more successful in the area of childbirth practices than in other areas of traditional medicine. Green (1988) notes that this success has often been attributed to traditional birth attendants' not posing any serious competition to physicians in terms of their professional status, power, and resources. In other cases, when governments have attempted to incorporate traditional healers into modern sector projects or programs, these attempts almost always involve some kind of training for the healers to upgrade their knowledge. Unfortunately, the healers often receive training in the most basic and mundane tasks, such as mixing oral rehydration solutions, even though the healers would like to learn how to give injections and read X rays.

A training session designed for integration should be one in which both allopathic providers (particularly physicians) and traditional healers are trainers and trainees, because both have information to contribute and to gain. Integration should mean the involvement of healers in the planning, implementation, and evaluation of health services delivery to foster cooperation and participation. This does not necessarily mean moving the traditional healer to a hospital setting, any more than it should mean moving the physician to the healer's practice setting. Integration, for example, may mean appropriate referral from a physician to a bone setter for fractures, as well as referral from an herbalist to an internist for appendicitis.

The second problem with integration is that of the often ignored differences between allopathic and traditional healers in methods of knowledge acquisition, as applied to proposed training programs. Paramount among these are differences in perceptions and beliefs in the method of knowledge production. Although both professions utilize some degree of both didactic and experiential learning, experiential learning is clearly more valued and weighted in traditional healing and less valued in the academy even though some degree of it is applied in allopathic training. Formal, didactic teaching is rarely applied to traditional healing practice because learning in the apprenticeship mode (experiential learning) is more appropriate and culturally customary.

The third problem with integration is that physicians have arrogantly requested that traditional healers share their knowledge about their treatments and medicines without establishing a systematic process to guarantee ownership of the information that is revealed. In Western culture, the protection of information, inventions, and discoveries and their revelation is guaranteed under copyright and patent laws. In a UN debate over how Southern nations are to be rewarded for contributions to plant species, Henry Shands, a U.S. delegate, argued that without a strong patent law, people have no incentive to investigate the possible superior medicinal properties of plant species (Simons 1989).

Although patent and copyright laws are not customary in oral tradition, revelation of information within this context has always been protected. One method of such protection has been for healers to reveal information only to one or two protégés who maintain the authenticity as well as secrecy of such information as a part of their own practice. Thus, open, widespread revelation is an allopathic phenomenon and should carry with it the protection and rewards that go with it or, alternatively, a culturally appropriate modified version. When traditional healers possess the knowledge to discover, create, and use compounds of effective medicinal properties, such information should not be shared with others in the absence of some systemic guarantees that the original sources of such information or medication are protected and/or appropriately rewarded for its revelation. Although healers may not articulate such a right, it is a basic human desire to receive the comfort and protection of these fundamental principles regarding information sharing and proprietorship, regardless of the pattern of knowledge acquisition.

Such protection and rights of ownership are paramount in promoting open information sharing and true reciprocity between and among health providers and policymakers. The resistance of physicians to sharing information with traditional healers could be considered an example of such protection. It should, however, be noted that such reluctance about integration is not unique to physicians. It is also true of medical anthropologists, medical sociologists, health educators, and other public health professionals. However, the stakes are much higher for the public when healers, both allopathic and traditional, do not cooperate with each other to maximize health coverage for the people so that the public might benefit from the best of both worlds.

International health professionals will have a better appreciation of international health problems if they understand that treatment modalities, like diseases and disease patterns, are intricately tied to beliefs and values within cultures. As long as Africans successfully seek treatment from both allopathic and traditional healers, it is prudent to strive for mutual collaboration based on respect and trust between the two types of health providers. Perhaps the word should be *cooperation* instead of *integration*. The latter tends to conjure up resistance among those who interpret this process as an encroachment on their territory. This has been my experience during workshops and lectures on traditional medicine.

IMPLICATIONS FOR NATIONAL HEALTH POLICY

An important factor contributing to successful national health policy in African countries is clear definition of the healing modalities. Such a definition should involve people from both allopathic and traditional healing systems. In many countries, such as South Africa, traditional healers have organized themselves and attained professional status to assert their professional identity and be assured of government recognition and support. Integration, registration, and professionalization, however, may be possible only after a period of official government recognition. Such recognition may take various forms, at various levels, in various contexts. By *recognition*, I mean an array of relationships among traditional healers, government officials, and medical personnel that may range from private meetings to licensure. Healers, traditional or modern, are human and therefore may interact and exchange information as family members, friends, and professionals.

Policymakers should decide on communities' unmet health needs and then involve social and behavioral scientists, as well as community members, in health program planning, implementation, and evaluation. The community thus helps to define acceptable healing practices based on indigenous reasoning, which may be inexplicable in the Western context. Cultural diversity among peoples of different nations and the impact of such diversity on program replicability cannot be overemphasized. Community involvement is one strategy for acknowledging the impact of culture on a national health system. This is often realized when the individuals, families, and communities for whom a program is intended, as well as service providers (traditional healers), have the opportunity to be a part of the team that defines the health problems to be targeted and formulates their solution through design of a particular health program. Sensitivity to traditional customs and social norms, and thus cultural appropriateness of a program, is ensured through the participation of community members.

Allopathic health providers can learn from traditional healers, just as traditional healers can learn from allopathic practitioners. Understanding the components of a system of healing is critical to the ability to influence the health behavior of those who subscribe to that system. Some allopathic physicians have already started to utilize what they have learned from traditional healers. Some now place an amulet around a child's neck to ensure that the child returns for a follow-up visit, so the physician can maintain continuity of care until the patient is cured. Reciprocally, some traditional healers now send their fracture patients to have their bones X-rayed in a hospital.

FINAL THOUGHTS

One of the key primary health care providers in most African countries is the traditional healer. Because traditional medicine is based on cultural and traditional values, it is important for health educators to affirm and legitimate this modality within the formal health care system. Ignoring traditional medicine is tantamount to ignoring the cultural relevance of health and disease in these societies. After all, one cannot sincerely address health care delivery in Africa without giving adequate coverage to traditional medicine. Social and behavioral scientists who are interested in health care delivery in African nations should devote adequate time to an exploration of the past, present, and future contributions of traditional healers to health care delivery in these countries.

Communication and cooperation must prevail if there is to be an optimal working relationship between these forms of health services. Therefore, social and behavioral scientists have critical roles to play in improving global health care policies and systems, and it is vital that they work with traditional healers to ensure the provision of adequate health care systems in African nations.

9

The Future of Health Promotion

The Legacy of Paulo Freire

Since the English translation thirty years ago of his widely read book *Pedagogy of the Oppressed*, Freire's work has suffered the misreadings of well-meaning educators who have interpreted his work as a "brilliant methodology," a kind of manual for teachers who would bring out the best in their otherwise indifferent students. Such characterizations are undoubtedly fed by the common identification of pedagogy merely with compassionate teaching: What is taught is unproblematic; the only issue is how to teach on the basis of caring.

—Stanley Aronowitz (in Freire 1998:19)

I always say that the only way anyone has of applying in their situation any of the propositions I have made is precisely by redoing what I have done, that is, by not following me. In order to follow me it is essential not to follow me!

—Paulo Freire (Freire and Faundez 1989:30)

FREIRE AND THE RIGOR OF LEARNING

The passing of Paulo Freire, in 1997, to "the unforbidden," as the Edos of Nigeria would say, touched many in the education and the social and behavioral science communities. The celebration of his life through his theory of practice and practice of theory is best remembered by his insistence that critical consciousness become a vital part of education discourses. His bold and triumphant remapping of community as a terrain of conscientization and transformation has forever given hope to educators and other cultural workers for whom "learning to question" is a more powerful and richer pedagogical process than "seeking the answer." For Freire, discovering complexities in the ways of everyday life through authentic dialogue demonstrated his conviction that all persons be seen as subjects and, given adequate supportive context, have the power to transform the world and not merely as objects and thus acted upon by more powerful agents.

Health education and health communication are two of the many disciplines that have come to embrace the foundation of Freire's work that will continue to be celebrated by educators and cultural workers internationally. However, although it is important that we respect and pay tribute to Freire and his work, we must continually engage in the critical reanalysis and re-creation of that work while we use it as a foundation for our work, for this is what Freire would insist upon. Although many health workers have taken up Freire's challenge of cultural absorption, Freire (1993) believed that "to open up to the culture's soul is to allow one to become wet, to become soaked in the cultural and historical waters of those individuals who are involved in the experience" (106). He never believed that such a practical grounding eschews a theoretical and intellectual thoroughness. For him, "the liveliness of the conversation, the lightness of the spoken word, the spontaneity of the dialogue are not in themselves a denial of the serious intent of this work or its requisite intellectual rigor" (Freire and Faundez 1989:3). In fact, it is the rigor of his scholarly enterprise and his ability to ground this enterprise in cultural realities that have given many educators, public health workers, and the communities they work in and with the vibrant space they needed to come to claim and/or reclaim their agencies as thinking and knowing subjects. Freire explicitly said that "the starting point for a political-pedagogical project must be precisely at the level of the people's aspirations and dreams, their understanding of reality, and their forms of action and struggle" (Freire and Faundez 1989:27). Unfortunately, many have misinterpreted this to mean to start where people are rather than mapping where people aspire to be and connecting their collective aspiration to their present situation. Starting where people are does not mean material assessment of a people's economic condition but rather a higher level of consciousness to which they aspire and that should begin the process of education. This also holds true for a pedagogical exercise in the classroom that challenges educators to begin with where students aspire to be rather than where their material presence would suggest.

Freire triumphed in educating and reeducating many of us that the critical consciousness and human sensibility of those consigned to being the "wretched of the Earth" must not be measured by their material worth or the degree to which they are lettered. Put simply, literacy and numerical competence do not equal critical decision-making abilities and human transformation in and of themselves. Freire reminded us that both the haves and the have nots are inherently capable of either liberatory or oppressive practices. After all, when it comes to culture, there are no have nots, because everyone belongs to a culture or a combination of cultures. Each aspect of this complex human equation involving power, opportunity, ownership, belonging, subjectivity, and dignity is culturally and spatially acquired, produced, and nurtured or denied according to the peculiarities and social arrangements.

Many educators demand simplicity so they can avoid complexity, request closure when the debate has not started, and focus on a common denominator when the evidence suggests that the denominator is not common—hence the importance of the numerator. Others bemoan their lack of professional recognition while foreshortening rigorous philosophical enterprise within their profession by invoking such homilies as "those of us in the trenches" or "give me practical, guaranteed solutions." As a cultural crusader whose work transcended the trenches of the local, Freire believed that a rigorous philosophical enterprise is a necessary precondition for a meaningful practical project that informs as it transforms. To allow one's intellectual curiosity to be dwarfed by the belief that the proximity of one's professional space to the downtrodden is sufficient to work with "these people" is a limitation of interventions that Freire challenged for many years. In other words, many subscribe to Freire's notion of critical consciousness as long as it is the consciousness of the "targeted community" that is being examined rather than that of the interventionists. This is particularly true as it relates to the interventionists' philosophical and theoretical imagination. This is to say that to be a community health educator/communicator, if one embraces Freire's philosophy, means to embrace the spirit of his unquenchable desire for continuous philosophical engagement in ways that interrogate, deepen, and enrich the theory that guides our practice, allow the practice to in turn reshape the ideological contours of our philosophy and theory. This is what Freire meant by praxis reflection and action. Never before has the issue of philosophy, ideology, theory, and practice converged to encourage debates concerning the cyclical nature of health issues and social problems as with the question of empowerment to prevent HIV and manage AIDS.

HEALTH EDUCATION AND EMPOWERMENT

Cultural empowerment in health promotion and education can be an effective tool that enriches the production and acquisition of knowledge for interventionists and their audiences. The emphasis on participation of people in group action and dialogue is critical to the extent that interventionists do not assume the population is powerless at both the micro and the macro levels of decision making. The process must not assume that the community lacks confidence in its ability to change the lives of its members. Participation as a tool for cultural empowerment is an important health education approach that is an essential foundation for the kind of learning opportunities that empower both students/audiences and teachers/facilitators.

To realize fully the benefits of empowerment as a process that situates students/audiences as actors rather than factors, subjects rather than objects, and spectators rather than spectacles, cultural and educational theorists must examine and analyze the historical genealogy of classical pedagogy that disempowers the learner in a manner that Freire refers to as the "castration of curiosity" (Freire and Faundez 1989:35). Classical pedagogy places patriarchy, White and middle-class, at the center of discourse, and at the same time maintains Others—non-Western cultures, racial and ethnic minorities, women, and low social economic classes—at the margin. Ultimately, a pedagogy of culture is needed to centralize and affirm differences in cultural expressions, thus empowering learners to be actors and subjects in the production of knowledge and their social and cultural identity.

In *Learning to Question* (Freire and Faundez 1989), Freire relates an incident that took place in Mexico: an agronomist who was engaged in agricultural education through extension activities decided to help the Mexican peasants by proposing that the farmers replace their simple variety of maize with a hybrid variety to achieve greater yield in productivity. The farmers tried the hybrid successfully but subsequently changed back to their original maize variety. Had the agronomist engaged the farmers in the production and acquisition of taste, meaning, and pleasure in what was to be their new cultural reality, he would have learned, as he did later, that this simple variety of maize was grown for home consumption only and not for sale, as he had erroneously assumed. Most important, the farmers grew the simple variety of maize "to eat in their *tortillas* and the taste of the hybrid variety of maize was completely different from the other and thus represented a basic change in the culture of that community in the form of the taste of their *tortillas*" (93).

Another example comes from my experience as a health education consultant for USAID in Nigeria in 1990. As part of the community's income-generating activities, the farmers were encouraged to grow their yams with fertilizers for higher yield. They tried fertilizers successfully for a year, but then discontinued their use. The yams that were grown with fertilizers rotted after two months of storage, whereas the nonfertilized yams could be stored successfully for the six months that would elapse before the planting of yams in the new season. Yet another example is the distribution of oral rehydration solution packets. According to David Werner (1989), these packets eventually create dependency instead of empowering people who should be taught to prepare their own solution using local ingredients and implements. "The 'technical aid' conception of education 'anesthetizes' the educatees and leaves them a-critical and naive in the face of the world" (Freire 1973:152).

Empowerment in health promotion is often defined as a process of helping people to take control over their health. It has also been used synonymously with such indices as coping skills, mutual support, community organization, support systems, neighborhood participation, personal efficacy, competence, self-esteem, and self-sufficiency (Rappaport 1984). This concept of empowerment evokes the notion that the control of environmental forces is the ultimate goal. Although this may be true, understanding those forces to strategize on how to transform their reality is also a legitimate outcome of empowerment. Thus, the objective changes resulting from empowerment are different because they reflect the varied needs of individuals, groups, organizations, and communities, and the contexts where empowerment occurs.

The major difference is that Freire is primarily concerned with environmental and social constraints that must be exposed, whereas some health educators and other health professionals are focused on giving power to individuals. The question then becomes, What happens when such efforts fail? In fact, the word *empowerment* has no meaning in Spanish or Portuguese. Indeed, it has no meaning in Edo or Yoruba of Nigeria. In Edo and Yoruba, it is represented as a process that embraces notions of wisdom and maturity, which are considered to be a much more meaningful state of being "powerful." Freire focused more on raising critical consciousness that helps to problematize the interaction of a collectives within their social political contexts. Instead, Freire's work has become a form of a movement on self-empowerment.

What is quite telling is how a concept in its modern appropriation originates from a region, travels the world, and takes on a new name and meaning only to return home to find that it has no meaning in the region that gave it birth. It is no wonder that although Freire saw the possibilities in the disenfranchised and was committed to a collective notion of knowledge production, the new self-empowerment movement is concerned with the deficits in individuals and how to remedy by teaching them how to acquire power.

Whereas Freire was addressing the centrality of politics in knowledge production, the new self-empowerment is concerned with the question of what is wrong with individual bodies in their population of interests. Whereas Freire was promoting what could be referred to as education as a social political process, the new self-empowerment is focused on celebrated linear behavior theories and models to chart how "these unfortunate souls" can be "empowered" to overcome the forces that have circumscribed their potential for "normal well-being." Thus, the new discourse on individual empowerment is based on the hallowed pretext that one (usually all-knowing academics) can empower another (the disenfranchised). In the PEN-3 model described in chapter 12, I propose cultural empowerment as a way of reinscribing the positives and strengths in cultures as a collective process at the beginning of health promotion intervention. Cultural empowerment takes into account how health knowledge, beliefs, and actions are produced and interpreted at both micro (personal, family, and community/ grassroots) and macro (national and international power and politics) levels. Thus, the decision making of individuals and families must be situated within its proper political, historical, and cultural contexts. Empowerment should begin with educational institutions, so as to enlighten every student about the experiences and histories of diverse national and international communities. Such institutionalization of empowerment is the hallmark of critical pedagogy.

Freire (1970, 1973) revolutionized pedagogical approaches four decades ago by bringing to the fore the debate over European-centered versus multicultural pedagogy. Classical pedagogy disempowers students and audiences by, among other things, assuming that students can only acquire knowledge, not produce it. This pedagogical approach is what Freire (1970) refers to as "banking education." The pedagogical manifestations of this monocentric all-or-nothing discourse have been challenged in cultural studies. Larry Grossberg (1994) offers an alternative approach to cultural studies that is a confluence of hierarchical practice, which assumes the role of the all-knowing teacher; dialogic practice, which allows the silenced to speak; and praxical pedagogical practice, which offers people the skills they need to change their destiny. Grossberg's alternative approach refuses to assume intellectual claims to authority even though the teacher does not have to abandon the position of authority.

CRITICAL PEDAGOGY AND CULTURE

In *Pedagogy of Freedom*, Freire (1998) states that "to know how to teach is to create possibilities for the construction and production of knowledge rather than to be engaged simply in a game of transferring knowledge" (49). In other words, the teacher/interventionist refuses to assume ahead of time that he or she has the appropriate knowledge, language, or skills; instead, he or she engages people in a contextual practice in which he or she is willing to risk making connections, drawing lines, and mapping articulations between different domains, discourses, and practices, to see what will work, both theoretically and practically. In his seminal work, *Pedagogy of the Oppressed*, Freire (1970) writes that many political and educational plans have failed because their authors designed them according to their own personal views of reality, never once taking into account the people to whom their programs were directed.

Freire and Henry Giroux—as well as other cultural critics and educational theorists, such as Stuart Hall and Cheikh Anta Diop—have challenged political, educational, and social systems that valorize the hegemony of the Western culture while at the same time marginalizing women and people of other races and cultures. Critical theories and the discourse of difference must become central to pedagogical reformation (by this I mean the production of knowledge and social and cultural identity in schools, communities, and work sites as well as domestically and internationally) in health and education. This rethinking of health and educational intervention approaches is particularly timely given the global currents of deconstruction (rejection of universal truth) of past existential boundaries and construction of new alliances based on politics of representation (inclusive of health projects that represent diverse races, ethnicities, nationalities, and genders). Given the link between cultural expressions and health behaviors (Airhihenbuwa 1995b), it is critical that public health and health communication scholars revisit the politics of its professional location in the world.

Crossing the boundaries of educational discourse, we must transcend the possibilities of learning opportunities by engaging students, audiences, and teachers in the production of knowledge, meaning, pleasure, and value. In *Stealing Innocence*, Henry Giroux (2000) posits that culture is a foundation for pedagogical and political issues and thus must be central to schools' functions in the shaping of particular identities, values, and histories, by producing and legitimating specific cultural narratives and resources. Although crossing cultural borders is advocated, it should be borne in mind that the border crosser is not a race-effacing agent. U.S. ethnic minorities cannot assume White identity in terms of representation. Therefore, crossing borders may be subject to conditions of race, gender, and nationality, to mention but three.

CULTURE AND HIV/AIDS INTERVENTIONS

HIV/AIDS remains one of the predominant health issues and social problems of our time. Although there is no doubt that the HIV and AIDS epidemic in the United States is slowing in some population groups while increasing in others (UNAIDS 2005), and at the same time, antiretroviral therapy is offering hope to many who are HIV infected, there is still much to be done, and the epidemic is far from over.

Freire (1973) believed that "education is communication and dialogue. It is not the transference of knowledge, but the encounter of subjects in dialogue in search of the significance of the object of knowing and thinking" (139). The social and contextual nature of HIV and AIDS is evidenced by the peaks and valleys of interest and alarm as shaped by media coverage, the politics of identity, historical experiences, the social climate, and the cultural contexts, as well as the proliferation of new issues. There is no doubt that culture is at the center of HIV and AIDS prevention, both as a health and a social issue. Furthermore, although HIV and AIDS are typically viewed in individualistic terms, it is imperative to recognize that the interpretation of these conditions resides in the varied and specific cultural and identity contexts where it is found. That is, that although no community is exempt from this epidemic, it is vital to heed Freire's insistence, echoed by many scholars, that each effort aimed at prevention or amelioration be designed in consultation with each community. Although the politics of identity are central to understanding behavior, their relation to culture have been debated for several decades. The rejuvenation of this issue can be credited in part to the need to understand the dynamics of behaviors and their contexts that enable or threaten HIV and AIDS prevention and education strategies. A significant body of research has addressed the importance of contextualizing values and meanings and thus interpretation of diseases and their treatment in general and HIV/AIDS in particular especially in the context of stigma. Interestingly, HIV and AIDS prevention has become the template for gauging the role of culture in health promotion and disease prevention. It is no surprise that Freire's work has been applied in HIV/AIDS intervention in communities.

Culture, as taken up in planning interventions, often means specific cultural traits—qualities that are unique to the community in curious ways. We believe it is vital to view culture as a dynamic concept that is multiaccentual and seamless. Freire (1973) believed that "inheriting acquired experience, creating and recreating, integrating themselves into their context, responding to its challenges, objectifying themselves, discerning, transcending, men [*sic*] enter into the domain which is theirs exclusively—that of History and Culture" (4).

Perhaps more important, Freire's notion of culture is based on humanity's unique knowledge of temporality. Freire (1973) stated, "The dimensionality of time is one of the fundamental discoveries in the history of human culture" (3). Particularly as this concept relates to HIV and AIDS, one can see how knowledge production is *the* defining aspect of how a culture responds to the epidemic.

Culture is also an important component of how a people define selfhood. Western cultures, to varying degrees, tend to view the self in individualist terms (see chapter 12)—that is, the self as fixed, as unitary, and as the locus of all action. However, Freire challenged this notion and argued that the self is a relational entity located in a variety of contexts that both acts on and is acted on by those contexts. More generally, the debate over the construction of the self can be viewed within the context of identity and difference. Robert Crawford (1994) believes that "the heart of the cultural politics of AIDS is a contestation over the meaning of the self" (1347). A large part of this contestation involves the definition and construction of a person living with HIV/AIDS as "other." In its most basic sense, health is associated with those who are *not* infected with HIV and unhealth with those who are infected with HIV. Again, Freire's focus on critical consciousness comes into play as it reminds us that regardless of HIV status, each person has the right to be a subject and not an object.

I believe and do advocate that cultural sensitivity be central to public health theory and practice. This position is evident in the UNAIDS communications framework for HIV/AIDS and the PEN-3 model (discussed in chapters 11 and 12, respectively), which has as a central theme an emphasis on the context before the units within the context. To Freire, this meant reading the *world* before reading of the *word*. He believed that "reading the world is an antecedent act vis-à-vis the reading of the word. The teaching of the reading and writing of the word to a person missing the critical exercise of reading and rereading the world is, scientifically, politically, and pedagogically crippled" (Freire 1994:78). It is important to explore all domains of human behavior so as to promote the positive, recognize and affirm the existential, and contextualize the negative such that opportunity costs and benefits for change are understood and appreciated—whether the project is health related or not.

What has become increasingly apparent is that these discussions that are mostly centered on the need to understand how the context or environment (a culture) shapes individual and group actions tend to almost always revert to individual differences which are believed by some to be independent of their environment. On another level, there is a noticeable resistance to engaging a dialogue that will centralize the celebration of difference. This resistance is founded on the fear that celebrating diversity somehow devalues the sanctity and sanctuary of sameness and "unity" as a privileged space for influencing health behavior. It is this resistance that fuels Freire's most compelling arguments in favor of understanding the totality of humanity rather than a focalized view of a problem.

CRITICAL CONSCIOUSNESS AND INSTITUTIONAL RESPONSIBILITY

When issues of promoting culturally appropriate curricula are raised, many faculty members and university administrators commonly express an interest.

Institutional responsibility toward cultural diversity expressed in curriculum reformation often yield to episodic programs designed to provide remedial (read: remedy) support for those whose identity is different from that of the mainstream culture in society. By showcasing programs designed for the neediest of the oppressed, cultural sensitivity is believed to have been achieved because culture is often used as a proxy for SES. These episodic remedial interventions becomes an opportunity for some "bleeding hearts" to propose offering the shirt off their back to a poor disenfranchised student because the institutional disengagement denies this same student the opportunity to be motivated to learn so he or she can get a job to buy his or her own shirt. This absence of systemic curriculum reform has perpetuated a form of institutional racism. Such institutional racism is embedded in structural discrimination as exemplified in the omission of critical texts that can seriously prepare and challenge students to engage in critical thinking and emancipatory education such as that inspired by the works of Chiekh Anta Diop, Frantz Fanon, Wole Soyinka, Paulo Freire, Ngugi wa Thiong'O, Ben Okri, bell hooks, Henry Giroux, Oyeronke Oyewumi, Paul T. Zeleza, and many others. Of particular importance are contemporary scholars addressing critical theories of race and identity such as Michael Eric Dyson, Cornel West, Charles Mills, Lucious Outlaw, and Emmanuel Eze. In the absence of the necessary curriculum reformation that will ensure critical reading and evaluation of these texts, cultural sensitivity in public health and health education/promotion is reduced to an expression of empathy for the marginalized without the commitment to engage in the challenge for a meaningful education for critical consciousness. The noninclusion of critical texts from the curriculum has resulted in the miseducation of our students thus raising questions about the preparation of our students for the future. The resulting miseducation or undereducation significantly contributes to what Michael Brown and colleagues (2003) refer to as "disaccumulation" of opportunity and resources. *Disaccumulation* refers to societal selective investment of wealth in certain institutional structures that lead to economic and social advantages (accumulation) for Whites and a simultaneous economic and institutional disinvestments resulting in economic and social disadvantages (disaccumulation) for Blacks.

Refusal to welcome the challenge of raising critical consciousness often causes individuals to reduce discussions of cultural sensitivity into a mechanism that is designed to police political correctness (PC). Although conservatives have often been criticized for their negativity around PC, some liberals are equally guilty of truncating issues of cultural sensitivity to PC as a way of legitimizing their desire to engage in the discourse on cultural diversity at an incipient level. In the words of Dyson (1995), "'PC' has become the common rallying cry of conservatives, liberals, and radicals, many of whom harbor resentments against the assertive presence and practices of formerly excluded minorities who no longer need representation by proxy. When these minorities show up to speak for themselves and often in terms that are radically different from how stereotyping for scapegoating has made them appear, there is resistance from friend and foe alike" (x). Indeed, the new wave of political conservatism has ushered in a new form of PC in what Dyson refers to as "patriotic correctness." Intellectual capital and national commitment are now measured by the size of the national flag one displays. Program effectiveness is no longer based on interventions that address "what is," such as condom use, but rather on "what ought to be," such as abstinence only. The increasing acceptance and application of abstinence-only programs by educators who actually do not believe in its effectiveness comprise an important example of how the social and political contexts regulate individual behavior. Knowledge does not lead to behavior change—not even among those who should know better. Abstinence is as true of its innocence of behavior as it is of its innocence in its programmatic effectiveness to promote health and prevent disease. Its effectiveness as an exclusive strategy for pregnancy or HIV prevention has been seriously limited. Yet, educators still believe that they can change individual behavior independent of the contexts of these behaviors particularly when a program focuses on intervention for those who are vulnerable and economically disadvantaged in society.

For those who believe that it is their birthright to forever liberate the disenfranchised, it is not readily apparent that such "ever-lasting" commitment is a partial endorsement of an ever-lasting consignment of their "beneficiaries" to being "the wretched of the Earth" and to being "faces at the bottom of the well." In other words, the goal of critical theory and emancipatory education should be for the privileged interventionists and advocates to disengage over time so that those who must benefit from programs can take charge of their destinies. For those who have been marginalized, liberation is a process that begins at that phase when the ways they produce and acquire knowledge and construct meanings not only for themselves but for everyone are affirmed and legitimized. In order to fully engage this discourse, one needs to engage a dialogical education that is designed to provide a space for these voices at the conception of the learning/teaching process. This is the beginning of raising critical consciousness. This is where the legacy of Paulo Freire will remain ever compelling.

FINAL THOUGHTS

The need to accent the importance of culture has converged with the importance of critical consciousness and dialogical education as a process of understanding social contexts of health beliefs and actions. We have begun to appreciate the importance of "learning to question" as a critical learning-teaching process that does not totally rely on providing answers. Although Freire's philosophy and practices provide a clear foundation for engaging dialogical education in the classroom, each educator must begin by unlearning personal and professional practices that may provide him or her comfort but which at the same time contribute to the silencing of others. To constantly question and challenge one's privileged space and location by moving beyond the borders that have hitherto circumscribed one's professional practice is to learn *to be comfortable with being uncomfortable*. This is where Freire's work has been particularly instructive because he believes that true learning takes place when we allow ourselves to step out of our familiar and comfortable professional space.

Freire was emphatic in cautioning educators and interventionists that his work is *not* a model or curriculum that can be slavishly applied to any situation. Rather, Freire's work is an example of a critical process engaged in by human subjects who reject the objectification that has become such an overwhelming feature in contemporary scholarship. To best honor Freire's legacy of hope and possibility is not merely to follow in his practical footsteps but to continue embracing his philosophical and spiritual consciousness even as one may choose a different path but to continue asking critical questions so that human rights, freedom, and social justice for all become a central goal in global health.

3

REMAPPING THE TERRAIN ON HEALTH

10

Spirituality

The Site of the True Otherness

What is Africa about religious intolerance and deadly fanaticism? The spirituality of the black continent, as attested, for instance, in the religion of the ORISA, abhors such principles of coercion or exclusion. . . . Tolerance is synonymous with the spirituality of the black continent, intolerance is anathema!

—Wole Soyinka (1999:48)

The recorded history of the separation of mind and body dates back to the fourth century (Paulsen 1926). Since these divergent values emerged, the two tracks have evolved almost exclusively along the line of the body for medicine and the mind for spirituality. According to Richard Dyer (1991), "Christianity maintains a conception of a split between mind and body, regarding the latter as at the least inferior and often as evil" (16). The post-Hippocratic modern medicine focused on the body to the exclusion of the mind, while at the same time modern theology focused almost exclusively on the mind (Paulsen 1926). Having followed these paths for some time, medicine and theology have begun to embrace values that, at least, recognize that mind and body are connected in health values and health behavior. Yet, African spiritual ethos such as Orisa has always been anchored in the coexistence of the mind and body even though its principles were never centralized in the discourse on mind and body.

In recent years, researchers have reviewed published work in public health and religious literature and concluded that there is a positive association between religion and health. In a review of more than two hundred empirical studies in epidemiology dating back to the nineteenth century, J. Levin and Schiller (1987) found positive findings associating religion with positive health outcomes. Subsequently, Levin (1994) found these associations to be valid and may be causal, and in either case deserving of further study. In a review of more than two hundred empirical studies on the relationships between religious commitment and mental health (Gartner, Larson, and Allen 1991), measures of religious participation such as church attendance were found to be more strongly related to mental health than were attitudes about religion. Moreover, most of the studies that found positive relationships between religion and health measured real-life behavioral events such as alcohol use, suicide, and mortality, whereas most of the studies that found negative or conflicting relationships were based on paper-and-pencil personality tests measuring such qualities as humility, altruism, assertiveness, and so forth. Similarly, a comprehensive review of two hundred articles published in psychiatric and psychological literature through 1989 (Larson et al. 1992) concluded that religion was associated with positive mental health outcomes. These studies and many more (some of which are not published) have been influential in providing the foundation for some of the important work currently being done in examining the relationships between religion and HIV/AIDS.

SPIRITUALITY AND AFRICAN IDENTITY

Religion in much of Africa today is often thought of as either Christianity or Islam. Until recently, much of the attention of the role of health and positive living (coded in morality) has been based on Christianity. Christianity in turn was deployed mostly through missionary activities. The more one examines the history of missionaries in Africa, the more difficult it becomes not to identify it with Western cultural hegemony that often becomes a cornerstone for further commercial interests. According to Mudimbe (1988:45), the missions' program is indeed more complex than the simple transmission of the Christian faith.

What has never been studied has been the role of African spirituality (independent of traditional healing) in HIV prevention. It is as though African spirituality is a nonfactor where spirituality is connected to daily events. For example, the question of attendance for organized worshipping will be moot because African spirituality is not restricted to institutional contexts that are marked by organized weekly institutional gatherings. African spirituality is a decentralized medium to which family can schedule times of worship and devotion. Indeed, where success in African responses to illness has been recognized, African spirituality is never acknowledged. The success of the Aro psychiatric hospital in Nigeria has been hailed by international mental health scholars as a model for all countries. However, none of the explanatory factors advanced for the success has ever been credited to African spirituality that is produced through the communal sense of belonging that was the hallmark of Aro hospital. The spiritual foundation of childhood is likely to influence future behavior even when the person no longer actively participates in events that nurture these values.

This chapter is not meant to describe religion. It is focused on addressing the character of African spirituality that I consider to be necessary if we are to fully understand values, beliefs, and behavior that occasion a pandemic such as HIV and AIDS. Stigma is considered to be a major obstacle to controlling the pandemic. Spiritual leaders within organized religions are considered to be key gatekeepers in reducing and/or eliminating HIV/AIDS-related stigma. Central to the debilitating force of stigma are the moralization of behavior (particularly sexual behavior) and the condemnation of persons living with HIV/AIDS as religious deviants. The common spiritual doctrines on which stigmatization has been problematic, however, are mostly on Christianity and Islam. However, a doctrine conspicuously absent from this discourse is that of African spirituality. Scholars such as E. Bolaji Idowu (1962) addressed Yoruba spirituality as an anchor and organizing principle of Yoruba beliefs. Yet Yoruba spirituality is absent from the discussion of the role of spirituality in the discourse on HIV/AIDS in Africa. A central theme of the spirituality of Orisa (among the Yorubas) is openness and tolerance. In *Yoruba Beliefs and Sacrificial Rites*, Joseph Omosade Awolalu (1979) offers a scholarly analysis of Yoruba spirituality as the foundation on which an understanding of Yoruba values and beliefs must be studied and understood. A central point that must be understood in Yoruba spirituality, which holds true for many others in Africa, is that there is no dualism of good and evil as is represented in God and the devil in Christianity. "In other words, the Yoruba world does not know of totally opposing forces—one representing evil and the other good" (28). In fact, the concept of sin, as constructed in theocracy, does not exist in the Yoruba spirituality. It must be noted that such absence of the concept of sin in no way suggests that there is an absence of right and wrong. In the absence of a codified and moralized language of deviance, as in sin, the Yoruba spirituality enjoys a level of tolerance and openness that promotes a communal value of oneness rather than a moral duality.

These values were easily reinforced through mores of community sharing and reciprocity. Among the Edos of Nigeria, for example, these values of sharing are mostly anchored in a common belief that the *oba* (king or queen) owns the land from Benin City (Nigeria) to overseas. The expression that the oba owns the land was meant to convey a common value that no one owns the land even though there are parcels of land on which generations of the same family farmed and raised crops for cash and consumption. The Oba owns the land in trust. This is the value on which my childhood was nurtured in Benin City. Thus, having a space to farm was a privilege rather than a right. In the same token, that a space was a privilege did not mean that a neighbor could encroach on your space, because the boundaries of one's privileged space were always respected. Social and communal justice was central to the values inherent in sharing and labor. According to Emmanuel Eze (2001), "Because the typical African society posits social harmony as a goal, labor relations are marked by cooperation rather than competition" (34). In revisiting Senghor's negritude, Eze established the link between Senghor's interpretation of African labor practices with the socialist forms advanced by Karl Marx. Because private ownership of land is prohibited in most traditional African societies, Senghor concludes that it is labor as defined by the privilege of using the land that defines ownership rather than capital as defined by actual ownership of the land.

HEALING AND SPIRITUALITY

This same principle regarding sharing and communal justice underscores the ethical practice in traditional healing. Traditional healers, for the most part, believed that a healer should not commodify her or his gift of healing. In fact, it is believed that healing for money will render meaningless their gift of healing to the community. For example, some healers believed that if one were to be paid, it should be after the healing has yielded positive result to the satisfaction of the patient and family rather than before. Two stories shared by scholars in health research should illustrate this point.

The first story is from Senegal and was shared by Chiekh Niang, professor of anthropology and sociology at the Cheikh Anta Diop University in Dakar. When Cheikh was an undergraduate student in Dakar, his sister fell ill and was taken to several hospitals for treatment. After visits to many hospitals, her condition did not improve until someone suggested that Cheikh take his sister to a traditional healer in a village. As a young student who had just began to learn of the value of Western ways of knowing, he was initially reluctant to subject his sister to this "unscientific" healing modality. Fearing that he was out of options to help his sister, however, he decided to try this modality as a last resort. They journeyed and finally arrived in the village, where an informant immediately directed him to the healer. When he met the healer, Cheikh explained his sister's condition and sought his help. To Cheikh's amazement, the healer acted very surprised and said to Cheikh that he was not a healer and that Cheikh was mistaken. Frustrated and confused, Cheikh went to his informant thinking that he had gone to the wrong person. Cheikh was reassured that he in fact had met the right person and should go back and plead his case. Cheikh went back to the man asking for his help. After much discussion and pleading, the healer reluctantly agreed to attend to the sister. After a month of treatment, she was cured of her illness. When Cheikh offered the healer money, the healer took a fraction of the money and told Cheikh that no true healer heals for money. Moreover, according to the healer, Cheikh was a student and needed the money more than he did. Cheikh finally asked why the healer had refused to attend to him when he first approached the healer. The healer responded that he could not consider himself a healer. The moment he starts to do so, cautioned the healer, he could lose the special gift of healing. Thus to have agreed at the outset that he was a healer would have meant that he really took himself seriously as a healer. Central to traditional healing in this case is the spiritual sense of humility and being humble about one's "gift" of healing and healing for humanity rather than money.

The second story came from Ilesa, Nigeria, and was shared by a leading professional in HIV/AIDS communication, Bunmi Makinwa. For years when Bunmi would visit his father, Papa Makinwa, in Ilesa during the summer holidays, it was not unusual for elders in the town to stop Bunmi to express their gratitude to his father for healing them or someone in their family for one condition or the other. Of particular note was the testimony of his father's success in "treating" women who were having problems becoming pregnant and who eventually had babies. Each person offering this unsolicited testimony was always adamant that it was the father's treatment that had led to the baby being conceived and brought to life. Bunmi was not always convinced because his father never acknowledged his healing skills. As a young man receiving his university education "under Western eyes," Bunmi had also begun to develop certain measures for judging what constitutes actual healing. None of these seemed to be evident in his father's case, particularly because his father denied that he was a healer.

Bunmi had a friend whose wife was having difficulty becoming pregnant. The couple had exhausted all the biomedical procedures at the leading hospitals in Lagos and Ibadan. In part, out of desperation to offer help to his friends and also to somewhat "test" the so-called prowess of his father with helping women to conceive a child, Bunmi asked his friend to talk with his father about their situation. As soon as they agreed, Bunmi spoke with his father and asked whether he would agree to see his friends. His father agreed to talk with them but nothing else because "I am not a healer," the father reminded Bunmi. The couple met with Papa Makinwa and he listened to them intently. At the end of their story, Papa Makinwa started to laugh. This rather curious response prompted Bunmi to ask his father why he found their story amusing, to which the father responded that there was nothing wrong with the couple. He proceeded to caution the wife that "she worries too much" and needs some hot tea to help her relax. Papa Makinwa proceeded to provide the tea for the wife with instruction on how often it should be drunk. He insisted that there was no medicine in the tea. It was just a tea like any other. He also scheduled a weekly meeting with her for conversation (it was actually for him to monitor the progress). After the couple left, he asked Bunmi to impress on his friend (the husband) to do all he can to keep the wife's mind at ease because "she worries too much." Apparently, drinking the tea (which he insisted was not medicinal) and counseling her to relax did the trick. Today, the couple has three children. Up to his death, Bunmi's father insisted that he was not a healer. He also never accepted money for healing people because he never acknowledged that what he did was to be rewarded with money. Again, humility was the spiritual code that guided his practice.

SPIRITUAL IDENTITY CONFLICTS AND THE TRUE BRAIN DRAIN

The cultural landscape of healing and its spiritual foundation have been changing and continue to change. What is clear is that healing as a spiritual experience in these separate African contexts engenders selfless dedication to helping with no expectation for reward. One could surmise that if the land belongs to no one and is here so that the herbs and trees (e.g., plants such as "medicineless" teas) are grown, the benefit from using community properties cannot be claimed for personal gain. Although much has been written about the spiritual code of Christianity, expressed in values of various helping profession, little or nothing has been said about the African spiritual codes. Moreover, Christianity continues to maintain its orthodoxy over values celebrated by Africans often at the devaluation of African spirituality. Richard Dyer (1991) observes:

> If Christianity as observance and belief has been in decline in Europe over the past half-century, its ways of thinking and feeling are none the less still constitutive of both European culture and consciousness and the colonies and ex-colonies (notably the USA) that it has spawned. Many of the fundamentals of all levels of Western culture—the forms of parenting, especially motherhood, and sex, the value of suffering, guilt, the shock of post-Enlightenment materialism—come to us from Christianity, whether or not we know the Bible story or recognize the specific items of Christian iconography. (15)

Marginalization can be said to have been effective at the point when the oppressor no longer has to be involved in holding firmly the instrument of oppression because the oppressed has assumed the position of the oppressor by advocating rules that negate his or her own beliefs. Spirituality is an area that has been so central to the Nigerian psychic that when he or she engages in it, it is done unquestionably. What is considered an extreme form of religion, such as fundamentalism, might be a matter of one's spiritual location. However, what is not in question is how Nigerian Christians have come to exalt their faith based on how far they distance themselves from traditional African spirituality. African spirituality, like African culture, has come to represent for these Christians the retrogressive values from which one must depart and deprecate as a sign of one's Christian devotion. It would appear that the more advanced the African level of education, the farther the distance that is believed must be established between themselves and African traditional spirituality. Indeed, the true medium through which messages can reach the heavens has been constructed to be in the image of one truth. Jesus for Christians, Mohammed for Muslims, Buddha for Buddhists, and indeed a syncretic religion like Hinduism can claim a singular identity. However, African spirituality is rejected in part because of the multiple media through which the heavens can be reached. Sango, Oronmila, and other media often referred to as deities represent multiple truths, which is a total anathema to the notion of universal truth represented in a single medium. The language of paganism and animism has helped to nurture a demonic representation of African spirituality. Pouring libation is shunned as a backward spiritual practice because it has not been sanctioned for Africans by the arbiters of their fate. An African Christian will bemoan the Western obsession with individuality of identity and the limitation of the West's focus on a singularity of solution except when it comes to spirituality. In the Western culture, sin is about "what you do" rather than "who you are." Among some Nigerians and Africans (whether at home or in the diaspora), sin is "who you are" because of your agency as a cultural and traditional subject. Indeed, political leaders have not been immune from this self-cultural deprecation. Most political leaders would not even acknowledge any belief in traditional spirituality while keeping their traditional spiritual guidance a hidden activity, carried out at night when no one could see them. Like traditional healing that remains on the margin of the state-controlled health system, traditional spirituality is being maintained on the margin of culture by many African elites, preventing the level of cultural interrogation of its values so that its acknowledgment can only be left at the level of romanticism rather than critical examination of its philosophical logic.

As we deal with the global surge of the HIV/AIDS epidemic, it would appear that, as Soyinka's excerpts have indicated, the spiritual foundation on which stigma can be erased and tolerance embraced is in African spirituality. It will clearly not be erased in the moral devaluing of sexuality practiced in the doctrine of Christianity. Indeed, if there is one area where Africans could provide moral leadership in dealing with diseases of marginalization, it is in the centrality of humility and tolerance in African spirituality.

SPIRITUALITY AND THE TRADITION OF COLLECTIVITY

If Wande Abimbola (1990) is correct in declaring that "a continent that cannot claim an indigenous religious tradition and system of thought can hardly be described as independent" (17), the silence and indifference that cast a shadow over Africa traditional spirituality are quite problematic, even more so in the context of HIV/AIDS. The reality of the role of spirituality in health outcomes is more evident in healing modalities. Healing modalities are very much anchored in spiritual values of a society. By this I am referring not only to the choice of remedy and the process a healer follows to arrive at a prescribed regimen but also to the prescribed and proscribed practices. From proscribing a male physician from attending to a female patient (as in some Islamic cultures) to the dominance of male physicians over female physicians (Christian cultures), religion and spirituality have played and will continue to play (women are still not allowed into priesthood in the Catholic Church) a crucial role in how illness is represented and treated in a given culture. HIV and AIDS have actually magnified the fissure between Western religious and spiritual values professed and the actuality of those values. It has also unveiled the hollowness in cultures where spirituality has been demonized and thus rendered dependent on others for interpretation of humanity. The point here is not to suggest that Africans should not subscribe to other forms of spirituality whose origin remains outside their cultural realm but rather to make the case that the absence of a spiritual identity, either in a syncretic sense (as in Hinduism) or in multiple traditions (as in Orisa/Yoruba), has rendered certain discourses on African identity rather incomplete, particularly in the context of health values and behavior.

   The challenge of humanizing HIV and AIDS as a part of our community has led to a discourse (infected and affected by) that locates HIV not only in the body of those infected with the virus but also in the entire community as a result of the inescapable connectedness of everyone in the community. The famous words offered by Martin Luther King in the letter from the Birmingham jail—"We are caught in an inescapable network of mutuality tied in a single garment of destiny. What affects one directly, affects all indirectly"—may very well represent the emblem for humanizing HIV and AIDS in our world. The centrality of community collectivity in defining individuality has been addressed by African philosophers. Kwame Gyekye (1997) has considered the meaning of *person* as opposed to *individual* (more on this in chapter 12). Gyekye quotes John Mbiti, who concluded that for Africans, the individual can be said to be defined as "I am, because we are; and since we are, therefore I am" (37). For example, when applied to HIV/AIDS, we can no longer ignore its impact on us all. Issues around the modes of transmission and behaviors related to transmission of HIV have forced us to confront how to reconcile the spiritual value of "what ought to be" with the public health mission of "what is" (Airhihenbuwa 1995b). This seeming binarism is not mutually exclusive. It is based on the principle that prevention efforts offer the potential and possibility that people want the best for themselves, their family, and their community. This combination of trust and hope is often referred to as faith.

Faith has always been at the core of spirituality and religion. Increasingly, public health and the medical community have come to realize the value of faith in human behavior and have been turning to spirituality for an understanding of this human value. Indeed, faith is considered to be "one of the miracles of human nature which science is as ready to accept as it is to study its marvelous effects" (Osler 1910:1471). Faith is also present in today's practice of medicine such as a physician's praying before surgery, a traditional healer's prayer during treatment, or physicians and healers leaving prognosis up to the patient's will to live (Airhihenbuwa 1995b).

SPIRITUALITY AND HIV/AIDS

Spirituality is a much broader and a more inclusive concept than religion even though the two terms are often used interchangeably. According to M. Relv (1997), "spirituality encompasses hope; faith; self-transcendence; a will or desire to live; the identification of meaning, purpose and fulfillment in life; the recognition of mortality; a relationship with a 'higher power,' 'higher being' or 'ultimate'; and the maintenance of interpersonal and intra-personal relationships" (2). Evidence from HIV/AIDS literature shows that there is a relation between spirituality and HIV/AIDS (Gray 199). This and the increasing urgency for solutions created by the epidemic have prompted the World Council of Churches' (1997) Executive Committee to issue a challenge to all churches to respond to the urgent call for actions resulting from the spread of HIV/AIDS worldwide.

In fact, some authors have been critical of the limited role played by churches in HIV/AIDS prevention. F. Symth (1998) believes that the influence of the church and the role of the national culture hinder the delivery of

HIV education, prevention messages, and programs. Moreover, it fosters "fatalism about the avoidance of infection" and reinforces feelings of guilt and shame that discourage self-empowerment with regard to sexual activities. Although I do not claim or promote an unquestioning acceptance of African spirituality or any other spirituality, it is evident that its central doctrine is the key quality we seek in the leadership of organized religion in the fight against HIV/AIDS—tolerance and unquestioning and a nonjudgmental support of all.

Researchers have studied the role of HIV and spirituality and have come up with recommendations for caregivers to consider in their work with persons living with HIV/AIDS. According to J. Barroso (1997), although the role of spirituality in the lives of people with AIDS is complex and multifaceted, health professionals should always be ready to support HIV/AIDS patients with their spiritual needs by helping them utilize their spirituality in a way that will be fulfilling for them. The author also suggests that intervention for HIV/AIDS patients in the context of spirituality and social support are individualized, culturally sensitive, and focused on the person's disease progression stage. There should be a shift in perspective where health care professionals develop or foster patients' spiritual beliefs, especially when their patients have illnesses for which there is no known cure. To accomplish this, a thorough understanding of African spirituality is needed.

FINAL THOUGHTS

There is a popular story about a devout Christian whose town was flooded but refused to evacuate because he was waiting for God to come to him and rescue him. The first rescuers who came to rescue the man were unsuccessful as he refused to leave his house while insisting on waiting for God. As the floodwaters rose to the man's chest, a second group of rescuers came by boat, but the man refused to budge; because he had been a good Christian and had obeyed all of the laws of God, he was convinced that God would come directly to rescue him. As the water continued to rise, covering his house, he climbed onto his rooftop, at which point the third group of rescuers came by a helicopter, but the man was steadfast in his conviction of seeing God directly. Of course, the man drowned and went to heaven. At heaven's gate he was furious at God for not coming to rescue him. God chided the man, asking him what else he expected since He had sent him three groups of rescue workers, first on foot, then by boat, and finally by helicopter. The story usually amuses as its moral is meant to reflect a man who misunderstood the multiple media through which God communicates with people. My question was always one of examining who the rescue workers were and what their message was to the man. In the context of HIV/AIDS, is it possible that these rescue workers blamed the man for the flood even as they were attempting to help? Could it be that the rescue workers' message was to question the man's individual behavior rather than understanding the context that bred his vulnerability? What if the boat was constructed as a condom? Is it possible that the man had learned in church to stay away from such boats? Suppose the man found out that the helicopter pilot was gay. Is it possible that the man has learned in church to demonize gays and lesbians such that his refusal to be rescued was due to the jaundiced information he received from the church rather than the importance of accepting the rescuers as messengers of God? What if his neighbors who evacuated without question were African spiritualists? Do we credit their spirituality for promoting the value of coexistence and tolerance, in which case one ought not to base the veracity of a message on the spiritual identity of the messengers?

Spirituality encompasses beliefs and value systems that range from organized religion to individual and/or collective values whose beliefs represent a guiding principle on which meanings are based. These values have proven relevance for HIV/AIDS prevention, care, and support. The obvious neglect of African spirituality makes the discourse on spirituality and health incomplete. HIV and AIDS programs should focus on forging alliances with communities so that efforts to confront HIV and AIDS can gain from different forms of spirituality. Interpersonal communication, which is discussed in chapter 11, is indeed a form of communication for which African spirituality has a wealth of experience.

11

In the Valley of Selfhood and Mountains of Cultures

Contextualizing HIV/AIDS Communications

Aghase Edo, Edo ye re: When you arrive in Edo, know that Edo is still far.

—Edo proverb

The Greek mythical Sisyphus ceaselessly pushed the proverbial rock up toward the mountaintop, but he failed (or so it was conventionally reasoned), as the rock always rolled back down. Where others saw failure and hopelessness in the plight of Sisyphus, the French writer and Nobel laureate Albert Camus saw courage and triumph. For Camus, Sisyphus's success lay not in reaching the mountaintop but rather in continuing the effort despite knowledge of the repeated similar outcome. Only a profound understanding of the relations of the rock to its physical and social environment could have led to a reasoning that locates the site of success not in the rock reaching the mountaintop but in providing an alternative interpretation of the context of Sisyphus's journey with the rock.

Like the pre-Camus interpretation of Sisyphus, success in health communication and public health programs tends to be based on changing particular individual behaviors through approaches that are almost oblivious to the structure and context in which such behaviors occur. When individuals fail to adhere to or fulfill the goal of the prescribed regimen and expected behavior change, the structure and context is hardly examined for the meaning of such behavioral outcomes. The limitation of individual behavior change has been lamented by several researchers in the context of public health (McKinlay and Marceau 2000; Kelly 1999), communications (Freimuth 1992; Rogers 1995; Singhal and Rogers 2003), bridging the racial gaps in health (Williams and Collins 1995; Gabriel 1998; Krieger and Sidney 1996), centralizing culture in health behavior (Airhihenbuwa 1995b; Airhihenbuwa and Obregon

2000; Lupton 1994; Hahn 1995; Spencer 1999), and HIV/AIDS (Airhihen-buwa, Makinwa, and Obregon 2000; Parker 2002). HIV/AIDS prevention continues to be anchored in the old banking model of education and social policies that were debunked by Paulo Freire, Frantz Fanon, and many others several years ago. The result has been the formation of a generation of managers of human behavior and technocrats and administrators of the epidemic who have provided us with elegant but acultural and acontextual recipes for judging risky or deviated behaviors (Parker 2000). Although the outcry for addressing root causes continues to grow, the anchor of the behavior change model on a focalized view of the individual prevents health professionals from being able to translate what has been learned (individual as the focus of change) to what should be done (social change to eliminate root causes).

WHAT HAS BEEN

One reason that health and communication professionals are unable to translate their knowledge into action is rooted in their inability to see program failure as a limitation of their learning methodology rather than in the response by the people. For example, a common image for inculcating a focus on the individual rather than the context is often represented graphically with an illustration that locates an individual at the core (i.e., bull's eye) of a concentric circle (figure 11.1).

The outer layers have contextual factors that are arranged to represent influences of family, community, culture, vocation, policy, environment, work, racism, and other factors that are the root cause of the negative (sometimes positive) individual health behavior to be changed. The visual image this graphic represents is one that focuses attention on the person at the core. It is thus reasoned, and would appear to be linearly logical, that because the person, at the core, is the ultimate repository of all these influences, the point of entry for behavior change ought to be this person. Thus, the continuous focus on the individual even as one bemoans the limitation of such a focus.

The challenge for public health communication addressing behavior change today is to engage in a serious analysis whereby we debunk the simplistic notion of individual-based preventive models and embrace a focus on the confluence of factors in the concentric outer circles that collectively circumscribe the health decisions of the individual. As we presented in the UN-AIDS report (UNAIDS/Penn State 1999), the common social psychological theories and models include the health belief model, theory of reasoned action and planned behavior, and social cognitive theory. It should be noted that the notion of collective efficacy has gained increased attention in social

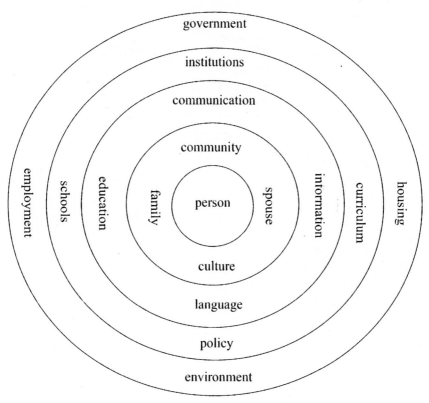

Figure 11.1. Traditional Model Focused on the Individual at the Center

cognitive theory even though the focus remains on individual rational volition to change. Focusing on the outer circles addresses the root causes of individual problems. It helps us to move away from engaging in "target group
intervention" whereby the response to negative individual health behaviors
is to "shoot good intentions into the target"—that is, on the individual at the
core of the concentric circles. Stated differently, the outer layers are stran-
gulating the individual at the core. Thus, the outer layers should be transformed into protective cushions rather than the iron ring they often represent.

The need to address preventive health strategies at the contextual level
rather than focusing narrowly on individual behavior has been increasingly
recognized by researchers, including Vera Paiva (2000) on issues of
HIV/AIDS in Brazil, Margaret Spencer (1999) on issues of social psychological contexts of health among African Americans, and organizations including the Rockefeller Foundation (1999) on social contexts of communication
interventions, and the Institute of Medicine (2003). For example, Paiva sees

HIV/AIDS as a social problem that goes beyond specific individual sexual behaviors. Rather, these behaviors are quite complex and vary according to partners, context, and especially, culture or subculture. Similarly, to speak of individual sexual behavior is seen as limited given that a sexual encounter, for example, involves two people, a relation that may imply unequal relations of power (between passive and active; old and young) and between man and woman among heterosexuals. Cultural codes, symbols, and values embody the essence of meaning that people bring to the production and acquisition of knowledge. These forms of cultural expression are accented in the meanings that participants bring to the communication of health messages. The dialogic process necessarily accents verbal and nonverbal exchange such that participants' behaviors are culturally meaningful.

Health workers and those who design health promotion and disease prevention programs must examine health behaviors in particular cultures in terms of whether they are rooted in the cultural values and beliefs of the people. For example, it has been demonstrated that in several African countries, person-to-person communication (through home visits) has been more effective in changing negative health behaviors than have messages distributed through the mass media. This finding is undoubtedly related to the oral tradition that is the customary bedrock for the production and acquisition of knowledge, as well as the construction of meanings around which daily events are anchored in African cultures.

HEALTH PROMOTION AND CULTURAL COMMUNICATION

In *Decolonizing the Mind*, Ngugi wa Thiong'O (1986) indicates that if the bullet is the means of physical subjugation, language is the means of spiritual subjugation. For this author, learning about the use of language is important; however, it is even more important to understand how language has been used to define identities, cultures, and behaviors. It is through this process of interrogating language as an instrument of power and marginalization that we begin to understand the role of imperialism relative to how we view ourselves and others as discussed in the previous chapters. Such initial interrogation should precede forms of learning and communication that we may choose to employ in health communication projects. Examining forms of learning requires an examination of the meaning of senses in the learning process.

It has long been established that the most effective method of learning is through demonstration, because the learner uses all the senses—hearing, smell, vision, taste, and touch (Fuglesang 1973). Unfortunately, most of the health communication programs that have been implemented in African nations have emphasized only visual learning. It should also be noted that visual literacy is an acquired skill. This means that learning based on what is seen whether on billboards or television must be skillfully acquired with repeated exposures.

Central to the issue of cultural variance in the production and acquisition of knowledge is how the notion of visual literacy constructed to be a "superior form of learning" devalues orature and orality, as theorized and practiced in many African countries, as forms of cultural production. Seeing and/or visualizing, as expressed in such idioms as "You see what I mean" and "Get the picture?" are more symbolic of mental imagery than of visual learning, although visualizing can serve as a reinforcer. The notion of knowledge production and acquisition through what one sees suggests a physical vision as opposed to a mental vision. Mental vision has transformative possibilities that should be promoted in oral cultures such as those found in many African societies.

In societies in which cultural production is realized primarily through orature, the ability to engage in the production of individual and collective mental imagery in learning is superior to visual or physical abilities. This process of cultural communication is unacknowledged in many health programs being implemented today in most African countries. Instead of focusing on encouraging the production of mental vision that engages individuals by affirming their own space and voice, institutions of higher learning (which for the most part provide training instead of education), as well as development agencies, have institutionalized the production of standardized learning based on physical vision. The result is a push for physical learning, such as the use of transparencies and slide projectors as the ultimate form of sharing and communicating with audiences and students. In fact, some institutions in both Northern and Southern nations have gone so far as to require that those who share knowledge, whether students making classroom presentations or professionals presenting conference papers, use physical or visual materials as the primary tool of communication, with the speaker's voice serving only a secondary function.

This form of learning has been promoted even though not many educators can effectively and efficiently use slides, transparencies, and other materials to engage their audiences in the production and acquisition of knowledge. For the majority, effectiveness in sharing information is increasingly being measured by the fanciness of the audiovisuals. Less attention is paid to the importance of the speaker's voice in communication. The speaker no longer has to aspire toward acquiring a voice that can transport the audience and/or student to undertake an independent cultural journey that leads to production of meaning. Rather, professionals have settled for a uniform, often voiceless and male-centered meaning—the ultimate form of what Freire refers to as "cas-tration of curiosity" in learners. The paradox in this case becomes evident in how we reward speakers and affirm leadership in education. In certain cir-cumstances, it is the individual who is able to "stand and deliver," in the ab-sence of visual support, who is commonly deemed to be deserving of recog-nition. For Molefe Asante (1987), the spoken word occupies a central place in communication, particularly among African Americans:

> The scholar, rhetorician, or historian who undertakes an analysis of the Black past without recognizing the significance of vocal expression as a transforming agent is treading on intellectual quicksand. . . .What is clear is that leaders who articulated and articulate the grievances felt by the masses have always under-stood the power of the word in the Black community. . . . Their emergence has always been predicated upon the power of the spoken word. (86)

The power of the spoken word has always been recognized by people of African descents as the hallmark of the varied interpretations and value of sto-rytelling. Such interpretations are sometimes encoded in songs of a story, such that the wisdom of the story is recalled in the song. The Edos of Nigeria always begin a story by singing a song that captures the spirit and the message of the story. Songs and dances are central to nearly all Edo rituals celebrating rain, birth, circumcision, and marriage, as well as funerals and more routine cere-monies. For Ngugi, songs and dances are not just decorative additions to an oc-casion; they are an integral part of the conversation, the drinking session, the ritual, and the ceremony. Indeed, the power of the spoken word becomes even more central to everyday rhetorical endearments as well as rhetorical resistance. Misinterpretation of the function and meanings of verbal expressions often re-sult from social scientists attempting to either read more into forms of expres-sion than there is or simplify them and rid them of their cultural meanings.

Although songs and dances are central to the Edo form of cultural produc-tion, individuals need certain skills to navigate the terrain of meanings and codes enshrined in the cultural landscape. Such skills are often acquired through experiential education and training. Indifferent and sometimes obliv-ious to the significance of songs and dances, as well as storytelling, in many African countries, Westernized or Eurocentric intellectuals have often engaged themselves in these media of expression even though they have no training, skills, or understanding of these forms of cultural production. Such culture-effacing acts are an extension of the belief that orature and oracy as a form of cultural production is simplistic, premodern, and easily engaged in by anyone with training in the more "modern" (read: written tradition) form of cultural production. Untrained in oral communication, and acting from their incorrect perceptions of the simplicity of the oral genre, these individuals produce simple stories and songs that are indifferent to any cultural code, interpretation, and meaning. Chinweizu, Jemie, and Madubuike (1983), in their classic book *Toward the Decolonization of African Literature*, challenge the prejudices that are often espoused by Eurocentrists when evaluating African literature and oral tradition:

> In evaluating African literature and matters related to it, they [Eurocentrists] start out by taking outstanding written material from Europe as their standards; they gather whatever African material they find convenient, usually of middling quality or worse, and compare them adversely with the best from Europe, and thereby unctuously confirm themselves in their initial prejudice that Europe is "good" and Africa is "bad." When it comes to the African oral tradition, their anti-African prejudice is reinforced by their anti-oral prejudice. They therefore gather the most grossly inadequate versions of African oral material they can find, and proceed, once again, to unctuously confirm themselves in their double-barrelled prejudice against things both African and oral. (87)

The use of language in any culture is designed to mirror the worldview— better yet, the world sense—of the culture. Every culture has a name for what is considered important to its reproduction and identity. It is often wrongly suggested that African languages have limitations in their usage. This myopic conclusion uses Western standards to evaluate the lexical functions of all languages and their cultural relevancies. According to Chinweizu et al. (1983), the "issue of parity and reciprocity has implications for the matter of making comparisons between the oral and written modes. Cognizance ought to be taken of the diversity of genres within the oral and the written forms, so that only comparable forms are compared" (35). The possibilities of the oral genre include the mystification of reality and the reality of myths, the spontaneity of communication and communicating spontaneously, and the extension of the interpretive potentials of cultural codes and meanings even when invoked for the first time.

Cultural practices relating to patterns of knowledge production and acquisition, in this case oral tradition, must be seriously considered in health communication interventions in cultures in which orature is the primary basis of communication. Health communication projects conducted in Africa to date have tended to operate on three key assumptions:

- Health information can reach the populace through the media.
- This health information can change negative health practices if Africans have the requisite health knowledge. Therefore, the health information should focus on the acquisition of the relevant health knowledge.

- If African do not acquire the relevant health information, it means that their skills for acquiring these messages must be "developed" as in development of literacy programs.

The problem with these operational assumptions is that they place all of the responsibility for program outcomes on the actions or Africans, particularly those in the rural areas. Therefore, if a program fails, it is always reasoned that the villagers' ("villagers" is often a common code used to describe either fondly or derogatorily Africans who are less Western in their expression and mannerism) community lacked the requisite knowledge and/or motivation to initiate the expected health actions that would lead to positive health outcomes. The health interventionists absolved themselves of any responsibility and accountability for the failure of the community to attain the expected health outcomes. Most health communication interventionists refuse to interrogate their complicity in the formation and imposition of their cultural hegemony on Others as constructed in the interplay of language and culture.

WHAT SHOULD BE

In September 1999, UNAIDS in collaboration with the Pennsylvania State University published a communication framework for HIV/AIDS, which highlighted the influence of the social and environmental context on individual health behavior (UNAIDS/Penn State 1999). Developed through a participatory process that involved 103 health communications practitioners and researchers, the framework espoused approaches to HIV/AIDS prevention, care, and support that are grounded in the meanings and values of the infected and affected populations. In developing the framework, five consultative workshops were held in Geneva; Washington, D.C.; Abidjan, Cote d'Ivoire/Ivory Coast; Santo Domingo, the Dominican Republic; and Bangkok. The framework identified five contextual domains that should be the focus of health and communications approaches to HIV/AIDS prevention, care, and support. The domains are (1) government policy, (2) SES, (3) culture, (4) gender relations, and (5) spirituality. Since its development, four African countries (Ethiopia, Lesotho, Ghana, and Malawi) have held planning meetings to begin the implementation of this framework as part of their national strategic plans. Similarly, national AIDS programs in countries like Colombia and Mexico in Latin America are incorporating the framework into their national strategic communication plans. In this chapter, I describe this UNAIDS contextual framework for communicating HIV prevention, care, and support using cases to illustrate the relevant domains. Recommendations are offered for effectively implementing and evaluating programs for HIV/AIDS prevention, care, and support in countries of Africa, Asia, and Latin America and the Caribbean.

THE VIEW FROM THE MOUNTAIN

A focus on individual health behavior (the person at the core of the concentric circle) is akin to being located in a valley with a deluded belief that inhabitants can be empowered to move the mountains. In the valley, one's sense of the mountain is mostly appealing in part because it is unmovable and rationality succumbs to its omnipresence while normalizing its indisputable power over the valley. Past approaches to HIV prevention, care, and support have been anchored in the valley with only occasional reference to the presence of surrounding mountains but with no systematic approach to transform its circumventing force and defining influence. Yet, it is only from the sides of the mountain, or from a journey toward its summit, that a broader view of the valley's identity and limited ability to define and regulate its knowledge, attitudes, and practices can be understood.

Thus, the traditional information, education, and communication programs are developed at the mountains for implementation in individual valleys, rather than focusing on the contextual factors that facilitate or hinder individual behavior in the valley (see Airhihenbuwa et al. 2000). Issues of time, meanings, and language are critical to identifying the valley even though they are often ignored in programs. Most communication interventions utilize campaigns, which are time-bound and target-specific groups of individuals in specific geographic locations. They lack sustainable activities, the involvement of communities and linkages with macro-/national-level initiatives. Integration of mass media and interpersonal communication strategies is also lacking, and insufficient attention is given to the role of emotions, orality, and interpersonal communication in national HIV/AIDS communications strategies (Singhal and Rogers 1999). Communication and health interventions, unfortunately, have tended to focus on the tree, not the forest. To use a cultural approach to health promotion is to recognize that the forest is more important than the tree. It is the understanding of the forest that allows us to appreciate the ways in which the individual trees are shaped by the meanings constituted in the forest—the context. In fact, the forest defines the identity of the tree, particularly in terms of order and seniority. Indeed, seniority (as will be discussed in the next chapter) is perhaps the most important single determining factor of the cultural production of relationships and behavioral expectations among the Edos and Yorubas of Nigeria.

In one effort to redress this programmatic deficit resulting from the afore-mentioned social psychological models, the new communications framework was developed in 1999. The UNAIDS Communications Framework offers an opportunity for a multisectoral and multidisciplinary approach to health and communications for social and behavioral change that could be measured and evaluated at multiple levels but with an emphasis on the outer layers of the circle—focusing on mountains and forests rather than valleys and trees.

BACKGROUND ON THE FRAMEWORK

The UNAIDS/Penn State framework offers five contextual domains as an interrelated network of influences for health decisions and actions. The frame-

Figure 12.1.   The PEN-3 Model

work is represented as a house with the structures designed in response to environmental conditions and social historical traditions of the region or country. The idea was to provide a basic structure of a house (the framework) and each country will transform it into a home (country strategy) based on its unique and shared strategies for defining and responding to the epidemic. Thus, the framework is a "house to home" (see figure 11.2) approach to HIV/AIDS prevention, care, and support (UNAIDS/Penn State 1999). I will discuss each domain in the context of HIV/AIDS in African countries.

Contextual Domain 1: Policy

Government policy, arguably, exacts the most impacting influence on social change that can transform the outer layers for the benefit of individual health outcomes even when individuals have no intention of changing. The need for government policy is often most appreciated when it is absent as in the case of absence of policy to protect against HIV and AIDS stigma. Although the tendency has been to focus solely on government policy, policies of institutions outside government such as universities, bilateral donor agencies, and other civil society organizations are also central to transforming the outer layers.

In 2000, the international conference on HIV and AIDS was held in Durban, South Africa, with the theme of "breaking the silence." This silence was believed to be unbearably endemic in circles of government and communities. More than twenty years into the epidemic, many governments have yet to assume leadership in promoting policy that protects the human right of persons living with HIV/AIDS in their countries. Two major conferences in Africa, the first in Addis Ababa, Ethiopia, in December 2000 and the second in Abuja, Nigeria, in April 2001, were convened specifically to call heads of nations into action for HIV and AIDS. In many instances, persons living with HIV and AIDS are stigmatized and left without protection while being asked to disclose their status. For instance, Gugu Dlamini was stoned to death by her neighbors in South Africa when she disclosed her HIV status on a radio station in Kwazulu Natal Province on World AIDS Day in 1999. In 2001, out of fear of being infected by sharing the same courtroom space with a person living with HIV, a judge in Lagos, Nigeria, refused to hear a case of a person living with HIV suing her employer for illegally terminating her appointment following the disclosure of her HIV-positive status.

On the part of the community, stigmatization abounds in ways that undermine prevention strategies and deny basic human rights to those living with the disease. Unfortunately, breaking the silence has not been extended to donor communities, training institutions, and private sector companies. These major institutions continue to maintain an audible silence by directly or indirectly continuing to promote approaches to health and development behaviors that are known to have little impact on health behavior outcomes. These individual-based strategies (that eschew the contexts) continue to be advanced by colleges and universities with the support of bilateral and multilateral donors.

It should be noted that individual behavior change continues to be important, particularly on the part of policymakers and organization leaders, in bringing about what Peter Piot, executive director of UNAIDS, often refers to as institutional behavior change. When individual behavior change is most important, it is for changes in the behavior of individual leaders in government and institutions. In Uganda, Senegal, Thailand, and Cambodia, the national government, NGOs, and other civil society institutions dealt with HIV and AIDS issues openly and directly (Diop 2000; Phoolcharoen 1998). In Uganda, the political will to openly address HIV and AIDS, under President Yoweri Museveni (individual behavior), provided an environment conducive to creating and sustaining a national response. Unfortunately, the gain in Uganda has witnessed a reversal due in large part to the new rhetoric in an almost exclusive focus on abstinence as opposed to the combination of abstinence with behavior change and condom use as was openly promoted and supported in the past.

In Thailand, the prime minister is the chairman of the AIDS commission, which coordinates a comprehensive AIDS Action Plan through fourteen different ministries, over two hundred NGOs, and various private sector institutions (Singhal and Rogers 2003). There are also some bold leadership decisions that have had positive impact on reducing HIV in other countries. In 1993, when the World Bank decided to support Brazil with a large loan aimed at curbing the growing AIDS epidemic in Brazil, President Itamar Franco decided to accept this loan (AIDS I), a decision that became critical in Brazil's response to the epidemic. Subsequently, President Fernando Henrique Cardozo accepted a second loan (AIDS II) that solidified Brazil's successful management of HIV/AIDS, including the provision of antiretroviral therapy to all persons living with HIV and AIDS in Brazil.

Contextual Domain 2: SES

SES has a significant impact on success and failures on many public health interventions even though it does not explain independently, inequity in health outcomes (Williams and Collins 1995; Airhihenbuwa, King, and Spencer 2001). Individuals and communities that constitute the bottom rung of the socioeconomic ladder are the most vulnerable to HIV/AIDS: they have the least power, the least access to information, and few resources to fight HIV/AIDS (Melkote, Muppidi, and Goswami 2000). They also have poor nutritional status, have little access to health care, and are least able to afford medical services.

SES is influenced to a great degree by government policy. For example, the Asian market crash of the late 1990s negatively impacted the consistency with which sex workers in Thailand were able to adhere to the 100-percent condom adoption policy in brothels. This policy was quite effective until this contextual event over which sex workers had no control but had to cope. However, a 100-percent condom policy can be effective only in contexts where the risk of transmission is concentrated in an organized population such as sex workers in brothels. When cases of AIDS are classified according place of resident, as in South Africa, living in informal settlements presents the highest risk environment. Living in an informal settlement is more of an indication of economic conditions than individual behavior.

Contextual Domain 3: Culture

The role of culture in understanding the contexts of preventive health behavior cannot be overemphasized. Rather than focusing exclusively on the negative aspects of culture as is often done in intervention programs, we insist on addressing the positive aspects of culture as well. Culture is most important when interventionists understand the strengths that reside in a particular community so that interventionists are able to identify the "cultural strength" as they examine cultural barriers (see the PEN-3 model in the next chapter). The goal is to assess the positive and negative in a culture rather than focusing solely on the negative. For example, *ukhusoma* is a Zulu word that refers to the traditional practice of young people courting and engaging in nonpenetrating sex. To focus prevention intervention on the high incidence and prevalence of HIV/AIDS in Kwazulu Natal Province (where Zulu culture is predominant) without also recognizing some health promotion practices that are traditional to the people will be overlooking a cultural strength of the Zulus in health behavior practices.

Waly Diop (2000) observes that several sociocultural and spiritual dimensions of Senegalese society have strengthened the nation's response to HIV/AIDS: for instance, the cultural norms with respect to universality of marriage; the rapid remarriage of widows(er)s and divorced persons; and extended social networks of parents, cousins, relatives, neighbors, and others who control sexual irresponsibility. A more detailed discussion of culture is presented in chapter 12.

Contextual Domain 4: Gender Relations

The impact of HIV and AIDS on women remains one of the most challenging aspects of the epidemic. Women are more vulnerable to HIV, more stigmatized, and the least empowered to control their environment. The tendency has been to focus on women without equal focus on men even though most women become infected through their sexual intercourse with men. For example, heterosexual intercourse is responsible for 80 percent of HIV among African American women compared with 30 percent for men (intravenous drug use and men having sex with men accounts for 70 percent of transmission among African American men). In fact, at the Asian and Pacific Regional Conference on HIV/AIDS in Kuala Lumpur in 1999, a scholar from India concluded that marriage was the single most significant risk for HIV transmission among Indian women. We preach monogamy, but 90 percent of women who are HIV positive are monogamous. Yet programs tend to focus on what wives should do about condom use rather than what husband should do about initiating and encouraging condom use. Also, although women sex workers are blamed for the spread of HIV, sex workers exist because of the demand from men. Furthermore, men usually determine whether sex takes place and whether a condom is used.

If an orphan in Africa is a motherless child, then it should not be surprising that authors have concluded that children's health status is dependent on their mothers' race/ethnicity and educational status. However, what is not clear is whether the mother's educational status is the result of instruction received in school or the result of employment gained by virtue of her education. In other words, could a woman without the certificate or diploma, but with the same job and salary, be able to impact her children's health? What about the impact of educational status on buying and using condoms consistently or discussing the use of condoms with one's spouse or partner? An examination of contextual factors will reveal how government policies sometimes help perpetuate women's economic and social subservience to men. For example, in Kenya, women cannot apply for a passport or open a bank account without the husband's or male partner's approval.

Contextual Domain 5: Spirituality

Spirituality is a much broader and a more inclusive concept than religion, even though the two terms are often used interchangeably. As discussed in chapter 10, spirituality includes values and beliefs about love, tolerance, compassion, sacrifice, hope, courage, patience, and faith; reflections on what is right and wrong, fair and unfair; and ponderings on the meaning and purpose of life, the inevitability of mortality, and the relationship between mind, body, and soul (Relv 1997). Evidence from HIV/AIDS literature shows that there is a relationship between spirituality and HIV and AIDS (Gray 1997). This and the increasing urgency of the epidemic have prompted the World Council of Churches' (1997) Executive Committee to issue a challenge to all churches to respond to the urgent call for actions resulting from the spread of HIV/AIDS worldwide. Churches are to be a healing sanctuary in the community by truly being there for their members in times of need. Because of the global extent of the disease, churches should face the realities of the epidemic and address issues of prevention while confronting and dispelling stereotypes and false information, which often dominate discussions of HIV/AIDS. In Uganda, more than eight thousand Islamic religious leaders (Imams) have launched a spiritually motivated grassroots movement to charge HIV-related behaviors of Muslim communities, declaring a spiritual war on HIV and AIDS. Although the call to organized religion to become engaged in preventing HIV and caring for persons living with AIDS is laudable, it is equally lamentable that African spirituality has not been actively engaged in the fight against HIV and AIDS.

CASE STUDIES FROM COUNTRY EXPERIENCES

The following case studies illustrate the key issues and problems in implementing HIV and AIDS programs. Case studies, through their narrative approach, deal with the real-life experiences of real people and help to anchor the discussion about HIV and AIDS, including possible solutions, in the given context. Case studies also encourage active participation. In each case, the entry point for problem analysis is the person (the core). However, the entry point for addressing the problem is the context (the outer layers). I offer these cases to encourage an open dialogue (better referred to as a "polylogue"; see Airhihenbuwa 1995b) on the contexts of HIV and AIDS prevention, treatment, and support.

Case 1

A physician is asked by a man to help him secure AIDS medication for his wife. There is no drug available in this country. The wife is sick and it is suspected that she may be HIV positive. The physician requests to meet with the wife for testing. The husband initially refuses and wants this to be done without his wife knowing about her suspected condition. Fearing the negative outcome of inaction, the physician agrees to the condition that the wife is not told that she is being tested for HIV. The wife is tested at the hospital and is found to be HIV positive. The attending physician would like to inform the wife of her status but is unable to do so due to a hospital policy. What are the implications for policy, SES, gender relations, and culture?

Case 2

A commercial sex worker meets with a client over dinner. During dinner, the client pays for services to be rendered. Before service could be rendered, the sex worker asks the client to use a condom. The client refuses, claiming that he does not like to "eat candy with paper" (suggesting that a condom takes away pleasure). The sex worker refuses to provide service unless the condom is used. The client becomes angry and physically threatens the sex worker if she does not return his money. The sex worker continues to insist that a condom must be used as a preventive measure. The client calls the police station to complain. A policeman is sent to the scene and, after listening to the client's complaint, arrests the sex worker for refusing to provide service for which she has been paid. What are the implications for gender relations, policy, SES, culture, and spirituality? Suppose the police officer were a female—might the outcome be different?

Case 3

An NGO conducted a series of workshops to train women in condom use because data showed that there was a low rate of condom use in the community. On the last day of the workshop, a rather reserved woman who said hardly anything during the workshop approached the facilitator for advice. She tells the workshop facilitator that before coming to the workshop, she knew how to and wanted to use condoms, but the problem is that she does not know how to bring up the issue without getting her husband angry. The husband is a mineworker and away from home for months at a time. She suspects that he probably has lovers in the mining town where he works. She is less concerned that he may have lovers and more concerned with the possibility that he may infect her with HIV. She is very worried and wonders when the NGO facilitator plans to have similar workshops for husbands like hers. What are the implications for gender relations, culture, and spirituality?

Case 4

A female employee of a construction company goes for a HIV test. Her result is positive. She returns to work devastated, only to find out that her supervisor at work already knows about her HIV status. Her employment is terminated. She later discovers that the clinic physician had called one of his friends at her company and informed him of her test result, without her consent. It is on this basis that her supervisor found out about her HIV status and that she lost her job. What are the implications for policy on stigmatization as well as for addressing the counseling needs of health workers?

Case 5

A newspaper story describes one of the largest corruption cases in country history. The story focuses on one individual who happens to have one of the largest work pensions in the country due to a corruption ring. The writer points out that this person is on the run and that his salary and his health benefits have been suspended, "which are both very important to him because he has AIDS." Persons living with AIDS (PLWAs) react critically to the emphasis on the man's HIV status, pointing out that this is an example of how the media stigmatize PLWAs by associating them with punishment, corruption, and other negative aspects of society. What are the implications for policy and SES?

These cases are presented to offer opportunities to question the questions as a way of developing strategies for overcoming the contextual issues that circumscribe personal efforts to change and/or maintain positive behavior. Rather than focus on these broader issues, interventionists tend to focus on personal behaviors such as teaching adults to read and write. Adult literacy still continues to be a focus on many health projects in African countries. Although the benefits of literacy are acknowledged, the contextual nurturers that must be in place for the newly acquired level of literacy to be sustained are often ignored.

LITERACY AND EDUCATIONAL INTERVENTIONS

Unfortunately, literacy has been equated with education nd, ultimately, stages and levels of development. Although literacy is usually a by-product of Western formal education, education (acquisition of the skills and information needed to make informed decisions) is not always the outcome of literacy. In fact, some of the traditional literacy programs were designed to provide unsuspecting consumers with the skills to understand and purchase certain commercial products. This is not surprising, given that literacy is believed to be the springboard to national development.

The misguided notion of literacy as a precursor for national development is based on Anderson's (1966) claim that a society requires a 40-percent adult literacy rate for economic "takeoff" (cited in Street 1984). This paradigm resulted in the widespread development and promotion of adult literacy programs, particularly in Southern nations. Many aspects of this practice continue today, in light of the fact that people tend to lose literacy skills if their daily engagements do not involve reading and/or writing. In fact, a number of the illiterate adults in some African countries today were once able to read and write as a result of completing primary school education. The ability to read and write is like many other skills, such as computer literacy. It requires a continuous and active engagement to maintain the skills that have been acquired. You can learn it, but if you do not use it, you lose it. Thus, most of the current literacy programs are simply reinventing the wheel—or, worse, reinventing the flat tire.

Three decades ago, UNESCO attempted to improve the sustainability of literacy skills by creating what it called a "literacy environment" (Street 1984). This meant that certain features in the environment of a community would be transformed to fit the needs and desires of those promoting the literacy program, rather than the program's being modified to fit with the community environment. Challenging UNESCO and others who perpetrate this acultural and acontextual model of learning, Paulo Freire and other cultural workers proposed adult literacy programs that engage the participants as subjects rather than objects. Using this approach, participants are engaged in the construction of sociopolitical issues that shape their collective reality, in a "process of consciencization." In Freire's adult literacy model, the participants are exposed to social and political issues that affect them so that they can become involved and have input into the decisions that affect them. "No program of literacy-training can exist—as the naive claim—which is not connected with the work of human beings, their technical proficiency, their view of the world" (Freire 1973:157), because "literacy involves not just the reading of the word, but also the reading of the World" (Freire 1993:59).

Even when the goal of a literacy program is sensitive to the cultural reality of the people the program is designed to benefit, the methods and techniques of implementation are often not culturally sensitive. In this respect, it is important to examine the methods employed in health communications. Specifically, we should examine the level of congruence between the traditional mode of learning (oral—mouth to ear) and the Western mode of learning (visual—eye to object) that is being introduced. In other words, to what degree does the use of posters and flyers, which are visually dependent, conflict with the traditional method of learning in an oral tradition? Literacy is critical to the degree that it problematizes the very structure and practice of representation by focusing attention on the fact that meaning is not fixed and that to be literate is to undertake a dialogue with others who speak from different histories, locations, and experiences (Giroux 1992a). Literacy is yet another development index that has been used to pursue the notion of universal truths.

As a consultant to the WHO in 1991, I was asked to develop a health education curriculum in Geneva (this request did not come from the Division of Health Education). This guideline was to be used in the development of health curricula in several African countries, without the involvement of participants from those countries. I protested and registered my objection to being a party to a process that totally disempowers the teachers, administrators, and students in these countries. Such is a Geneva hegemony (in spite of the fact that some WHO programs have been effective) that marginalizes Africans by denying them the opportunity to be subjects and actors in the systematization of educational processes that will shape their future. This institutionalized model of neocolonialism is practiced by using a credentialed member of the marginalized group to sustain Western hegemony in the name of inclusion and pluralism. It has become a common practice for national and international institutions to recruit unsuspecting credentialed Others (including third-world nationals and members of minority groups in the first world) to pursue and promote what are believed to be universal solutions to the problems of the Others' people. Although an increase in the representation and involvement of disenfranchised Others is welcome, it does not absolve institutions' decision makers of their responsibility to ensure that they do not contribute to the marginalization of identity and ideas.

FINAL THOUGHTS

We are challenging the assumption that individual behavior change interventions based on individual behavior change theories have very limited use in health communication for HIV and AIDS. If the person is at the center of the concentric circle, it does not follow that the person must be the entry point for intervention. Understanding this basic principle is the health communication challenge of the twenty-first century. Cultural sensitivity in health communication, health promotion, education, and development programs can be realized only when we centralize the cultural experiences of those who have hitherto been marginalized in the production of knowledge and cultural identity. To be specific, it is counterproductive to target individuals for most health risk reduction efforts without considering the effects of those individuals' cultures, languages, and environments. In this chapter, I have presented the UN-AIDS contextual framework for health and communication in HIV/AIDS. This framework resulted from a participatory discourse that recognizes the centrality of the physical and social environment in HIV and AIDS prevention, care, and support.

In his book *Quantum Healing*, Deepak Chopra (1990) relates the story of a man and a scorpion. A man was leaning over a gutter to rescue a scorpion that was drowning in mud, but he kept getting stung by the scorpion each time he tried to rescue it. This repeated occurrence exasperated an onlooker, who chided the rescuer for engaging in this seemingly hopeless exercise. The rescuer responded that it is the nature of scorpions to sting, and it was his nature to rescue it. Like Sisyphus, the rescuer understood that success is less about the individual action and more about an understanding of the context and relationships that gives meaning to such action. We are products of our contexts and the expectations of our roles within them. Our contexts shape our reality, expressed in individual behavior. Whether our efforts are considered failure or triumph depends on the context that gives meaning to events.

There has been a global response to the AIDS pandemic represented in the special session of the UN general assembly in June 2001 and the mobilization of a global AIDS fund by UN secretary-general Kofi Annan. Some serious questions have been raised about the good intentions but weak results represented in the report of the June 2001 UN special session on HIV/AIDS (Gruskin 2002). However, the academic and donor community must be challenged to go beyond good intentions to become resolute in focusing on the context that circumscribe and could liberate individual behavior. Mountains shape and define valleys like forests shape and define trees. To assume otherwise or to fail to recognize the contexts, unfortunately, is promoting a different form of an epidemic.

12

Of Culture and Multiverse

Renouncing the Universal Truth in Health

Western man [*sic*] has created chaos by denying the part of his self that integrates while enshrining the parts that fragment experience. These examinations of man's [*sic*] psyche have also convinced me that the natural act of thinking is greatly modified by culture. Western man [*sic*] uses only a small fraction of his mental capabilities, there are many different and legitimate ways of thinking, we in the West value one of these ways above all others—the one we call "logic," a linear system that has been with us since Socrates.

—E. T. Hall (1976:9)

At the center of health and education initiatives is the ability to look to our past, not only for historical continuity but for understanding about the trials, failures, and possibilities that shape our individual and collective experiences. This is the beginning of the framing of a social cultural infrastructure on which African identity and behavior can be understood. Affirming the ties of the past allow us to bond the present to the future by relearning our history while nurturing our unique and our shared sensibility to subvert domination and transform our world (hooks 1992). As Stuart Hall (1991) notes, the relation that people of the world have to their own past is a part of the discovery and affirmation of their own ethnicity: "The past is not only a position from which to speak, but it is also an absolutely necessary resource in what one has to say" (18). These past and present experiences constitute a group's cultural identity.

The recognition that culture should be a critical focus in health programs continues to gain currency. Increasingly, health educators and public health and health communication researchers and practitioners have realized that past failures of many preventive health intervention programs are blamed conveniently on the individual, to the exclusion of the context that shapes and nurtures the individual. Many African scholars have called for a focus on knowledge production that are anchored in African cultural ways of knowing.

KNOWLEDGE AND KNOWING

Knowledge is culturally produced through forms of direct and indirect exchange between parents and children, teachers and students, speakers and audiences, and families and their environment. To embrace Western paradigms is to embrace a cultural production, a Western cultural production. The reluctance to represent the Western ways of knowing as cultural has resulted in the binarism of the West and the rest of the world. Such a binarism almost always privileges the West in the discourse on globalization. As much as the focus of this chapter is on African ways of knowing about health, a comparison with the role of Western influence in African knowledge production is inevitable. This form of relationship continues to exist even though it has taken different forms and shifting direction over the years. Regardless of the nature and texture of the relationship, the outcome tends to always privilege the West and suppresses African thoughts at the margin.

This relationship of the West to Africa and the world can be illustrated by the relationship between the egg and the coconut—it does not matter whether the egg falls on the coconut or the coconut falls on the egg; it is the egg that will break. The coconut and egg represent different identities that, allowing for some possibilities of hybridization, in principle affirm each other's particular space. Unfortunately, the relationship of the West to Africa has been a relationship in which the West positions itself as the coconut always poised to clash with and crush the egg. In fact, when considered side by side, the egg and the coconut represent different forms of cultural production and meaning on the global landscape. They echo the philosophy that searches for multiple truths because, according to Chinua Achebe, when one thing stands, another thing stands beside it. Neither the egg nor the coconut is static in its cultural representation. In other words, whereas a culture may symbolize the egg in one instance, in another it may be the coconut. For example, although many African cultural codes and meanings (the coconut) were impervious to assault during colonialism and postcolonialism (i.e., the introduction of traditional medicine), these same societies have yielded (the egg) to the adoption and often valorization of non-African languages for political, educational, personal, and business/market exchanges. By the same token, although the Western cultures have maintained their religious traditions (the coconut), these same cultures have yielded to other cultural codes (the egg) that are now being shaped by music and clothing constructed by the ethnic minorities that their dominant cultures tend to marginalize.

Cultural identity is anchored in an affirmation of a collective sense of consciousness. Culture is not a symbol of unquestioning reverence but a fluid terrain of ideological and material relations that are endless, multilayered, and always open to questions (Giroux 1992a). For Ngugi wa Thiong'O (1993), culture embodies moral, ethical, and aesthetic values in the form of spiritual eyeglasses through which people come to view themselves and their place in the world. Language as an expression of culture is the collective memory bank of a people's historical experiences. Those who develop health, education, and communication programs must examine carefully the differences as well as the similarities in cultural perceptions, so as to understand the contexts of health beliefs and practices more fully and to address them appropriately within their particular cultures. Such understanding should not be based on market economy and buying power, the traditional indices of development. Culture develops within the process of a people wrestling with the natural and social environment, and thus it embodies the moral, aesthetic, and ethical values that are manifested in the people's consciousness (Ngugi 1993).

Important aspects of cultural expression in African countries are found in aesthetic values and meanings as evident in arts, music, and clothing. Such values and meanings are laden with desires, emotions, and expectations that are not meant to be discernible through Westernized code. For example, "the notion of religion is hardly ever used [by Westerners] to designate African beliefs and religious practices" (Mudimbe 1988:76). In an attempt to show "the ways things really are" in the non-West, we have become engaged in discourses that produce a non-West that is deprived of fantasy, desires, and contradictory emotions (Chow 1991). It is the omission of these aesthetic values from the analytic framework used to examine African cultures that renders external approaches to African experience often Eurocentric. Even when certain non-African intellectual traditions have been favored by Africans, important limitation still should be noted. At the very least, ownership of history and idea is central to the question of identity in framing health solutions. Some literary criticism, such as Marxist, is limited by its insistence on the tendency to base aesthetic assessment solely on how the market economy shapes the political struggle of the proletariat. This market-driven analysis tends to make Marxist literary criticism thin on what are commonly considered aesthetic concerns in African traditions, thus ignoring or denouncing as "formalism" questions of beauty, style, technique, sensibility, and appropriateness, which are at the core of African aesthetics (Chinweizu and Jemie

1987). These aesthetics must be evident in ways of knowing and feeling of health and behavior programs conspicuously absent from conventional health behavior models of today.

I have argued (see Airhihenbuwa 1994, 1995a, 1995b) that group- or community-based interventions must begin with a focus on culture. Indeed, it is the focus on the individual (independent of the context) that prevents us from addressing the problems of inequity and discrimination such as racism and structural discrimination in the United States. The tradition of social science and public health has been to focus on the individual rather than the social context, even though the playing field is uneven. Because race is recognized by many researchers as a social construction, culture, which is a more appropriate representation of group ways of knowing, has become a more critical domain within which programs should be understood in developing health interventions. Besides deflecting attention away from issues of group inequity, the focus on individual behavior has also enshrined the moralization of behavior, particularly in the United States. Criminalization is very much tied up with race and the attendant "demonization and immoralization" of the Black body. An example is the way federal and state laws penalize Blacks and Whites, differentially, for the use of crack cocaine and powder cocaine, respectively. The extensive news coverage of Blacks using crack cocaine (compared with the relatively low coverage of Whites using powder cocaine) led to new legislation for a mandatory sentence for a first offence of possessing crack cocaine, whereas possession of powdered cocaine is a mere misdemeanor. Because moralizing over a group's behavior is easily seen as too obvious a claim to moral superiority of one group over another, a focus on individual behavior remains the strategy for deploying moralization while at the same time making it appear inconsequential. It is thus more plausible to ground the discourse around negative health behavior on moral foundations even though such foundations may not be self-evident when targeting behaviors of interest. In this case, the difference that makes a difference has meant a disturbingly legal difference.

As Michael Brown, Martin Carnoy, and colleagues (2003) have argued, the solution to eliminating racial disparities does not lie in individual intentions and differences, but rather in institutional policies and practices that create and maintain these disparities. Some of these institutional policies and practices are often shrouded in the politics of morality and historical lineage. J. Morone (1997) argues that representational politics and the moralizing of Americans are founded in the Puritan cultural ethos of early New England communities. Indeed, he contends that these early notions of individualism and behavioral morality presage the present public health discourse on negative health behavior. "Health care reformers sometimes wonder why they have not been able to find more political support for their causes—universal health insurance for children, expanded protection for the uninsured, or funding for treatment of drug abuse. One answer lies in a most unlikely place: the way in which Americans view the morals of their fellow citizens" (1017).

My point here is not to focus on moralization over behavior as a cultural byproduct of the American experience but to point out the way in which individual behaviors (positive or negative) are grounded in cultural values in ways that do not render themselves either obvious or optimally promoting health. In fact, the most commonly employed mechanism for "overshadowing" the role of culture is to individualize behaviors and target them for change. I argue that a more effective strategy is to focus on contextual domains (such as culture) that give meanings to behaviors of interest and thus must become the focus of public health, health education/promotion, and health communication training programs.

THE PEN-3 MODEL

The training of any person for an occupation requires an understanding of culture as a superstructure that can maintain memories of the past alive trough its substructure. Health beliefs and actions should be examined within the context of culture, history, and politics. In this chapter, I present the PEN-3 model (figure 12.1), a cultural model that I developed in 1988 and that was first published in 1989 to be used in planning and evaluating culturally appropriate

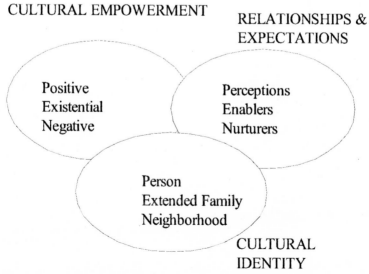

CULTURAL EMPOWERMENT

RELATIONSHIPS & EXPECTATIONS

Positive
Existential
Negative

Perceptions
Enablers
Nurturers

Person
Extended Family
Neighborhood

CULTURAL IDENTITY

Figure 12.1.　The PEN-3 Model.

health interventions. PEN-3 has been modified and presented in subsequent publications, including in *Health and Culture: Beyond the Western Paradigm* (Airhihenbuwa 1995b). With new information and application of the use of PEN-3, an updated version is presented in this chapter. I present not only the model but the process for applying it in the community.

Culture is best understood as a people's shared history, language, and psychological lineage. Moreover, culture dictates structure in a society. For example, architectural structure symbolizes the cultural norms and values of a people expressed in physical spaces. Because traditional houses are cyclical in many African cultures, this leads me to the observation that most African cultures believe in circles of relations that are seamless (more on this later). To illustrate the centrality of culture in health behavior outcomes, I will focus on cultural production among the Edos of Nigeria.

Any conceptual approach for health promotion programs should be anchored in what I referred to in *Health and Culture* as a polylogue—a community conversation. This process allows members of the culture of interest to be a part of the conversation and the decision to appropriate what may be culturally sensitive and culturally appropriate in their community and society. Although I refer to PEN-3 as a model, my intent is not for it to be applied in some prefabricated box or matrix but for it to offer a space within which cultural codes and meanings can be interrogated and allocated. In this way, the range of possibilities of cultural values and practices could be either encouraged, acknowledged, and/or discouraged as process of program development, implementation, and evaluation.

The PEN-3 model allows the kind of flexibility that encourages intracultural diversity such that the process should be engaged each time a program is conceived. Health workers should employ a polylogical process that ensures affirmation of different cultural expressions in different locations. Moreover, this model also challenges health promotion and communication workers to address health issues at the macro (policy, government, societal, and international) level as well as the traditional micro level of health program interventions. The utility of this model therefore relates to its amenability to modification and extension of its limits and possibilities such that the production and acquisition of knowledge in a given culture is sensitively and sensibly represented in the project. In addition, this model incorporates salient elements, notably knowledge, perceptions, and beliefs, that feature in health education and health promotion models, theories, and frameworks even though it is firmly anchored in African and African American philosophy and history with insights from critical theory in fields such as cultural and gender studies. Thus, PEN-3 consists of three dimensions of health beliefs and behavior that are dynamically interrelated and interdependent: relationships and expectations, cultural empowerment, and cultural identity.

I will discuss why and how the current discourses on health education/ promotion and public health should be transformed to focus on the cultural experiences. In every society, in every community, in every family, in every individual, there is this tripartite entity· of positive, existential, and negative that coexist to define the individual and his or her contextual identity. Society produces (either through its government or educational institutions) policy to address negative values and explicate existential values through the arts and humanities while seeking ways to promote the positive through spiritual codes and doctrines. Persons, as products of community and society, use the spiritual to address the negative, engage in the pursuits of the positives particularly in its manifestations in morality, and express the existential through relationships and expectations that affirm the uniqueness of the culture. Communities and families become entities that have been subject to studies because our understanding of these entities has been based on how we see either the individual or society but never from both ends (individual and society) at the same time. The PEN-3 model thus offers an opportunity to examine the tripartite entity in cultural identity and by extension the behaviors that are believed to manifest those value within these entities.

The next section begins with the domains of relationships and expectations followed by cultural empowerment. The domain of cultural identity will be discussed last because this domain is the intervention point of entry. It is at this last domain that the question of identity becomes central to training meanings of and solutions to health problem.

RELATIONSHIPS AND EXPECTATIONS: WHEN RELATIONSHIPS ARE CENTRAL BUT CYCLICAL

When one thing stands, another thing must stand besides it. . . . This saying "there is only one way" is something that is new to my people.

—Chinua Achebe (1988:161)

The construction and representation of health behavior are usually anchored in the interaction among the perception we have about the behavior, the resources and institutional arrangements that promote or discourage actions, and the influence of family, kin, and friends in nurturing the behavior. Relationships and expectations also represent many of the traditional domains of interest in conventional health behavior theories and models. The three categories of relationships and expectations are perception, enablers, and nurturers.

Perception

Perception here indicates knowledge and belief, values, in decision making that are focused on either persons or groups, highlighting the complementarity of emotion and rationality in behavioral outcomes. Unfortunately, emotionality is overlooked in a discourse on health behavior that valorizes rational volition in preventive health decisions. In the introduction to *Pluralistic Universe*, Henry Samuel Levinson (1909) reminds us that William James concluded in 1890 (in his *Principles of Psychology*) that normal intelligence or thought is based on emotion, interest, and motivation, and that truncated intelligence is unemotional. For example, some Nigerian mothers believe that a healthy child does not need to be protected against illness, and this view may affect immunization programs, because preventive injections are often considered to be a treatment. Or, when there is a cultural belief that consuming sweet foods causes diarrhea (a belief held by the Edos, Yorubas, and Igbos of Nigeria), it becomes a serious challenge to promote the use of homemade oral rehydration solutions, which contain sugar, as therapy for diarrhea. Existing perceptions can lead to the need to resolve conflicts that might arise in people's minds, because to them it might seem as though the causative agent of a disease is also its treatment or cure.

For example, many years ago, when African Americans answered yes to the question "Can someone get AIDS from donating blood?" some researchers misinterpreted this to mean they have poor AIDS knowledge. In fact, this response indicates a strong negative distrust of White health care providers, reflecting a belief that they may intentionally infect Blacks with the AIDS virus—a perception that is, according to Vanessa Nothingham Gamble (1997), the result of a historical legacy of medical atrocities visited on the bodies and minds of African Americans in the United States commonly emblemize in the Tuskegee syphilis experiments.

Another example of perception is on the subject of body weight between African Americans and Whites. Several researchers have reported that being overweight is not necessarily associated with negative body image for many African Americans. Shiriki Kumanyika found in her studies that African Americans who are overweight are likely to be less concerned about their body size than are their White counterparts (Kumanyika, Wilson, and Guilford-Davenport 1993). However, such perceptions about body image should not compromise the seriousness of overweight and obesity as a condition that often lead to chronic diseases such as type 2 diabetes and heart disease. It does speak to different perceptions about what is considered to be attractive body shape and size among healthy adults.

Knowledge and beliefs are the key elements that shape our perceptions of reality, and thus of health and illness. Quite often, knowledge and beliefs are placed on two ends of a continuum with knowledge enshrined and beliefs denigrated. Even though belief is the community knowledge and experience, it is seldom considered a valid aspect of positive perception until it has been certified as knowledge by health professionals. Scientific health knowledge has become the collection of information and values that have been certified to indicate positive health action. For example, the etiology of chicken soup as an effective remedy for the common cold has always been a production of cultural beliefs as constructed by grandparents even though never acknowledged as knowledge.

However, now, to drink chicken soup for the common cold is considered to be knowledge because physicians have now certified its effectiveness. Medical and health researchers and practitioners are now "knowledgizing" beliefs by (1) patenting herbal medicines and (2) legitimating the need for more dialogue between healer and patient, as practiced by traditional healers (Airhihenbuwa 1995b). Indeed, the importance of spirituality in healing, hitherto scorned as part of healing because it was belief based, has now found a home in physicians' "knowledge-based" practice.

In our pursuit of adequate health behavior outcomes, knowledge has come to mark the point of departure, the foundation, the requirement that must be acquired because it is believed that it predicts behavioral outcome. Behavioral outcomes are often appropriated as a change in health behavior from what was negative to what is positive. The process for reaching this goal entails employing theories and models that allow us to dismantle behavior, change it, calibrate it, and grease it to produce the expected quantifiable health outcomes. It is assumed that improved knowledge and a change in attitude are the twin engines that generate expected outcomes in behavior. The result is that we diagnose behavior as a problem that needs to be fixed and proceed with a regimen that we believe is necessary for a positive prognosis. In fact, we approach the individual and the community as diseased entities that must be diagnosed—hence our focus on behavioral and community diagnosis.

Enablers

Enablers refers to resources and institutional support, SES, and wealth (assets over liabilities) as measures of resources and power, and costs and availability of services such as drugs for treating HIV. An example of this category may be the absence of antiretroviral therapy and a culture of activism that have led to a social movement to force drug manufacturers to reduce the price of AIDS drugs. At a child survival workshop in Nigeria, several mothers cited being asked to pay for the treatment of abscesses (a side effect of vaccination) as a major reason for not taking their children for immunization through the Expanded Program on Immunization, even though they know the injections are free. Paulo

Freire (1989) discovered that mothers' reluctance and/or refusal to give eggs to their children started when colonial settlers told the indigenes that eggs were bad for them (the indigenes), so that eggs would be sold cheaply (because they were of little use to those who produced them) to the colonizers.

The focalized view of behavior also blinds the gazing health professional to the totality of the context and the factors that influence the behavior of interest. This could be illustrated by the story of the rescue workers who were so "focalized" on resuscitating drowning victims that they failed to look up to see the perpetrator on the shore who was pushing the unsuspecting victims into the river. The totality of the relational pattern of behavior is conditioned and nurtured by culture. This pattern must be understood in the context of resource sharing, policy formulation, power structure, and how these relate to the family, the community, and its politics. In fact, politics is often treated as a separate entity apart from the cultural context.

Nurturers

Nurturers refers to family eating traditions, community and events, spirituality and soul, values of friends (e.g., about drinking), and marriage rules and expectations. Examples of this category may be a culture of caring for the sick at home and wife inheritance. Another example relates to the challenge of promoting immunization. The fact that older siblings who were never immunized are in good health tends to suggest to some parents and families that immunization and other modern preventive actions against childhood diseases are unwarranted for their young children. The concept of nurturers emphasizes the importance of increasing significantly the number of underrepresented groups in the health professions who understand and respect their culture and communities.

It is also important to promote an understanding of cultural beliefs and practices among majority groups. After all, the goal of employing a cultural model is not to discourage persons from outside the culture to engage in health interventions but rather to provide everyone with a framework that will guide effective health intervention outcomes. Indeed, that one is from a given culture does not confer an automatic expertise for implementing a culture-based project in the absence of a model or framework. Thus, PEN-3 encourages border crossings in health interventions both intra- and interculturally. For example, because of the disproportionately high level of cardiovascular disease in the African American population, special emphasis has been placed on eating practices and weight control. However, PEN-3 provides the framework to analyze the cultural elements of African American eating practices, particularly those foods that are shared by other Americans. Because food is a cultural symbol and eating is a symbolic act through which people communicate, perpetuate, and develop their knowledge and attitudes toward life, an understanding of cultural influences on eating habits is essential for the health educator (regardless of the educator's cultural identity) who wants to provide realistic educational interventions designed to modify dietary practices.

The most important cultural dynamics among the Edos are the relationships between families and within the family. Relationships and interactions among persons and groups are based on the expectations of one's role in the culture. Among the Edos, once relationships are formed, loyalty is expected. Indeed, relationships define roles and expectations that are maintained over time. One's identity is thus formed, reformed, and nurtured through these networks. Among the Japanese, Hall (1976) notes that "once a relationship is formed, loyalty is never questioned. What is more, you have no real identity unless you do belong" (113). Group identity is considered to be more important than individual identity. For the Edos, seniority often dictates the direction and flow of information. As Oyeronke Oyewumi (1997) has explained, seniority is based not simply on birth order in the family but also on the responsibility assumed within the family and broader community. Thus, acquisition of values based on beliefs and knowledge are conditioned by one's position and responsibility in the family and the community. For example, the cyclical nature of the relationship and the ways of knowing inscribes emotionality (such as seeing a family member dying from AIDS) as a valid form of human experience that often triggers action to adopt a preventive health action such as using a condom when previous knowledge could not. Relationships and expectations are products of culture.

CULTURAL EMPOWERMENT:
BEFORE CORN, WHAT DID THE CHICKEN FEED ON?

Cultural empowerment is better understood within the lived experience of Africans insofar as the coexistence of all forms of life that is shared in the communication tradition of oralcy. This is a critical aspect o' what has been referred to as oral traditional culture by scholars. Amadou Hა nპate Ba (1982), the Malian historian, captures this notion of oral tradition as follows: "Oral tradition is the great school of life, all aspects of which are covered and affected by it. It may seem chaos to those who do not penetrate its secret; it may baffle the Cartesian mind accustomed to dividing everything into clear-cut categories. In oral tradition, in fact, spiritual and material are not dissociated."

Culture and *empowerment* are two words that are almost never coupled. Culture is often represented as a barrier, whereas empowerment is often represented as strength. The domain of cultural empowerment affirms the possibilities of culture as an embodiment of the tripartite entities of positive, existential, and negative. The cultural empowerment domain is thus composed of three categories.

Positive

This category includes values and relationships that promote the health behavior of interest; healing modalities given that each culture has its strategy for dealing with health problems, including sexually transmitted infections; and nonmarket values to the extent that cultural values cannot all be subsumed into measurable parts that are quantifiable in monetary gain or loss. Examples include the promotion of such traditional practices as breastfeeding and the eating of green vegetables. There is a tendency on the part of some upwardly mobile African American professionals to disengage slowly from eating green vegetables, as was done traditionally, because such foods are not believed to be associated with progress and affluence. As I have recommended and now insist, all programs developed for a community must begin with the positive. It is the responsibility of the interventionist to find out what those positive values are. If none can be found, it may indicate that the interventionist is incapable of working in such a community and he or she must leave before he or she becomes a part of the problem.

According to Wole Soyinka (1996), the Nigerian Nobel laureate,

> In a more fundamental sense, however, man [*sic*] is first a cultural being. Before politics, there was clearly culture. Only man [*sic*] the producer could have evolved into the political being, which, to pare away all mystification, is the evolutionary stage related to the development of society and the consequent sophistication acquired in the management and protection of resources. This hierarchy of evolution also explains why man [*sic*] resorts to his cultural affiliations when politics appear to have failed him, never the other way round. (129)

Existential

Existential refers to the qualities of a culture that makes it unique. These qualities are mostly ill understood by outsiders and often are blamed for program failures. Language is clearly a form of cultural expression where a difference makes an important difference. I have used the term *language elasticity* to represent these necessary differences. *Language elasticity* refers to the different forms of expressions, codes, and meanings of a language, even if the same language, such as English, is spoken in different regions and countries.

Face saving is another existential quality of a cultural capital that families are expected to invest in the actions of everyone. All personal behaviors are believed to be representative of the family name. Indeed, an Edo parent would often emphasize the importance of face saving by threatening to disinherit their child of his or her family name if the child continues to "shame" the family.

Beyond language and face saving, there are other cultural practices that are existential. An example is the differential meaning of adoption. In the Western context, one's nephew or niece (even one's spouse's child) needs to be considered "adopted" to gain family legitimacy and all the rights that are accorded. In many African cultures, because of the family context, beyond the nuclear boundary defined in the West, assuming a full parental responsibility for one's nephew, niece, and cousins (even children of close friends) does not require a process of adoption to gain full family legitimacy. This difference in the process of gaining legitimacy in family membership has often led to confusion of whether adoption is a part of African tradition.

Other examples of existential qualities include the use of palm oil and indigo as a soothing lotion for a child with measles and the placing of an amulet around a child's neck to ward off evil spirits. In fact, some physicians have actually used this practice with their pediatric patients, telling them that only the physicians may remove the amulets. This helps to guarantee that patients will return for follow-up visits. Public health educators should address what *is* and not what *ought to be*. They should refrain from moralizing over behaviors that are unfamiliar to them and that they do not understand. The programmatic thrust of public health, health education and promotion, and health communication should be to address what is in terms of matching intervention with current health practices, such as sexual activities among teenagers, rather than what ought to be, such as abstinence. Understanding these existential beliefs is where African American theoreticians have made significant contributions. For example, these researchers link African American lifestyles, at least in part, with African values to produce a holistic worldview, as opposed to an abstract construction of personality assessment that sees the individual as pathologic.

Negative

Negative refers to the conventional objective of program interventions that focuses on what is wrong that should be changed. However, rather than focus exclusively on negative behavior, we should examine the contexts of behavior to include policy environment, wealth rather than the exclusive focus on income of persons, communities, and society; the position of women in society relative to decisions about sexuality; and the spiritual contexts of the health behavior in question. Examples of this category include social arrangements that lay a foundation for the present inequity and inequality such as racism and differential housing and education as has been documented in the United States by scholars like David Williams and Chiquita Collins (2004). A parallel at the global level is the imperialism that produces power differentials in identities and nationhood as documented in the work of Cheikh Anta Diop,

Frantz Fanon, Edward Said, Chinweizu, Wole Soyinka, Michel Foucault, and Noam Chomsky.

In PEN-3, the *Es*—extended family, enablers, and existential behaviors— are the most powerful influences on and for cultural production. The enablers speak to power, politics, and history; the existential speaks to affirmation of humanity and cultural empowerment; and extended family speaks to the vitality of sustained positive traditions and influence as well as a major contribution to global production of knowledge, meaning, and interpretation. The dynamic interrelatedness of these three levels must be balanced to demonstrate the degree to which politics, policy, power, and culture shape and are being shaped by persons within their family.

Public health and health communication programs focus on health beliefs and behaviors. These programs must reflect the cultural perspectives of the people for whom they are designed. Health educators and communicators should focus on both positive (cultural empowerment process) and negative behaviors in a health program. Very often, too much attention is focused on negative behaviors, with few or no acknowledgements and/or rewards offered for positive behaviors. In some instances, educators arrogantly blame the failure to change negative behaviors on the presence of existential behaviors.

This process of empowering individuals in health education programming is often based on the assumption that individuals, primarily because of their limited economic resources, are powerless. Eurocentrists often consider silence, which makes some Westerners uncomfortable, to indicate voicelessness and weakness. They thus believe that knowledge can be measured using economic or development indices such as income level and fluency in a Western language. The authoritarian connotation of participation obviously reduces it to a presence of the popular classes in the administration of development programs even though such participation is encouraged to support only what has been planned and decided. This silencing of Others through development participation foregrounds the impetus for the construction of a culturally appropriate programmatic framework that involves Africans at the initial discussion of the project for health promotion programs in Africa. It is in addressing these program deficits that PEN-3 has been particularly useful to researchers and practitioners in learning to involve communities in health behavior interventions.

The process of culturalizing health knowledge, attitudes, and practices does not assume that people are powerless or ignorant. The process affirms diversity in the way people construct their individual and collective realities within the possibilities of their locations. What is positive or negative cannot be based on a universal notion promoted in economic development. In fact, the process challenges many shortcomings of empowerment as advanced in the economic and development paradigm. M. Rahnema (1992) illustrates these shortcomings in the following:

When A considers it essential for B to be empowered, A assumes not only that B has no power—or does not have the right kind of power—but also that A has the secret formula of a power to which B has to be initiated. In the current *participatory ideology*, this formula is, in fact, nothing but a revised version of state power, or what could be called fear-power. The crux of the matter is that populations actually subjected to this fear-power are not at all powerless. (123; emphasis added)

Because empowerment has become the new focus of health promotion discourse, its use continues to maintain currency in social and behavioral science. I have proposed "cultural empowerment" as a way of reinscribing the positives and strengths in cultures as a collective process at the beginning of health promotion intervention. Cultural empowerment takes into account how health knowledge, beliefs, and actions are produced and interpreted at both micro (individual, family, and community/grassroots) and macro (national and international power and politics) levels. Thus the decision making of individuals and families must be situated within its proper political, historical, and cultural context.

Cultural empowerment allows the interventionist to look at the totality of the context rather than to focalize on the limitations (particularly negative behaviors) of individuals as though these were independent of the context. Any project based on cultural empowerment must begin with some of the positives and strengths of the culture and community. Every culture has something positive that must be recognized and promoted. In fact, I believe that if an interventionist goes into a community and is not able to identify something positive about the community, he or she has no business being there.

We must transform the "medical negativization" of behavior inscribed in behavioral and community diagnoses into a humanization of community relationships, expectations, and assets anchored in its cultural world sense. Promoting positive values must become central to all health promotion and disease prevention programs.

Two examples will illustrate this point: first, a relative lack of physical activity may be noted in African Americans, but the belief in a "rest ethic" (see Airhihenbuwa, Kumayinka, Agurs, and Lowe 1995) has long been valued as a form of preventing cardiovascular risk reduction before relaxation came into vogue. Second, although *fatalismo* (fatalistic outlook) is often noted as a negative cultural norm among Latinos, the role and centrality of family in successful smoking cessation programs (as has been reported by the CDC [1998]) should be recognized as a positive Latino cultural norm. I have also noted elsewhere that spirituality and fatalism are two sides of the same coin. Appealing to a higher power for positive health decision is hailed as a spiritual fulfillment. When the same heavenly appeal assume the tone of acceptance of negative health outcome as a condition of one's fate, one is often said to be fatalistic.

Cultural empowerment allows health educators to identify not only the positive aspects of culture but also what is unique about the culture. These unique cultural qualities are what I refer to as "existential." Some educators may consider these qualities to be neutral. I contend that every aspect of a culture is active, and thus any perceived neutrality must be in the eye of the outsider beholder. Language elasticity is an existential feature of many cultures of oral tradition. Elasticity of language suggests that expressions are not linear but, rather, spiral. It is sometimes referred to as language of indirection, but "indirection" locates linear languages as the point of departure, on the one hand, while suggesting that these languages lack direction, on the other.

Jazz is an example of cultural production based on elasticity of language. The suggestion that jazz is based on improvisation mislabels this form and structure of cultural production with classical music as the point of departure. In oral tradition, the richness of oral expressions provides visual images on which learning and imagination are founded. Proverbs, adages, and riddles are the structure on which the direction of communication is based. These forms of language elasticity hold important implications for health education and health communication interventionists who invest an inordinate amount of capital in what we see as opposed to what we hear. In other words, the use of visual messages, such as posters, flyers, and visual aids, such as slides at lectures, may have limited utility in cultural contexts where world sense (demonstration in a small group is effective because all the senses are used) is more appropriate than worldview. On the other hand, even when these visual messages are used in appropriate contexts, such use is often a poor substitute for the billboards and mass media commercials against which the messages compete.

Another important issue around language elasticity is the representation of senses. What is learnable is believed to be based on what we can see, because Western discourse privileges sight over all other senses. According to Oyewumi (1997), "The term 'worldview,' which is used in the West to sum up the cultural logic to a society, captures the West's privileging of the visual. . . . It is Eurocentric to use it to describe cultures that may privilege other senses. The term 'world-sense' is a more inclusive way of describing the conception of the world by different cultural groupings" (2–3). Studies are often cited to show how what you see is more important than what you hear, touch, smell, or taste. Indeed, what you see is touted as a universally dominant sense by invoking Chinese adages that suggest that sight is the most valuable sense in learning. We learn very early that seeing is believing, or, as the French would say, "Je suis comme St. Thomas: je ne crois que ce que je vois" (I am like St. Thomas: I only believe what I see), even though visualization requires more than the sense of sight; it requires imagination for which the sense of sight could be a distraction: Hence, some close their eyes to better visualize.

Even when sight is important, what we see is conditioned and given meaning by what we know and what we expect to learn. Indeed, acquired visual learning skills are what separate architects (experts in translating a two-dimensional drawing into multiple dimensional structures) from their clients. The clients can only experience dimension and space after the structure is completed. This often results in pain and agony for the clients because what was in the drawings was not how they visualized the structure (Hall 1976). It is this real ization of the limitation of sight as the "all-knowing sense" that prompted progressive architects to use structural models to demonstrate their visualization of proposed projects to their clients. Indeed, the production of knowledge is commonly expressed in architectural forms (Artless 1955), which led Kamau (1998) to conclude that the cyclical and spiral nature of the Agikuyu of Kenyan knowledge production is expressed in the round structure of "their nyunba (house), giti (stool), nyungu (clay cooking pots), and kiondo (basket)" (195). This cyclical and spiral philosophical world sense holds true for the Edos in the traditional construction of *owa* (house), *ukhuere* (stool), *egere* (cast-iron cooking pot), *akhe* (clay water pots), and *atete* (basket).

Our collective senses allow us to visualize and imagine the totality of experience in ways that will be impossible through only a single sense. Unfortunately, many health promotion and public health educators are slow to catch up to what architects have long recognized. Armed with the "universalist" (one truth for all humanity) predisposition enshrined in professionalism, an inordinate amount of professional capital continues to be invested in valuing sight as the all-knowing sense. Old visual learning techniques such as posters and flyers are being displaced by new techniques such as televised public service announcements and computerized messages—often subsumed under the rubric of social marketing. These approaches are rooted in the basic preventive health behaviorist premise that the tree is more important than the forest.

Finally, focusing on the context also means that interventionists must learn and adapt their methods of communication in ways that will make them and their message more acceptable in the community of focus. For example, when planning to address a group, the manner in which the interventionist is attired can further distance him or her from the audience.

To illustrate, a Caribbean friend recounted a story of his colleague who was visiting Senegal to give a lecture. Dressed in suit and tie, he sought his host's counsel about his outfit for the lecture and his host advised him to change into the *gandoura* (a traditional Senegalese outfit), to which he gracefully acceded. Unaware of the discussion about the outfit between the professor and his host, an elderly woman saw him leave the house for the lecture and remarked, "Now you are properly dressed." This example illustrates how presentation is not only about the appearance of the content of the material presented but also about the appearance of the presenter. Indeed, the appearance of the presenter, particularly when addressing culturally based health issues, may suggest to the audience that the message is foreign and consequently so is the meaning. Anyone who has a doubt should dress up in a wrapper, blouse, and head-tie or *boba* and *shokoto* (traditional Edo and Yoruba outfits) to lecture an American audience of strangers on the subject of American health behavior, such as poor eating practices, and then conduct an evaluation on how the message was received. Communicating the message is just as important as understanding the context. In fact, they are inseparable.

CULTURAL IDENTITY: WHEN SENSE MEANS MORE THAN "SIGHT"

Cultural identity in the African context has been represented in the notion of what has been referred to as *ubuntu*—"I am because we are." The notion that identity in the African contexts has meaning only within the community contexts. In its global representation, William James (1909), the renowned American philosopher, captures well the limitation of a unitary approach to understanding identity:

> Everything you can think of, however vast or inclusive, has on the pluralistic view a genuinely "external" environment of some sort or amount. Things are "with" one another in many ways, but nothing includes everything, or dominates over everything. . . . The pluralistic world is thus more like a federal republic than like an empire or a kingdom. . . . This world may, in the last resort, be a block-universe; but on the other hand it may be a universe only strung-along not rounded in and closed." . . . Our "multiverse" still makes a universe. (321)

Identity as a cultural marker has always been a contentious point for scholars. Because demographic variables, as identity markers, are commonly used to measure how individual differences may explain and/or predict problem behavior, identity is considered useful only in measuring problems and deviance. However, identity markers are critical in understanding the positive aspects of culture as well as the existential ones. For example, the role of ownership of the body and material goods is central to Western identity. The importance of ownership and territorial control is central to a requirement to define a child sojourning in one's home as adopted. Once adopted, there is a sense of ownership for the individuals that constitute that household. The same relationships and expectations may be experienced by an adopted child who finds a home with an African or an American family, but the definition of the child's sense of belonging in the family will be different. For the American parent, the child must be redefined as adopted to gain legitimacy, whereas for the African family, the child's essence in the home defines his or her legitimacy in the family with no new title. This has often led to the misunderstanding that African families do not adopt.

It is necessary to identify the point of intervention entry with the understanding that there could be multiple entry points. This process removes the assumption that all interventions should focus on the individual, thus leading to the development of billboards and other media messages that may not address the context of behavior change. The three components of the domain of cultural identity are person, extended family, and neighborhood.

Person

This component describes the degree to which the person may be dealing with the notion of multiple consciousness as an expression of a hybrid identity and also the degree to which the cultural context and language of the culture focuses on seniority (as with the Edo and the Yoruba of Nigeria) rather than gender (as in English and French) and qualitative reasoning, which means the learning is not based only on quantitative reasoning. For example, for intervention's point of entry, some program interventions on material health tend to focus on training wives for their new roles as a future new mother when the importance of motherhood in the culture requires that only another experienced mother in the family could offer such a training.

As has been mentioned, the term *individuality* has no cultural meaning in many African cultures. An individual is a person who has lost his or her singular identity because the person has violated certain community ethics and principle. In fact, because the individual has no identity value, an individual is a nonentity in most African languages. A person is considered to be a social being within a communal context, whereas an individual is one who is detached from the community. The singularity of identity is represented in a person in African languages and confers the status of personhood based on earned ethical standing in the community. To have violated those principles believed to be a precondition for personhood is to become an individual—one who no longer can be considered worthy of his or her community membership. According to the Ghanaian philosopher Kwame Gyekye (1997), the community provides the context for creating and developing the identity of personhood. "A person comes to know who she is in the contexts of relationships with others, not as an isolated, lonely star in a social galaxy" (43).

Although personhood is earned, it is assumed that everyone is entitled to it until one abrogates certain principles and ethics that are believed to be minimal in sustaining the rights and privileges of personhood. To violate such principles and ethics is to be considered a nonperson. Among the Edos of Nigeria, a person is referred to as *omwan*. The omwan who engages in action considered to be a model personality with high standards within the community and ethics is considered to be truly-omwan (truly a person). Conversely, the omwan who has violated what is considered to be minimal standard for a person in that community is often referred to as *'ni omwan* (one that is not a person). Indeed, this representation of personhood is captured in pidgin English in Nigeria, when someone who is considered to have violated certain communal rules is dismissed as "dat one no bi person" (that one is not a person)—he or she is an individual because he or she is not a social being and thus not a part of the community.

The critical lesson in this discourse on personhood is the role of the community and the larger society in defining what constitutes positive or negative behavior at the level of the person. Thus, intervention focusing on the behavior of the person is limited without a clear understanding of how the cultural community (or what Kwame Gyekye refers to as communocultural group) define, shape, and nurture personhood. Thus the question of the inadequacy of commonly used social psychological theories, discussed on chapter 11, is in large part due to their inability to represent the relationships between the person and their community in promoting health and preventing diseases.

Extended Family

This component entails the degree to which the family network privileges different persons within the family to influence key decisions in the family. Intervention points of entry may need to focus on gender and generation differences depending on the nature of the health problem, consumption patterns relative to the role of food in maintaining good health, and communication channels relative to the direction of communication particularly in cases where an older person believes that he or she cannot discuss sex with a younger person.

I have used the term *extended family* to specifically raise the question of the misreading of African identity. In Africa, what is considered extended family is simply family. Only from the location where the "nuclear family" is the point of reference could African family be constructed as extended. The definition of family in this case is what is often referred to in the West as the extended family. Among the Edos and Yorubas, there is no notion of a nuclear family, and thus the family (which is not constructed as "extended" because the Western nuclear family is not the normative reference) includes brothers, sisters, aunts, and uncles. Thus, as I discussed in *Health and Culture*, there is not word or a need for words such as *uncle*, *aunt*, or *cousin*. Indeed, brothers and sisters are not circumscribed by immediate natal bloodlines (see

Oyewumi 1997) but are included with relations that would be referred to as cousins in the West.

The family context that defines individual identity is broad, even though many programs that focus on family relations fail to take this into account. The resulting family relationships and responsibilities form the bases for communication on which preventive health programs should be anchored. The role and responsibility of individuals based on their seniority and position in the family have important implications for the community political and economic structure. Seniority dictates positions in the political and economic power structure. As an example, a husband's family may be the source of certain behavior manifested through the wife and husband so that any intervention should focus on her within the context of the family. Such a focus on the family should also take into account family lineage (e.g., patrilinear or matrilinear). However, when a program is designed to target a particular member of the family (e.g., the mother), the logic for her selection as the person to be the focus of the study must be so explained.

This domain of cultural identity in PEN-3 is critical to understanding how knowledge and beliefs are actualized in practice. For example, although persons and individuals are used interchangeably in the literature, there are important differences in their meaning in many African languages. As was discussed earlier, *person* is used in PEN-3 because of the cultural meaning of a person within a collective identity.

Neighborhood

Neighborhood is the capacity of a geographically and/or ideologically defined group (community, village, congregation, etc.) to influence decisions for its collectives. An example might be a community's capacity to decide on billboard advertising and communication in its community, representing the economic status and power structure of the community in dealing with HIV education from a culturally appropriate strategy. Overall, behaviors are reproduced through what children and adults are exposed to in the community. Neighborhood in this model is meant to connote the interconnectedness of families within a given village or communities within a city.

Assessing a community or neighborhood through the approval of a chief is not unlike what one should expect to find in any organized social structure with leadership hierarchy. For example, all government and private agencies require that all its members (employees) must have the approval of the "chief" (supervisor) before any oral or written representation of such person is approved. This is often done in the form of a clearance that must be acquired before an article can be published by an employee or an oral presentation can be made. All traditional communities often go through this structure of "chief" approval before information could be shared by members of the community.

APPLICATION OF THE PEN-3 MODEL

PEN-3 is designed to centralize voices of the community at the foundation of all health interventions. The first aspect is to develop a 3 × 3 table to produce a nine-cell possibility generated from two of the domains (table 12.1).

The following are the nine categories and HIV-specific examples from global lessons learned:

- Positive perception—HIV is about what you do rather than who you are
- Existential perception—Adoption occurs only within an extended family
- Negative perception—HIV is somebody else's problem.
- Positive enablers—100% condom policy and availability of ARV drugs
- Existential enablers—traditional healers in Senegal successfully treating HIV
- Negative enablers—racism, stigma, government not providing drugs
- Positive nurturers—*ukhusoma* (the Zulu word for nonpenetrating sexual acts)
- Existential nurturers—home-based care
- Negative nurturers—wife inheritance

With these nine categories, a collective decision must be made to prioritize the point of intervention entry given what research results shows about the context of prevention and which is likely to lead to a significant change in controlling the epidemic. In the examples cited earlier, a collective decision will be made based on whether changes in any of the examples given will take place at the level of a person, the extended family, or the neighborhood or community. In the conventional social psychological model, concluded to be inadequate for cultural interventions as discussed in chapter 11, we often begin intervention by discussing the individuals; in this model, the identity component is the last component because it is the nature and context of the issues that drives

Table 12.1.   Cultural Empowerment and Relationships/Expectations.

The Domains	Positive	Existential	Negative
Perceptions	1	2	3
Enablers	4	5	6
Nurturers	7	8	9

which of the identity categories would be most significant in reducing the spread of HIV and AIDS. In PEN-3, singular identity is represented in a person rather than the individual.

The implementation of interventions, consistent with PEN-3, should be based on whether health beliefs are long term and historically rooted in the tradition and culture or more recent, short-term beliefs. The reinforcement or changing of long-term cultural beliefs should be addressed through health education in the home (home visits) and/or through one-to-one contacts in the community, whereas more recent, nontraditionally entrenched health beliefs can be addressed through the mass media—posters, flyers, radio and television messages, and so on (Airhihenbuwa and Webster 2004).

It should be noted, however, that although home visits may also be appropriate for changing nonentrenched health beliefs, mass media have not proved effective for changing negative health beliefs that are historically rooted in cultural patterns and lifestyles. Researchers have shown that mass media channels are most effective for increasing knowledge, reinforcing previously held attitudes, and changing behaviors that were recently established or predisposed to change, as opposed to those that are tied to cultural values or are contrary to the attitudes and values expressed in the mass media. In child survival programs, despite the difficulty in organizing an outreach, face-to-face communication channels have been found to be most effective in oral rehydration therapy and HIV and AIDS education, as discussed in chapter 11.

When dealing with oral traditions, the focus should not be limited to "how to transform the learner," as is often the case; rather, attention should also be paid to whether the interventionist has the requisite skill to transmit knowledge in a culturally appropriate manner. It is important not only to understand the storyteller; it is equally important, if not more so, to understand the dynamics of the story listener. Oral tradition generally is not the heritage solely of the spoken or sung word; it is also the heritage of the ear (Faseke 1990). Stated differently, people in the oral traditional cultures of several African countries are accustomed to learning by what they hear. Learning by what they see is important to the extent that it is congruent with what they hear and who produces that information. The implication of this pattern of knowledge acquisition for the teacher must be understood and appropriately employed. In other words, if people in an oral traditional culture learn more by listening, the teacher (health and communication worker) should spend more time talking, discussing, and sharing insights than showing pictures or using other audiovisual aids. If talking and sharing ideas constitute the primary mode of learning, health providers (particularly those from other countries) must have adequate competence in oral communication to be able to impart knowledge effectively to individuals, families, and the community.

FINAL THOUGHTS

Several cultural factors can promote or hinder the success of public health, health education, and health communication programs in African countries. The future of public health, health education, and health communication lies in the ability to centralize these cultural factors within their proper historical and political contexts. For health promotion interventions, particularly in countries of Africa, Latin America, and Asia, as well as among ethnic minority populations in industrialized nations, health educators must employ culturally sensitive methods to examine varied health behaviors in terms of positive/beneficial beliefs that must be encouraged, existential/cultural beliefs and practices that do not threaten health, and negative/harmful health practices that should be changed. These domains are not independent of each other even though each plays a crucial role in the construction and maintenance of identity and behavior in a given culture. Although the person is still considered to be very important in health decisions, the person functions in relation to the role expectations embedded in the community; hence, the community must be understood in its totality. Moreover, the focus on culture and identity also means that the individual-based theories and models that are commonly used to inform HIV prevention and education are no longer considered adequate for understanding the context of health behavior.

The examples cited throughout the book are meant to generate more discussion, so that cultural dimensions of health can be assessed from positive, existential, and negative perspectives rather than from the sole perspective of negativity. Such negativity has led to the almost automatic coupling of the concept of cultural with that of barriers. The PEN-3 examples, therefore, are designed to promote empowerment by emphasizing strength rather than focusing exclusively on barriers. Finally, future program effectiveness will be based on the ability to effectively locate health in identity such that every arrival could be understood as a new departure in the cultural meanings of behavior.

13

The Way Forward

To Be Comfortable with Being Uncomfortable

We are on the threshold of a new era. The greatest responsibilities of our age rest not only with the big nation powers of the modern world, but also with the host of small nations, those whose ancient dreams are on the verge of extinction. The responsibilities of the unvalued, the unheard, the silent, are greater than ever. And the weight of this responsibility rests on one thing: we are essentially struggling for the humanity of the world. We are struggling to liberate the world into a greater destiny. We are struggling for world balance and justice.

—Ben Okri (1997:100)

This book echoes what has long been recognized: any attempt to provide health solutions for a given community or society must take into serious consideration cultural factors as well as the present stage of the transformation of the society. Thus, the degree to which new programs are adopted is dependent on the extent to which they are culturally appropriate. Interrogating questions of culture and context must begin with training programs that prepare students to understand the totality of behaviors. This means also that the students should be allowed the opportunity to retain their knowledge of the ability to know who they are without what they would eventually do. For this to occur, the health workers must understand, learn, and develop the skills they will need to reflect appropriately the cultural values of communities and societies. Doing so requires an understanding not only of the cultural significance of health behaviors but also of the interplay between culture and power relative to policy formulations and decision making at the multilayered levels of a society and its government. Such interplay of culture and power is commonly produced beyond the boundaries of health knowledge and health belief.

The dichotomy of knowledge and belief obscures the coexistence of both forms of cultural affirmation in production and adherence to values about learning and sharing. I contend that every accepted form of knowledge is a culturally sanctioned language of belief and of course every belief expresses a particular form of knowledge. I argue that the choice of applying a particular model or theory of behavior amongst a group of academically deified models of behavior is an expression of a belief. In the absence of a universally agreed-upon theory of behavior among the social science theoretical orthodoxy, an expression of belief (choosing one theory over another) tends to be normalized.

When knowledge assumes a frame that demands its independence in a form of identity, it also becomes an expression of belief. To insist that one's way of knowing is more relevant to another is a form of a belief deployed through institutions of knowledge production. On the contrary, when a belief opens up to transformation of its possibilities beyond the intellectual and cultural spaces that gave it birth, it becomes a different form of knowledge. Interrogating the interlocking partnership of belief and knowledge in a community has the potential of opening up safe spaces for the community and university, commonly referred to as "Town and Gown," to enter a dialogue on eliminating health inequities. Indeed, much of the university–community research partnership can benefit from embracing an approach that promotes the interplay and interdependency of knowledge and belief. It could also help to move beyond the "Othered" approach that typifies university–community research partnerships, which often has a subtext of a privileged cultural ethos seeking to "help" a disadvantaged cultural space with little or no interest in the identity and collective agency of those who people such disadvantaged cultural spaces.

The affirmation of "Otherness" invoked in the politics of representation also underscores a recognition that Others are torchbearers whose political and educational projects often lead to the discovery of new truths as well as the affirmation of old truths. Quite often, when scholars of oppressed races and nationalities insist that all writing is political, the claim has been dismissed as unscholarly or simply ignored. However, the reality of such claims in public health and health communication has been validated systematically in research on health disparity documents such as the ones produced by the Institute of Medicine reports in 2003 and by the Agency for Healthcare Research and Quality in 2004. Indeed, it is the apolitical analysis of some public health scholars anchored in universal applications that has misguided scholars into assuming acultural, ahistorical, and acontextual approaches to studying health and behavior.

Some educators and scholars today like to focus on individuality (at the exclusion of the contexts) as if it were the one key that would open all doors to

Black progress. Cornel West's (1993a) rejection of the approach of trying to open all doors with one key while closing one's eyes to all other doors except the one the key fits is most instructive of the limits of many conventional approaches to studying health and behavior. The question of identity, culture, and health is about recognizing the several doors that have always been open in the form of cultural expressions, but have been ignored until they no longer seem like doors but incidental windows. To understand health behaviors in its many expressions is to know that there are many open doors; they are simply not constructed in the usual, familiar shape, pattern, and structure.

The discourse on identity and global health is incomplete without the proper anchor on culture. Culture should be central to public health and health promotion intervention strategies in a manner that does not naturally couple the concept of barriers with culture. Intervention projects should draw on the possibilities offered in critical theories that lay bare institutional and Western hegemonies that continue to truncate efforts to address public health issues in Africa. Stuart Hall (1992) notes that cultural hegemony is about imbalance of power, and our responsibility, as echoed by Okri at the beginning of this chapter, is the struggle for a balance of power to achieve the best that our humanity exemplifies in social justice.

I have attempted to remap the terrains of conventional theories and cultural logics in health promotion, health communication, and public health by placing them within their particular cultural spaces. By so doing, it is possible to acknowledge that everyone has a culture and that all knowledge production is cultural, and thus all theory is cultural. Such a premise unveils the contextual anchors for theoretical assumptions and praxis so that behaviors are located within cultural spaces. These behaviors are then expressed through different forms of identity as expressed in different behavioral response to health and the lack thereof. What I have attempted in this book is to locate identity and behavior within cultural contexts of health. Thus, it was necessary to challenge existing public health epistemologies by decentering conventional views of health behavior and inserting and centering culture into their theories and practices.

As I have discussed throughout this book, a major requirement in engaging a health and culture project is that we begin with the interrogation of conventional assumptions and classical paradigms and their attendant Eurocentric and often patriarchal foundations. Such interrogation is meant to be a cleansing enterprise that must be engaged in by both the privileged and the marginalized as a liberatory process that allows questioning to become a form of answering. While the privileged interrogate the hegemonic tools of oppression that privilege them, the oppressed and marginalized interrogate their conscious or subconscious participation in promoting ways of knowing that evidently silence their own agency in policies of identity inscribed in the crisis of global health.

This is what Chinweizu (1987) refers to as decolonization of the mind. For him, decolonizing the African mind is as a collective enterprise, a form of communal exorcism engaged through an intellectual bath in which one needs another's help to scrub and cleanse the nooks and corners of our minds that we are not able to see by ourselves.

Perhaps more critical in this collective interrogative enterprise is the interrogation and transformation of the minds of the knowledge producing powers in the citadel of knowledge production in Western academies. Toni Morrison (1992) and Frantz Fanon (1958) believe that as we examine the scholarship that explores the minds, imaginations, and behaviors of the oppressed, it is equally critical that we examine what racial ideology does to the minds, imaginations, and behaviors of oppressors. Understanding the psychosocial functions of the role of racism in the minds of the oppressors is critical to the development and operationalization of culture-centered research activities that should benefit both dominant and disadvantaged populations. Equally important is Nkiru Nzegwu's (1996) interrogation of the confluence of patriarchy and Eurocentrism that truncated Anthony Appiah's representation of African women's and specifically Ghanaian women's agency in the book entitled *In My Father's House*. In the same vein, Oyeronke Oyewumi (2003c) has deepened our appreciated of African women's agency by moving the analytic frame from victim to agent and from sisterhood to motherhood. By emphasizing the importance of the unconscious and questioning the validity of a universal subject as the center of signification, Africans are demanding a new understanding of the social science and a transformation of public health and health communication.

People of African descent are challenging the oppressed to become engaged in politicizing and constructing health, education, and communication projects for the production of knowledge and practice that openly engage culture and identity. It also demands that the privileged conventional theories must be deconstructed such that research approaches to global health priorities such as eliminating health inequities can benefit from fresh theoretical approaches that promote linking health with cultural identity as political, practical, and theorizing enterprises. The politics of education, health, and identity must be understood in their symbiotic roles in the production, distribution, and acquisition of knowledge. Excising the political from the life of the mind, according to Morrison, is analogous to a trembling hypochondriac always insisting on undergoing unnecessary surgery in spite of the sacrifice and high cost. If politics is educational and education is political, health outcomes should be measured by the extent to which education in health is politically framed to better understand how identity- and culture-centered health behavior strategies can become central to global health.

A major aspect of this process entails an understanding of how people promote and/or challenge policies that affect them within their cultural contexts. In other words, one cannot assume that people are disempowered to make decisions based on their economically disadvantaged location. Marginalized groups have always devised active and passive resistance strategies to subvert oppression. This point can be illustrated by the story of the wise bird. There was once a man who found a beautiful bird, fell in love with it, and decided that he wanted it for a pet. He captured the bird, brought it home, and kept it in a cage. After some days, the man asked the bird if there was anything he could do for the bird. "Of course," the bird responded, "you can open this cage." "I am sorry I cannot do that," said the man, "but I can take a message to your family to let them know that you are in good health." The bird agreed, and off the man went to find the bird's family. He successfully located the family and delivered the message of the bird's good health and safety. Upon hearing the news, one of the bird's brothers fell down dead. The man was shocked at what had happened and could not wait to get home to relate the sad event to "his" bird. Upon hearing the news about his brother, and to the man's surprise, the bird that the man had imprisoned also dropped dead. The man, now filled with sorrow, opened the cage, and the bird quickly got up and flew out. As he flew away, he sang to the man, "Thank you for bringing me the wisdom of my people."

The collective consciousness of a people (the culture) prepares them to deal with and sometimes subvert and transform oppressive conditions in ways unknown to the oppressor. Such experiences and their resultant wisdom transcend levels of income, age, and generation. We must never assume that because a group is economically poor its members are also cerebrally, philosophically, and practically poor, nor should we assume that wisdom in and of itself will overcome economic oppression. Programmatic efforts must, therefore, be directed toward locating people's identity in their cultural spaces so that their philosophy informs the health practices that manifests in their health behavior.

The challenge for professionals in health education and promotion, health communication, and public health is to learn to question the questions. By this I mean to interrogate the cultural assumptions of health behavior. Identity as a cultural production can be understood when health is expressed in behavior through the process of critical intellectual engagement. Such a cultural production in contextualizing identity and behavior is a process whose liberating outcome anchors us *to learn to be comfortable with being uncomfortable*.

References

Abimbola, W. 1990. *Tradition and development in Africa today: Decolonizing African thoughts*. Paris: UNESCO.

Achebe, C. 1958. *Things fall apart*. London: Henneman.

———. 1987. *Anthills of the savannah*. Garden City, N.Y.: Anchor Doubleday.

———. 1988. *Hopes and impediments: Selected essays*. New York: Anchor Books.

———. 2001. *Home and exile*. New York: Canongate.

Ademuwagun, Z. A. 1974–1975. The meeting point of orthodox health personnel and traditional healers/midwives in Nigeria: The pattern of utilization of health services in Ibarapa Division. *Rural Africana* 26:55–78.

Airhihenbuwa, C. O. 1994. Health promotion and the discourse on culture: Implications for empowerment. *Health Education Quarterly* 21, no. 3:345–53.

———. 1995a. Culture, health education, and critical consciousness. *Journal of Health Education* 26:317–19.

———. 1995b. *Health and culture: Beyond the Western paradigm*. Thousand Oaks, Calif.: Sage.

———. 1999. Of culture and multiverse: Renouncing "the universal truth" in health. *Journal of Health Education* 30:267–73.

Airhihenbuwa, C. O., L. Jack, and J. D. Webster. 2004. Transforming scientific intervention research strategies to strengthen community capacity. In *Race and research: Perspectives on minority participation in health studies*, ed. B. M. Beech and M. Goodman. Washington, D.C.: American Public Health Association.

Airhihenbuwa, C.O., G. King, and T. Spencer. 2001. The global contexts of health behavior research: Implications for medicine and health. *Annals of Medical Education and Behavioral Science* 7:69–75.

Airhihenbuwa, C. O., S. K. Kumanyika, T. D., Agurs, and A. Lowe. 1995. Perceptions and beliefs about exercise, rest, and health among African-Americans. *American Journal of Health Promotion* 9:426–29.

Airhihenbuwa, C. O., S. K. Kumanyika, T. D., Agurs, A. Lowe, D. Saunders, and C. B. Morssink. 1996. Cultural aspects of African-American eating patterns. *Ethnicity and Health* 1, no. 3:245–60.

Airhihenbuwa, C. O., B. Makinwa, and R. Obregon. 2000. Toward a new communication framework for HIV/AIDS. *Journal of Health Communication* 5(suppl.): 101–11.

Airhihenbuwa, C. O., and R. Obregon. 2000. A critical assessment of theories/models used in health communications for HIV/AIDS. *Journal of Health Communication* 5(suppl.):5–15.

Airhihenbuwa, C. O., and O. Pineiro. 1988. Cross cultural health education: A pedagogical challenge. *Journal of School Health* 58, no. 6:240–42.

Airhihenbuwa, C. O., and J. D. Webster. 2004. Culture and African contexts of HIV/AIDS prevention, care, and support. *Journal of Social Aspects of HIV/AIDS Research Alliance* 1:4–13.

Amos, V., and P. Parmar. 1984. Challenging imperial feminism. *Feminist Review* 17:7–19.

Anderson, C. A. 1966. Literacy and schooling on the development threshold: Some historic cases. In *Education and economic development*, ed. C. A. Anderson and M. Bowman. London: Cass.

An-Na'im, A. A. 2002. *Cultural transformation and human rights in Africa*. London: Zed Books.

Arnfred, S. 2004a. African sexuality/sexuality in Africa: Tales and silences. In *Re-thinking sexualities in Africa*, ed. S. Arnfred. Uppsala: Almqvist & Wiksell Tryckeri.

——. 2004b. Re-thinking sexualities in Africa: Introduction. In *Re-thinking sexualities in Africa*, ed. S. Arnfred. Uppsala: Almqvist & Wiksell Tryckeri.

Artless, L. 1955. *Walking a sacred path*. New York: Berkley.

Asante, M. K. 1987. *The Afrocentric idea*. Philadelphia: Temple University Press.

Awolalu, J. O. 1979. *Yoruba beliefs and sacrificial rites*. London: Longman.

Barroso, J. 1997. Social support and long-term survivors of AIDS . . . including commentary by Buchanan, D., Tomlinson, P. & Van Servellen, G. with author response. *Western Journal of Nursing Research* 19, no. 5:554–82.

Beech, B. M., and M. Goodman. 2004. *Race and research: Perspectives on minority participation in health studies*. Washington, D.C.: American Public Health Association.

Bell, B. W. 1996. Genealogical shifts in Dubois's discourse on double consciousness as the sign of African American difference. In *W. E. B. Dubois on race and culture: Philosophy, politics, and poetics*, ed. B. W. Bell, E. Grosholz, and J. B. Stewart. New York: Routledge.

Bell, D. 1992. *Faces at the bottom of the well: The permanence of racism*. New York: Basic Books.

Bernasconi, R. 2001. *Race*. Oxford: Blackwell.

Bethune, M. 1933. *A century of progress of Negro women*. Address presented at the Women Federation Conference, Chicago, June 3.

Brown, M. K., M. Carnoy, E. Currie, T. Duster, D. B. Oppenheimer, M. M. Shultz, and D. Wellman. 2003. *White-washing race: The myth of a color-blind society.* Berkeley: University of California Press.

Centers for Disease Control and Prevention. 1998. *Tobacco use among U.S. racial/ ethnic minority groups: A report of the surgeon general.* Washington, D.C.: U.S. Government Printing Office.

Chinweizu. 1987. *Decolonizing the African mind.* London: Sundoor.

Chinweizu, O. Jemie, and I. Madubuike. 1983. *Toward the decolonization of African literature: Vol. 1. African fiction and poetry and their critics.* Washington, D.C.: Howard University Press.

Chomsky, N. 1989. *Necessary illusion: Thought control in democratic societies.* Boston: South End.

Chopra, D. 1990. *Quantum healing: Exploring the frontiers of mind/body medicine.* New York: Bantam.

Chow, R. 1991. *Women and Chinese modernity: The politics of reading between West and East.* Minneapolis: University of Minnesota Press.

Christian, B. 1987. The race for theory. *Cultural Critique* 6:52.

Clark, K. B., and M. P. Clark. 1939. The development of consciousness of self and the emergence of racial identity in Negro preschool children. *Journal of Social Psychology* 10:591–99.

Crawford, R. 1994. The boundaries of the self and the unhealthy other: Reflections on health, culture, and AIDS. *Social Science and Medicine* 380:1347–65.

Cross, W. E., Jr. 1991. *Shades of Black: Diversity in African-American identity.* Philadelphia: Temple University Press.

Davidson, B. 1969. *The African genius: An introduction to African social and cultural history.* Boston: Little, Brown.

Davis, A. Y. 1992. Black nationalism: The sixties and the nineties. In *Black popular culture: A project by Michelle Wallace*, ed. G. Dent (pp. 317–24). Seattle: Bay.

Davis, J. N. P. 1959. The development of scientific medicine in the African kingdom of Bunga-kitara. *Medical History* 3, no. 49:47.

Dawit, S., and S. Mekuria. 1993. The West just doesn't get it. *New York Times*, December 7, A27.

Dellenborg, L. 2004. A reflection on the cultural meanings of female circumcision. In *Re-thinking sexualities in Africa*, ed. S. Arnfred. Uppsala: Almqvist & Wiksell Tryckeri.

Diop, C. A. 1991. *Civilization or barbarism: An authentic anthropology.* Brooklyn, N.Y.: Hill Books.

———. 2000. From government policy to community-based communication strategies in Africa: Lessons from Senegal and Uganda. *Journal of Health Communications* 5:113–18.

DuBois, W. E. B. 1903. *Souls of Black folk.* Chicago: McClurg.

Dutta-Bergman, M. 2004. The unheard voices of Santalis: Communicating about health from the margins of India. *Communication Theory* 14:237–63.

Dyer, R. 1991. *White.* London: Routledge.

Dyson, M. E. 1995. *Making Malcolm: The myth and meaning of Malcolm X*. New York: Oxford University Press.

———. 1996a. *Between God and gangsta rap: Bearing witness to Black culture*. New York: Oxford University Press.

———. 1996b. *Race rules: Navigating the color line*. New York: Addison-Wesley.

Escobar, A. 1995. *Encountering development: The making and unmaking of the third world*. Princeton, N.J.: Princeton University Press.

Eze, E. C. 2001. *Achieving our humanity: The idea of the postracial future*. New York: Routledge.

Fanon, F. 1958. *Black skin, White mask*. London: Penguin.

Faseke, M. M. 1990. Oral history in Nigeria: Issues, problems, and prospects. *Oral History Review* 18:77–91.

Fassin, D. 2002. Embodied history: Uniqueness and exemplarity of South African AIDS. *African Journal of AIDS Research* 1:65–70.

———. 2003. Understanding AIDS in South Africa. *British Medical Journal* 326:495–97.

Fiske, J. *1993. Power works power plays*. London: Verso.

Foege, W. 1997. Arms and public health: A global perspective. In *War and public health*, ed. B. Levy and V. Sidel. New York: Oxford University Press and American Public Health Association.

Foreman, M., ed. 1999. *AIDS and men*. London: Panos/Zed Books.

Foster, E. V. 1963. *Treatment of African mental patients*. Paper presented at the Pan African Psychiatry Conference, Abeokuta, Nigeria.

Foucault, M. 1978. *The history of sexuality: An introduction.* Vol. 1. New York: Random House.

Freimuth, V. S. 1992. Theoretical foundations of AIDS media campaigns. In *AIDS: A communication perspective*, ed. T. Edgar, M. A. Fitzpatrick, and V. S. Freimuth (pp. 91–110). Hillsdale, N.J.: Erlbaum.

Freire, P. 1970. *Pedagogy of the oppressed*. New York: Continuum.

———. 1973. *Education for critical consciousness*. New York: Continuum.

———. 1993. *Pedagogy of the city*. New York: Continuum.

———. 1994. *Pedagogy of hope*. New York: Continuum.

———. 1998. *Pedagogy of freedom: Ethics, democracy, and civic courage*. Lanham, Md.: Rowman & Littlefield.

Freire, P., and A. Faundez. 1989. *Learning to question: A pedagogy of liberation*. New York: Continuum.

Fuglesang, A. 1973. *Applied communication in developing countries: Ideas and observations*. New York: Dag Hammarskjld Foundation.

Gabriel, J. 1998. *Whitewash: Racialized politics and the media.* London: Routledge.

Gamble, V. N. 1997. Under the shadow of Tuskegee: African Americans and health care. *American Journal of Public Health* 87:1773–78.

Garrett, L. 1994. *The coming plague: Newly emerging diseases in a world out of balance*. New York: Farrar Straus Giroux.

———. 2000. *Betrayer of trust: The collapse of the global public health*. New York: Hyperion.

Gartner, J. D., D. B. Larson, and G. D. Allen. 1991. Religious commitment and mental health: A review of the empirical literature. *Journal of Psychological Theology* 19:6–25.

Gates, H. L. 1999. *Wonders of the African world.* Alexandria, Va.: PBS Home Video.

Gilsselquist, D., J. J. Potterat, S. Body, and F. Vachon. 2003. Let it be sexual: How health care transmission of AIDS in Africa was ignored. *International Journal of STD and AIDS* 14:148–61.

Giroux, H. A. 1992a. *Border crossings: Cultural workers and the politics of education.* New York: Routledge.

———. 1992b. Paulo Freire and the politics of postcolonialism. *Journal of Advanced Composition* 121:1526.

———. 2000. *Stealing innocence: Corporate culture's war on children.* New York: Palgrave.

Gray, J. 1997. Spiritual perspective and social support in women with HIV infection: Pilot study. *Image: The Journal of Nursing Scholarship* 29:97.

Green, E. C. 1988. Can collaborative programs between biomedical and African indigenous health practitioners succeed? *Social Science and Medicine* 27:1125–30.

———. 1999. *Indigenous theories of contagious disease.* Walnut Creek, Calif.: AltaMira.

Greenbaum, S. D. 1992. Multiculturalism and political correctness: The challenge of applied anthropology in curricula politics. *Human Organization* 5, no. 4:408–12.

Grossberg, L. 1994. Introduction: Bringin' it all back home pedagogy and cultural studies. In *Between borders: Pedagogy and the politics of cultural studies,* ed. H. A. Giroux and P. McLaren (pp. 201–25). New York: Routledge.

Gruskin, S. 2002. The UN General Assembly special session on HIV/AIDS: Were some lessons of the last 20 years ignored? Editorials. *American Journal of Public Health* 92:337–38.

Guillory, J. A., R. Sowell, L. Moneyham, and B. Seals. 1997. An exploration of the meaning and use of spirituality among women with HIV/AIDS. *Alternative Therapies in Health and Medicine* 3, no. 5:55–60.

Guma, P. M. 1997. *The politics of Umoya: Variation in the interpretation and management of diarrheal illnesses among mothers, professional nurses and indigenous health practitioners in Khayelitsha–South Africa.* Chapel Hill: University of North Carolina Press.

———. 2002. *Throwing the bones: Divination, family structure and history in African healing traditions.* Bloomington: Indiana University–African Dialogue, Oral Heritage and Indigenous Knowledge.

Gwatkin, D. R. 2000. Health inequalities and the health of the poor: What do we know? What can we do? *Bulletin of the World Health Organization* 781:3–17.

Gyekye, K. 1997. *Tradition and modernity: Philosophical reflections on the African experience.* New York: Oxford University Press.

Hacker, A. 1992. *Two nations: Black and White, separate, hostile, unequal.* New York: Ballantine.

Hahn, R. A. 1995. *Sickness and healing: An anthropological perspective.* New Haven, Conn.: Yale University Press.

Hall, E. T. 1976. *Beyond culture*. Garden City, N.Y.: Anchor Books.

Hall, S. 1991. Ethnicity: Identity and difference. *Radical America* 23, no. 4:9–20.

Hall, S. 1992. The new ethnicities. In *Race, culture, and difference*, ed. J. Donald and A. Rattansi (pp. 252–59). London: Sage.

Hampte Ba, A. 1982. Approaching Africa. In *African films: The context of production*, ed. A. Martin. London: British Film Institute.

Harrison, I. E. 1984. *Colonialism, mealth (metropolitan health care) care systems, and traditional healers*. Occasional Paper No. 5. Urbana, Ill.: Association of Black Anthropologists.

Hernstein, R. J., and C. Murray. 1994. *The bell curve: Intelligence and class structure in America life*. New York: Free Press.

Hine, D. C. 1993. In the kingdom of culture: Black women and intersection of race, gender, and class. In *Lure and loathing: Essays on race, identity, and the ambivalence of assimilation*, ed. G. Early. New York: Penguin.

hooks, b. 1992. *Black looks: Race and representation*. Boston: South End.

———. 1993. Let's get real about feminism: The backlash, the myths, the movement. *Ms.* 4 (September–October):34–43.

Idowu, E. B. 1962. *African traditional religion: A definition*. New York: Orbis Books.

Ignatieff, M. 2001. *Human rights as politics and idolatory*. Amy Gutman (Ed.). Princeton, N.J.: Princeton University Press.

Illich, I. 1976. *Medical nemesis: The expropriation of health*. New York: Pantheon.

———. 1992. Needs. In *The development dictionary: A guide to knowledge as power*, ed. W. Sachs (pp. 88–101). London: Zed Books.

Imbo, S. O. 1998. *An introduction to African philosophy*. Lanham, Md.: Rowman & Littlefield.

Institute of Medicine. 2003. *Who will keep the public healthy? Educating public health professionals for the 21st century*. Washington, D.C.: National Academy Press.

Irvine, J. J. 1990. *Black students and school failure: Policies, practices, and prescriptions*. Westport, Conn.: Greenwood.

James, W. 1909. *A pluralistic universe*. New York. Longmans, Green.

Janzen, J. M. 1974–1975. Pluralistic legitimization of therapy systems in contemporary Zaire. *Rural Africana* 26:105–22.

Jones, C. P. 2000. Levels of racism: A theoretic framework and a gardener's tale. *American Journal of Public Health* 90, no. 8 (August):1212–15.

Jones-Lee, F. A. 2005. How did feminists miss this? The very public sphere of mothering in the United States. *Jenda: A Journal of Culture and African Women's Studies*, www.jendajournal.com/issues/jones.lee.htm.

Justice, J. 1987. The bureaucratic context of international health: A social scientist's view. *Social Science and Medicine* 25:1301–06.

Kamau, W. J. 1998. *Menopause: Perceptions and meanings of lived experiences of the Agikuyu post-menopausal women of Kenya*. Unpublished doctoral diss., Pennsylvania State University.

Kant, I. 2001. On the different human races. In *Race*, ed. R. Bernasconi. Oxford: Blackwell. (Originally published 1775.)

Keita, L. 2004. Philosophy and development: On the problematic of African development: A diachronic analysis. *African Development* 291:131–60.

Kelly, J. A. 1999. Community-level interventions are needed to prevent new HIV infections. *American Journal of Public Health* 89:299–301.

Kelly, R. D. G. 1997. *Yo' mama's disFUNKional! Fighting the culture wars in urban America*. Boston: Beacon.

Ki-Zerbo, J. 2005. African intellectuals, nationalism and pan-Africanism: A testimony. In *African intellectuals: Rethinking politics, language, gender and development*, ed. T. Mkandiware. Dakar: CODESRIA Books; London: Zed Books.

Knott, Y. C. 1843. The mulatto and hybrid: Probable extermination of the two races if the Whites and Blacks are allowed to intermarry. *American Journal of the Medical Sciences*.

Kozlowski, L., and R. J. O'Connor. 2003. Apply federal research rules on deception to misleading health information: An example on smokeless tobacco and cigarettes. *Public Health Reports* 118:187–92.

Krieger, N., and S. Sidney. 1996. Racial discrimination and blood pressure: The CARDIA study of young Black and White adults. *American Journal of Public Health* 86:1370–78.

Kumanyika, S. K. 2001. Minisymposium on obesity: Overview and some strategic considerations. *Annual Review of Public Health* 22:293–308.

Kumanyika, S. K., J. F. Wilson, and M. Guilford-Davenport. 1993. Weight-related attitudes and behaviors of Black women. *Journal of the American Dietetic Association* 93:416–22.

Lambo, T. A. 1961. Mental health in Nigeria: Research and technical problems. *World Mental Health* 13.

———. 1978. Psychotherapy in Africa. *Human Nature* 1, no. 3:32–39.

Larson, D. B., K. A. Sherill, J. S. Lyons, F. C. Craige, S. B. Thielman, M. A. Greenwold, and S. S. Larson. 1992. Associations between dimensions of religious commitment and mental health reported in the *American Journal of Psychiatry* and the *Archives of General Psychiatry*: 1978–1989. *American Journal of Psychiatry* 149:557–59.

Last, M. 1986. The professionalization of African medicine: Ambiguities and definitions. In *The professionalization of traditional medicine*, ed. M. Last and G. L. Chavunduka. Manchester: Manchester University Press/International African Institute.

Levin, J. S. 1994. Religion and health: Is there an association, is it valid, and is it causal? *Social Science and Medicine* 38:1475–82.

Levin, J. S., and P. L. Schiller. 1987. Is there a religions factor in health? *Journal of Religion and Health* 26:9–35.

Levinson, H. S. 1909. *Introduction: A pluralistic universe*. New York: Longmans, Green.

Lorde, A. 1984. *Sister outsider*. Trumansburg, N.Y.: Crossing Press.

Lott, T. D. 2001. Anthropological notion of race. In *Race*, ed. R. Bernasconi. Oxford: Blackwell.

Lupton, D. 1994. *Medicine as culture: Illness, disease and the body in Western societies*. London: Sage.

Macamo, E. 2005. Against development. *CODESRIA Bulletin* 3 & 4:5–7.

Malinowski, B. 1954. The rationalization of anthropology and administration. *Africa* 3:405–29.

Mama, A. 2005. Gender studies for African's transformation. In *African intellectuals: Rethinking politics, language, gender and development*, ed. T. Mkandiware. Dakar: CODESRIA Books; London: Zed Books.

Marable, M. 1993. Beyond racial identity politics: Towards a liberation theory for multicultural democracy. *Race and Class* 351:113–30.

Mazrui, A. A. 1986. *The Africans: A triple heritage*. Boston: Little, Brown.

McKinlay, J. B., and L. D. Marceau. 2000. To boldly go . . . . *American Journal of Public Health* 90:25–33.

McNeil, W. H. 1976. *Plagues and peoples*. New York: Doubleday

Melkote, S. R., S. R. Muppidi, and D. Goswami. 2000. Social and economic factors in an integrated behavioral and societal approach to communications in HIV/AIDS. *Journal of Health Communication* 5(suppl.):17–28.

Mills, C. 1997. *The racial contract*. Ithaca, N.Y.: Cornell University Press.

Minh-ha, T. T. 1991. *When the moon waxes red: Representation, gender and cultural politics*. New York: Routledge.

Mkandawire, T. 2004. *The spread of economic doctrines in postcolonial Africa*. Unpublished report, UNRISD, Geneva.

———. 2005. Maladjusted African economies and globalization. *African Development* 30, nos. 1 & 2:1–33.

Mohanty, C. T. 1991. Introduction: Cartographies of struggle. In *Third world women and the politics of feminism*, ed. C. T. Mohanty, A. Russo, and L. Torres (pp. 201–47). Bloomington: Indiana University Press.

Morland, K., S. Wing, and A. D. Roux. 2002. The contextual effect of the local food environment on residents' diets: The atherosclerosis risk in communities study. *American Journal of Public Health* 92:1761–67.

Morone, J. A. 1997. Enemies of the people: The moral dimension to public health. *Journal of Health Politics, Policy, and Law* 22:993–1020.

Morrison, T. 1992. *Playing in the dark: Whiteness and the literary imagination*. New York: Vintage.

Mudimbe, V. Y. 1988. *The invention of Africa: Gnosis, philosophy, and the order of knowledge*. Bloomington: Indiana University Press.

National Health Care Disparities Report. 2003. Rockville, Md.: Department of Health and Human Services, Agency for Healthcare Research Quality.

Ngugi wa Thiong'O. 1986. *Decolonizing the mind: The politics of language in African literature*. London: Currey/Heinemann.

———. 1993. *Moving the Center: The struggle for cultural freedom*. London: Currey.

Niang, C. I. 1994. The Dimba of Senegal: A support group for women. *Reproductive Health Matters*.

———. 1996. Integrating Laobe women into AIDS prevention strategies. In *Learning about sexuality: A practical beginning*, ed. S. Zeidenstein and K. Moore. New York: Population Council and International Women's Health Coalition.

Njoku, J. E. E. 1980. *The world of the African woman*. Metuchen, N.J.: Scarecrow.

Nkrumah, K. 1970. *Consciencism*. New York: Monthly Review Press.

Nnaemeka, O. 2005. Bringing African women into the classroom: Rethinking pedagogy and epistemology. In *African gender studies: A reader*, ed. O. Oyewumi. New York: Palgrave.

Nyamnjoh, F. 2003. O Africa: Gender imperialism in academia. In *African women and feminism: Reflecting on the politics of sisterhood*, ed. O. Oyewumi. Trenton, N.J.: African World Press.

———. 2005. From publish or perish to publish and perish: What "Africa's 100 Best Books" tell us about publishing Africa. *Journal of Asian and African Studies* 39, no. 5:2004.

Nzegwu, N. 1996. Questions of identity and inheritance: A critical review of Kwameh Anthony Appiah's *In My Father's House*. *Hypatia* 11:1.

Okri, B. 1997. *A way of being free*. London: Phoenix.

Oliver, M. L., and T. M. Shapiro. 1997. *Black wealth/White wealth: New perspectives on racial inequality*. New York: Routledge.

Olukoshi, A., and F. B. Nyamnjoh. 2003. Editorial. *CODESRIA Bulletin*, special issue 2, nos. 3 & 4:1.

Oruka, H. O., ed. 1990. *Sage philosophy: Indigenous thinkers and modern debate on African philosophy*. Leiden: Brill.

Osler, W. 1910. The faith that heals. *British Medical Journal*, June 18, 1470–72.

Outlaw, L. 1996. "Conserve" races? In defense of W. E. B. Du Bois. In *W. E. B. Du Bois on race and culture: Philosophy, politics, and poetics*, ed. B. W. Bell, E. Grosholz, and J. B. Stewart. New York: Routledge.

Oyewumi, O. 1997. *The invention of women: Making an African sense of Western gender discourses*. Minneapolis: University of Minnesota Press.

———. 2003a. Abiyamo: Theorizing African motherhood. *Jenda: A Journal of Culture and African Women Studies* 4.

———, ed. 2003b. *African women and feminism: Reflecting on the politics of sisterhood*. Trenton, N.J.: African World Press.

———. 2003c. Introduction: Feminism, sisterhood, and other foreign relations. In *African women and feminism: Reflecting on the politics of sisterhood*, ed. O. Oyewumi. Trenton, N.J.: African World Press.

Paiva, V., ed. 2000. *Fazendo arte com a camisinha: Sexualidades jovens em tempos de AIDS*. São Paulo: Summus.

Parker, R. 2000. Preface. In *Fazendo arte com a camisinha: Sexualidades jovens em tempos de AIDS*, ed. V. Paiva. São Paulo: Summus.

———. 2002. The global HIV/AIDS pandemic, structural inequalities, and the politics of international health. *American Journal of Public Health* 92:343–46.

Paulsen, A. E. 1926. Religious healing: A preliminary report. *Journal of the American Medical Association* 86:1519–22, 1617–23, 1692–97.

Phoolcharoen, W. 1998. *Partners in prevention: International case studies of effective health promotion practice in HIV/AIDS: Experiences from Thailand.* UNAIDS Best Practice Collection. Geneva: UNAIDS.

Radcliffe-Brown, A. R. 1952. *Structure and function in primitive society: Essays and addresses.* Glencoe, Ill.: Free Press.

Rahnema, M. 1992. Participation. In *The development dictionary: A guide to knowledge and power*, ed. W. Sachs (pp. 116–31). London: Zed.

Rappaport, J. 1984. Studies in empowerment: Introduction to the issue. In *Studies in empowerment: Steps toward understanding action*, ed. J. Rappaport, C. Swift, and R. Hess (pp. 1–7). New York: Haworth.

Relv, M. V. 1997. Illuminating meaning & transforming issues of spirituality in HIV disease and AIDS: An application of Parse's theory of human becoming. *Holistic Nursing Practice* 121:1–8.

Rogers, E. 1995. *Diffusion of innovations.* 4th ed. New York: Free Press.

Said, E. W. 1993. *Culture and imperialism.* New York: Knopf.

Senghor, L. S. 2001. *Negritude and modernity or Negritude as a humanism for the twentieth century race.* Robert Bernasconi (Ed.). Blackwell Readings in Continental Philosophy. Oxford: Blackwell.

Shisana, O., T. Rehle, L. C. Simbayi, W. Parker, K. Zuma, A. Bhana, C. Connolly, S. Jooste, V. Pillay, et al. 2005. *South Africa national HIV prevalence, HIV incidence, behaviour and communication survey.* Cape Town: HSRC Press.

Shisana, O., and L. Simbayi. 2002. *South Africa national HIV prevalence, behavioral risks and mass media household survey.* Cape Town: HSRC Press.

Shisana, O., D. Stoker, L. C. Simbayi, M. Orkin, F. Bezuidenhout, S. E. Jooste, M. Colvin, and J. van Zyl. 2004. South African national household survey of HIV/AIDS prevalence, behavioural risks and mass media impact: Detailed methodology and response rate result. *South African Medical Journal* 94:4.

Simons, M. 1989. Poor nations seeking rewards for contributions to plant species. *New York Times*, May 16, 18.

Singhal, A., and E. M. Rogers. 1999. *Entertainment education: A communication strategy for social change.* Hillsdale, N.J.: Erlbaum.

——. 2003. Communication strategies for AIDS. Thousand Oaks, Calif.: Sage.

Soyinka, Wole. 1975. *Death and the king's horseman.* New York: Hill & Wang.

——. 1976. *Myth, literature and the African world.* Cambridge: Cambridge University Press.

——. 1996. *The open sore of a continental: A personal narrative of the Nigerian crisis.* New York: Oxford University Press.

——. 1999. *The burden of memory, the muse of forgiveness.* New York: Oxford University Press.

Spencer, M. B. 1995. Old issues and new theorizing about African-American youth: A phenomenological variant of ecological systems theory. In *African American youth: The social and economic status in the United States*, ed. R. L. Taylor (pp. 37–70). Westport, Conn.: Praeger.

———. 1999. Social and cultural influences on school adjustment: The application of an identity-focused cultural ecological perspective. *Educational Psychologist* 3:43–57.

Stewart, J. B. 1989. *The state of Black studies: Perspectives from the first NCBS Summer Faculty Institute and implications of the NRC report: A common destiny.* Paper presented at Temple University, Philadelphia.

———. 1992. Reaching for higher ground: Toward an understanding of Black/Africana studies. *Afrocentric Scholar* 11:1–63.

———. 1996. In search of a theory of human history: W. E. B. Du Bois's theory of social and cultural dynamics. In *W. E. B. Dubois on race and culture: Philosophy, politics, and poetics*, ed. B. W. Bell, E. Grosholz, and J. B. Stewart. New York: Routledge.

Street, B. V. 1984. *Literacy in theory and practice.* Cambridge: Cambridge University Press.

Symth, F. 1998. Cultural constraints on the delivery of HIV/AIDS Prevention in Ireland. *Social Science & Medicine* 46, no. 6:661–72.

Teller, A. 1968. Studies on aspects of traditional medicine. *Lagos Notes and Records* 21:18.

Thiam, A. 1986. *Speak out, Black sisters: Feminism and oppression in Black Africa.* London: Pluto.

UNAIDS/Penn State 1999. *Communications framework for HIV/AIDS: A new direction.* C. O. Airhihenbuwa, B. Makinwa, M. Frith, and R. Obregon (Eds.). A UNAIDS/Penn State Project. Geneva: UNAIDS.

UNESCO. 1980. *Histoire general de l'Afrique.* Paris: Author.

United Nations Development Programme. 2005. *The Human Development Report: International cooperation at a crossroad: Aid, trade and security in an unequal world.* New York: Oxford University Press.

Webster, J. D. 2003. *Using a cultural model to assess female condom use in Mpumalanga, South Africa.* Unpublished doctoral dissertation, Pennsylvania State University.

Werner, D. 1989. *Health for no one by the year 2000: The high cost of placing "national security" before global justice.* Address presented to the 16th Annual International Health Conference of the National Council for International Health, Arlington, Va., June 18–21.

West, C. 1990. The new cultural politics of difference. In *Out there: Marginalization and contemporary cultures*, ed. R. Ferguson, M. Geverr, T. T. Minh-ha, and C. West (pp. 19–36). Cambridge, Mass.: MIT Press.

———. 1993a. *Keeping faith: Philosophy and race in America.* New York: Routledge.

———. 1993b. *Race matters.* Boston: Beacon.

Williams, D. R. 2002. Racial/ethnic variations in women's health: The social embeddedness of health. *American Journal of Public Health* 92:588–97.

Williams, D. R., and C. Collins. 1995. US socioeconomic and racial differences in health: Patterns and explanations. *Annual Reviews in Sociology* 21:349–86.

———. 2004. Reparations: A viable strategy to address the enigma of African American health. *American Behavioral Scientist* 47:977–1000.

Wilson, W. J. 1978. *The declining significance of race: Blacks and changing American institutions*. Chicago: University of Chicago Press.

Wiredu, Kwasi. 1980. *Philosophy and an African culture*. Cambridge: Cambridge University Press.

World Council of Churches. 1997. *The impact of HIV/AIDS and the churches' response facing AIDS: The challenge, the council's response*. Geneva: WCC Publications.

World Health Organization. 2003. *Expert group stresses that unsafe sex is primary mode of transmission of HIV in Africa*. WHO media release, April 4, 2003, http://who.int/mediacentre/statements/2003/statement5/in/ (accessed April 24, 2003).

Zeleza, P. 2003. *Rethinking Africa's globalization volume: The intellectual challenges*. Trenton, N.J.: African World Press.

———. 2004. Neo-liberalism and academic freedom. In *African universities in the twenty-first century: Vol. 1*, ed. P. T. Zeleza and A. Olukoshi. Dakar: CODESRIA.

Index

About the Author

Collins O. Airhihenbuwa is a professor in the Department of Biobehavioral Health at the Pennsylvania State University. He is also the director of the Center for Health and Culture, a private consulting firm; author of a cultural model (PEN-3) for health behavior with a focus on people of African descents; known internationally for his research on culture and the social contexts of health behavior; and author of *Health and Culture: Beyond the Western Paradigm* (1995) and *UNAIDS Communications Framework for HIV/AIDS: A New Direction* (1991). He is the 1998 Scholar of the Year of the American Association for Health Education and received the 2000 Symbol of HOPE Award of the *American Journal of Health Promotion* and the 2006 David Satcher Award by the Directors of Health Promotion and Education. He was the 2004/2005 president of the Society for Public Health Education.

0532 140